Thinker, Thought and Knowledge in East–West Perspective

Thinker, Thought and Knowledge
in East–West Perspective

V.N. Misra

PRINTWORLD
Publishers of Indian Traditions

Cataloging in Publication Data – DK
[Courtesy: D.K. Agencies (P) Ltd. <docinfo@dkagencies.com>]

Misra, V.N., author.

Thinker, thought and knowledge in East-West perspective / V.N. Misra.
pages cm
Includes bibliographical references.
ISBN 9788124610442

1. Thought and thinking. 2. Knowledge, Theory of. 3. Knowledge, Theory of (Hinduism) 4. Advaita. I. Title.

LCC BF441.M57 2021 | DDC 153.42 23

ISBN: 978-81-246-1044-2
First published in India in 2021

Printed and published by:
D.K. Printworld (P) Ltd.
Regd. Office: Vedaśrī, F-395, Sudarshan Park
(Metro Station: ESI Hospital), New Delhi - 110015
Phones: (011) 2545 3975, 2546 6019
e-mail: indology@dkprintworld.com
Website: www.dkprintworld.com

Preface

It is recently observed that thought has created thinker. Thought thinks itself. Each thought carries out with it the potential for self-consciousness. Thought is also treated as the source of nature and modern physics has a tendency to undermine the principle of causation. In another study it is stated that higher order thoughts (HOTs) are, themselves, conscious. This seems to prevent it from being able to explain our sense of unity of consciousness. As against these observations, the following observations of the present study, Thinker, Thought and Knowledge, are quite different:

i. Thought cannot create thinker. This is mainly because thought happens to be the object of self-consciousness which is embodied in human being. It may be noted here that only human beings can become thinker, because they have both mind and consciousness.

ii. Those who believe that thought creates thinker, they have taken into consideration only thinker and thought. This leads to duality under which it is difficult to know whether thinker has created thought or thought has created thinker. If one takes the triplicity of thinker, thought and thinking, in that individual experience takes place. This is mainly because in thinking, thinker and thought both are involved.

iii. Thinker, thinking and thought are not different but they are fundamentally one in self-consciousness. In reality,

I, the thinker, am consciousness which thinks, thinking is that consciousness myself operating; thought is also myself, a form or movement of the same consciousness. This shows that consciousness itself is unity. In this context, it is all the more important to quote Searle's observation that "consciousness is by its very essence qualitative, subjective and unified" (Searle 2004: 95). If consciousness itself is unity, how the atomic character of thought may prevent it from being able to explain our sense of the unity of consciousness.

iv. Thought as source of nature does seem to appropriate in the sense that it becomes the object of self-consciousness, which is embodied in human being. An inference may, therefore, be drawn that it is the self-consciousness rather than thought which becomes the source of nature. Self-consciousness, while knowing the objective world, it knows itself. There is no other entity which knows itself.

v. In the context of undermining the causation in the quantum physics, it may be stated that since the observer (i.e. human being) is involved how can he undermine the causation? The cause resides in the observer having causal body according to the Vedānta of Indian philosophy. The observer influences the properties of the quantum theory. In fact, it is the work of human consciousness which broke the tangible chunk of matter into ordinarily invisible atoms and the latter into absolutely invisible particles.

As regards the knowledge aspect of the study, it may be stated that perceptual knowledge concerning the relative existence and knowledge dealing with the Absolute Reality is discussed on the basis of Advaita Vedānta, and the Yogācāra Vijñānavāda of Buddhist philosophy. Kant's theory of knowledge is also discussed.

According to Kant, there are two main sources of knowledge.

In the first source, object is given to us. This is known as the faculty representations. The second one is the power of cognizing by means of representation. This is referred to as spontaneity in the production of conceptions.

In the Vedānta school of Indian philosophy, the higher knowledge is mainly concerned with *Brahman* which happens to be the Absolute Reality. It is pure consciousness. This is important because it is treated as the foundation through which the entire universe is known. Pure consciousness in itself is the Absolute Reality. Whereas, pure consciousness for itself is involved in the world affairs which have only relative existence. However, the perceptual knowledge is twofold: external and internal. The former is known by any of five sensory organs such as hearing, sight, touch, taste and smell. Whereas, the latter is the mental perception of pain and pleasure of knowledge, ignorance, love, hate, etc.

In the Buddhist philosophy, the self is represented by self-consciousness. This is involved in the internal perception. Whereas, the external perception depends on the images of the objects. However, the object of perception happens to be a unique particular meaning thereby an entity that is not shared by anything. The Buddhists have adopted the representative theory of perception under which everything happens as an inner episode with the mind. This is justified by the dream experience in which action also takes place.

The knowledge of Absolute Reality is treated as emptiness in the Buddhist philosophy. This has also been described as the Buddha nature known as *tathatā* (suchness), which is dependently co-arise. However, the *ālaya-vijñāna* happens to be the noetic aspect of *tathatā*. When *ālaya-vijñāna* returns to itself, it becomes the *dharmakāya* of the Buddha, the non-dual (*advaya*) principle, the Absolute. In order to achieve the stage of *dharmakāya*, one has to purify his consciousness by going through four stages: (i) *kāmāvacāra-citta-bhūmi* (sphere); (ii) *rūpāvacāra-citta-bhūmi;*

(iii) *arūpāvacāra-citta-bhūmi;* and (iv) *lokuttara-citta-bhūmi*. The fourth stage is the supramundane consciousness. This stage happens to be the realization of *nirvāṇa*, the Absolute Reality.

The changes in *ālaya-vijñāna* are momentary. Each moment, on the basis of the Buddha statement, has three sub-moments: arising, presence and dissolution.

It may, however, be stated that according to Sartre, the momentary instants of consciousness are unity in itself. Each instant of consciousness is a new existence, which does not arise out of a prior instant. This unity is treated as real and it is called the "unity within duration".

I am, indeed, grateful to Dr S.M. Pathak whose guidance in the research studies in economics has changed my entire life. His encouragement even in writing of philosophical books gives opportunity to express my feeling that his guidance has helped me in writing books even at the old age.

My gratitude is beyond words to Shri M.L. Pandit for encouraging me to write philosophical books.

I am indebted to Shri S.K. Sharma and Shri P.R. Sharma for their appreciation of my earlier books.

I express my gratitude to the authors from whose books the passages have been quoted in different chapters of this book.

I also express my gratitude to Shri Susheel Kumar Mittal, D.K. Printworld for his sincere efforts in publishing this book.

New Delhi **V.N. Misra**
5 January 2021

Contents

Introduction

THIS study attempts to examine thinker, thought and knowledge in East–West perspective with a view to provide substantial response in the sense that it is thinker who creates thought. Whereas in the following observations it is observed that thoughts creates thinker.

i. It is thought that has created the thinker;[1] thoughts themselves are the thinkers.[2]
ii. Each thought carries with it the potential for self-awareness.[3]
iii. The idea of a thinker is itself produced by thought and therefore cannot be separated from the process of thinking. Thought thinks itself.[4]
iv. Thought is treated as the source of nature.[5]
v. Modern physics has a tendency to undermine the principle of causation.[6]

The above first three observations can be justified on the basis of process philosophy, which has been started by the Buddha about 2,500 years ago, under which there is no being,

---

[1] Krishnamurti, J., 2007, *Choiceless Awareness*, p. 39.

[2] Chakrabarti, K.K., 2001, *Classical Indian Philosophy of Mind*, p. 75. This observation is based on O. Flanagon, 1992, *Consciousness Reconsidered*, p. 182.

[3] John, H., 2017, *Philosophy of Mind*, p. 72.

[4] Levy, P., 2019, *A Physics of Possibilities*, p. 268.

[5] Mukerji, A.C., 1957, *Self, Thought and Reality*, p. 214.

[6] Ibid., p. 224.

but only becoming exists. Everything is in process and flux. Now this process philosophy in the West has been revived again by A.N. Whitehead. It is stated that:

> Whitehead has said that philosophers who have started with being have given as the metaphysics of "substance" and those who have with "becoming" developed the metaphysics of flux. Whitehead points out the inseparability of the two.[7]

In this context, the following observation is worth stating:

> With all its organismic leanings, the process philosophy is predominating materialistic and mechanical and hence unmindful of the possibilities of consciousness. Had it become mindful of these possibilities of consciousness, it would not have been required to accord that independence to process as actually it has done. Process, indeed, is a product of consciousness proceeding from its concentricity of self-consciousness to the extensity of objectification.[8]

In the process philosophy, thinker and thought are not treated separately on the ground that are dependently co-arising as mutual causality. Therefore, it may be said that in the process system, there is no scope for storing the impressions in the mind because experiencer and experience cannot be relied separately. Further, with process philosophy the substance also cannot be separated from the flux as mentioned above.

Thinker and thought, however, become one in self-consciousness (*jīvātman*) of human being. This is mainly because thought becomes an object of self-consciousness. In other words, thought gets objectified of one's self-consciousness. Yet both thinker and thought may be distinguished. This is the Vedāntic interpretation.

The other fact is that thoughts are both quality (*guṇa*) and

---

[7] Matilal, B.K., 1997, *Logic, Language and Reality*, p. 283.

[8] Singh, S.P., 2004, *Vedic Vision of Consciousness and Reality*, vol. XII, part 3, p. xxii.

acts (*kriyā*), "they require the self as their supportive substance and the thinker. We note it as a ground of disagreement, then, that if the substance ontology is accepted, thoughts cannot be thinker."[9] This may further be supported by the observation that "thought exists only in relation to a conscious and abiding subject. Apart from this relation, it is an unreal abstraction."[10]

In view of the above facts this study attempts to examine, thinker, thought and knowledge covering the most significant divisions of philosophic study. These are: (1) Logic of the theory of thought; (2) epistemology or theory of knowledge; and (3) metaphysical or theory of being.[11] It may, however, be stated that theory of being is explained through thinking being in the Western philosophy, started by René Descartes. Whereas in the Eastern philosophy, being is known as conscious being, which is explained through self-consciousness because it happens to be *jīvātman* (self) according to the Vedānta school of Indian philosophy. Here, it may be pointed out that there is no difference between thinking being and consciousness being. Both have metaphysical notion.

However, thought has also been identified with the self. It is stated; "Thought is self, thought is the word which identifies itself as the 'me', and at whatever level, high or low the self is placed, it is still within the field of thought."[12]

The Yogācāra Vijñānavāda school of Buddhist philosophy has also divided consciousness into two aspects as stated below:

> When consciousness is born, its manifestation has two aspects: (i) that what discriminates the seeming subject (what can cause); and (ii) that what is discriminated, the seeming object (what is caused). As a seeming subject the aspect of

[9] Chakrabarti, K.K., 2001, op. cit., p. 75.

[10] Bowne, B.P., 1897, *Theory of Thought and Knowledge*, p. 30.

[11] Ibid., p. 6.

[12] Krishnamurti, J., 2007, op. cit., p. 97.

> consciousness is called perceiving division (*darśana-bhāga*). As a seeming object, the aspect of consciousness is called perceived division (*nimitta-bhāga*). There is another functional aspect of consciousness that what is the support of the perceiving and the perceived division, and may be regarded as their essential nature. This is called the "self-corroboratory aspect" (*sva-saṁvitti-bhāga*). It is the realization of the consciousness itself. If this was lacking, there would be no way of remembering the various manifestations of mind and its activities.[13]

It may, however, be pointed out that consciousness cannot be divided. Yet in the observations, the duality and triplicity aspects of consciousness are mentioned. This is mainly because of the following reason:

> The consciousness, although it is a complex entity, is only *one*. When we speak of its "parts" or "divisions", the only thing that we want to indicate is that it has diverse activities, diverse forms of manifestations, in the empirical reality – empirical reality that is created by the same consciousness when it manifests itself. It is not a real concrete division: it is only a theoretical division, a product of the conceptual analysis.[14]

Now coming to other observations like thought as the source of nature and modern physics undermining causation, it may be stated here that thought being the object of self-consciousness, cannot be the source of nature. In fact, it is human consciousness (i.e. self-consciousness) which itself is the source of nature. However, the quantum physics does not seem to undermine causality. It interprets the causality in different ways. The causal interpretation depends upon the quantum wave which carries information potentially active everywhere, but it becomes active in real sense when energy enters into the particle. This is, further, explained below:

> When a physicist observes an elementary particle – which,

---

[13] Ganguly, S., 1992, *Treatise in Thirty Verses on Mere Consciousness*, p. 139.

[14] Tola, F. and C. Dragonetti, 2004, *Being as Consciousness*, p. 201.

> from the quantum point of view, "causes" the particles to exist. …Before, the advent of quantum physics, the hallmark of "reality" was its measurability – for something to attain the status of being real, it had to be able to be measured. Quantum physics has startled the physics community by seeing through and dissolving this long-held and cherished notion. It is revealing that we ourselves are intimately involved in producing the results of our own measurements. Our discovery of a quantum entity in a very real sense "causes", it to be there, which implies that there is no physically real world independent of our observation of it. Before these entities are observed they do not really exist. There is nothing we can say about them; they are "unspeakable".[15]

Thinker as Thinking Being

(*Descartes Formula – Cogito, ergo sum* (I think, therefore I am))

In the *cogito, ergo sum,* one is affirming the existence of oneself as something which thinks. This is experienced below:

> The essence of the Cartesian self consists, therefore, only in thinking. I am, precisely speaking, only a thinking thing – that is, a mind that doubts, understands, (conceives) affirms, denies, wills, refuses, that imagines and also perceives. … This "thinking thing" is a substance and we do not know this substance immediately, in itself, but only because it is the subject of certain acts.[16]

This Cartesian *cogito* is interpreted in two ways as stated below:

i. Sometimes it is understood universally, implying the certainty of existence in all cases of conscious activity. Wherever there is consciousness there must be the ego as the subject of it.[17]

ii. It conveys the existence of a particular, contingent fact,

---

[15] Levy, P., 2019, op. cit., pp. 109-10.

[16] Roy, K., 2013, *Subjectivity in Science*, p. 28.

[17] Ibid., p. 29.

> namely that I in being conscious exist here and now. I cannot be conscious without existing at this moment; my very existence is implied in my thinking.[18]

It may be stated that these two ways of interpreting the *cogito* principle is necessarily interrelated. This interrelation is necessary for all truths of reason.[19] However, the most important aspect of the *cogito* principle is that existence and thinking are inseparably connected.[20] It means that my thinking reveals and guarantees my existence.[21] The *cogito* principle has been the best mode of discovering the nature of mind as evident from the following observations:

> Explaining the nature of mind, Descartes suggests that cognition or thought is the essence of mind and all other experiences like perception, imagination, emotion, volition, etc. are the "modes" of this thinking. Regarding the distinctness of this mind from the body, Descartes maintains that not only they possess different attributes but in some cases at least, the mind can function independently of the body, for clearly there can be no use of the brain for pure intelligence but only for imagination and sensation. The mind or soul is equipped with certain innate ideas, which it applies to but does not derive from external objects. These ideas are not always explicit in consciousness, but they are present in mind as latent potentialities at least. In any case, they have not originated in experience, which only can serve as an occasion of their explicit recall.[22]

However, Descartes' *cogito* principle has been influential, yet has been criticized and interpreted in different ways. These are stated below.

---

[18] Roy, K., 2013, op. cit., p. 29.

[19] Ibid.

[20] Ibid., p. 30.

[21] Ibid., p. 31.

[22] Ibid., p. 49.

Sartre's Interpretation of Descartes Formula: I Think, Therefore I Am

The above formula has been criticized by Jean-Paul Sartre on the following grounds:

(i) The consciousness which says "I am" is not actually the consciousness which thinks. Instead, we are dealing with a secondary activity.[23]

(ii) Descartes has confused spontaneous doubt, which is a consciousness, with methodological doubt, which is an act. When we catch a glimpse of an object, there may be a doubting consciousness of the object as uncertain. But Descartes' *cogito* has posited this consciousness itself as an object: the Cartesian *cogito* is not one with the doubting consciousness but has reflected upon it.[24]

On the basis of above observations, Sartre has concluded as follows:

> This cogito is not Descartes' doubting: it is Descartes' reflecting upon the doubting. " I doubt, therefore I am", is really, "I am aware that I doubt; therefore I am". The Cartesian *cogito* is reflective, and its object is not itself but the original consciousness of doubting. The consciousness which doubted is now reflected on by the *cogito* but was never itself reflective: its only object is the object which it is conscious of as doubtful. These conclusions lead Sartre to establish the *pre-reflective cogito* as the primary consciousness.[25]

Vedāntic Interpretation of Descartes' Formula: I Think, Therefore I Am

According to Vedānta school of Indian philosophy, consciousness

---

[23] Sartre, J.-P., 1984, *Being and Nothingness*, p. xi.

[24] Ibid.

[25] Ibid., p. xi. (This observation is based on translator's Introduction in the book of Jean-Paul Sartre, *Being and Nothingness*.)

is embodied in human being. It becomes self-consciousness because it manifests through the mind. That is why a person is spontaneously conscious of his own existence as "I am". Therefore, Descartes' formula has been interpreted by the Vedānta as "I am, therefore I think".[26]

The Cogito in Existential Philosophy of Jean-Paul Sartre

Sartre has started his existentialist theory of consciousness with an appraisal of Descartes' *cogito* – "I think, therefore I am". On the basis of this formula, Descartes has deduced the certainty of man's existence from his thought. "But Sartre's maxim – 'existence, precedes essence' may be interpreted as suggesting – I am, therefore, I think."[27] Sartre, in fact, "believes that man cannot act or think if he does not exist before hand. Consciousness, to him, is only a part of the encompassing structure of existence."[28] It may, however, be stated that the suggested formula of Sartre – I am, therefore, I think – is in complete agreement with Advaita Vedānta as mentioned above.

The Cartesian *cogito* has, however, not been accepted by Sartre mainly because it does not provide us the picture of the real consciousness – pure and simple. In this context, it is stated:

> The Cartesian *cogito* to Sartre is the consciousness of the "second order" or the reflected consciousness. Distinguishing the pure consciousness from the Cartesian one, Sartre makes a distinction between the two phases of consciousness, which

---

[26] Swami, Satprakashananda, 2001a, *Methods of Knowledge: According to Advaita Vedānta*, p. 83.

[27] Roy, K., 2013, op. cit., p. 129. In footnote, Krishna Roy has clarified about the formula. "It should be pointed out here that Sartre himself never explicitly declared that 'I am therefore I think'. It is only an implication of this saying 'existence precedes essence' which may be interpreted as I first exist and then subsequently think of something." – See p. 209, ref. 25.

[28] Ibid., p. 129.

> he calls the pre- reflective *cogito* and the Cartesian or reflective *cogito*.[29]

The *cogito* is treated by Sartre as reflective consciousness.[30] However, reflection has not been given any kind of primacy over the consciousness reflected on.

> It is not reflection which reveals the consciousness reflected on to itself. Quite the contrary, it is the non-reflective consciousness which renders the reflection possible; there is a pre-reflective *cogito* which is the condition of the Cartesian *cogito*.[31]

PRE-REFLECTIVE CONSCIOUSNESS OR COGITO

However, the main difference between pre-reflective consciousness and reflective consciousness is that in the former there is no ego, whereas in the reflective consciousness the ego appears.[32] It may be stated that, "unreflected consciousness must be considered as autonomous".[33] This is explained below:

> All unreflected consciousness, being a non-thetic consciousness of itself, leaves behind it a non-thetic memory that can be consulted. All that is required for this is to try to reconstitute the complete moment in which this unreflected consciousness appeared (and this is, by definition, always possible). For instance, I was just now absorbed in my reading. I am now going to try to remember the circumstances of my reading, my attitude, the lines I was reading. I am thus going to bring back to life not merely those external details but a certain thickness of unreflected consciousness, since it is only by this consciousness that the objects have been perceived, and they remain relative to it. This consciousness is not to be posited as an object of my

29 Roy, K., 2013, op. cit., p. 120.

30 Sartre, J.-P., 2012, *The Transcendence of the Ego*, p. 10.

31 Sartre, J.-P., 1984, op. cit., p. 13.

32 Sartre, J.-P., 2012, op. cit., p. 12.

33 Ibid., p. 19.

> reflection: quite the opposite, I must direct my attention to the objects I have brought to life, *but without losing sight of this consciousness*, I must maintain a sort of complicity with it, and draw up an inventory of its content in a non-positional way. The result is not in doubt, while I was reading, there was a consciousness of the book, of the heroes of the book, but the I did not inhibit this consciousness, it was merely consciousness of the object and non-positional consciousness of itself. I can turn these results, grasped athetically, into the object of a thesis and declare: there was no I in the unreflected consciousness. ... When I run after a tram, when I look at the time, when I become absorbed in the contemplation of a portrait, there is no I. There is a consciousness of tram-needing-to-be-caught, etc. a non-positional consciousness of consciousness. In fact, I am then plunged into the world of objects, it is they which constitute the unity of my consciousness, which present themselves with values, attractive and repulsive values, but as for me, I have disappeared. I have annihilated myself. There is no place for me at this level, and this is not the result of some chance, some momentary failure of attention: it stems from the very structure of consciousness.[34]

The reflective consciousness or cogito transcends itself in order to reach an object. This is stated below:

> The reflective consciousness posits the consciousness reflected on, as its object. In the act of reflecting I pass judgement on the consciousness reflected on; I am ashamed of it, I am proud of it, I will it, I deny it, etc. The immediate consciousness which I have of perceiving does not permit me either to judge or to will or to be ashamed. It does not know my perception, does not posit it; all that there is of intention is my actual consciousness is directed towards the outside, towards the world. In turn, this spontaneous consciousness of my perception is *constitutive* of my perceptive consciousness. In other words, every positional consciousness of an object is at the same time a non-positional consciousness of itself. If I count the cigarettes

[34] Sartre, J.-P., 2012, op. cit., pp. 11-13.

> which are in that case, I have the impression of disclosing an objective property of this collection of cigarettes; *they are a dozen*. This property appears to my consciousness as a property existing in the world. It is very possible that I have no positional consciousness of counting them. Then I do not know myself as counting. Proof of this is that children who are capable of making an addition spontaneously cannot *explain* subsequently how they set about it.[35]

According to Sartre, it is consciousness which serves as a link between me and the world. This is evident from the following observation.

> The world did not create the *me*, the *me* did not create the world, they are two objects for the absolute, impersonal consciousness, and it is through that consciousness that they are linked back together. This absolute consciousness, when it is purified of the I, is no longer in anyway a subject, nor is it a collection of representations; it is quite simply a pre-condition and an absolute source of existence. And the relation of interdependence that it establishes between the *me* and the World is enough for the *me* to draw all its content from the world.[36]

Sartre's theory of non-egological consciousness as mentioned earlier, is acceptable to Advaita Vedānta school of Indian philosophy. This is explained below:

> The view that the ego or "I" which is transcendent to consciousness arises only at the reflective level of consciousness is the echo of the Advaita view which holds that the ego (*ahaṁ*) arises when there is *cidābhāsa*, i.e. consciousness reflected in the internal organ; and this consciousness associated with the internal organ, which alone is capable of reflection, may be characterized in the terminology of Sartre as consciousness

[35] Sartre, J.-P., 1984, op. cit., pp. 12-13.

[36] Sartre, J.-P., 2012, op. cit., pp. 51-52.

> of in the second degree.[37]

However, according to Sartre, "ontological proof to be derived not from the *reflective cogito* but from the *pre-reflective* being of percipients".[38] This is clarified by the observation that "consciousness is consciousness of something. This means that transcendence is the constitutive structure of consciousness: that is, that consciousness is born *supported* by a being which is not itself. This is what we call the ontological proof."[39]

REFLECTIVE CONSCIOUSNESS OR COGITO

Reflective consciousness is positional. In that, "it transcends itself in order to reach an object and it exhausts itself in this same positing".[40] It is further explained:

> All that there is of intention in my actual consciousness is directed toward the outside, toward the table; all my judgments or practical activities, all my present inclinations transcend themselves; they aim at the table and are absorbed in it.[41]

UNITY BETWEEN PRE-REFLECTIVE CONSCIOUSNESS OR COGITO AND REFLECTIVE COGITO

The reflective consciousness or cogito cannot be separated from the pre-reflective consciousness. This is because "every positional consciousness of an object is at the same time a non-positional consciousness itself".[42]

It emerges that without the pre-reflective cogito (non-thetic, non-positional consciousness), the reflective cogito

---

[37] Balasubramanian, 2004, "Advaita Vedānta on the Problem of Enworlded Subjectivity", p. 87.

[38] Sartre, J.-P., 1984, op. cit., p. 21.

[39] Ibid., p. 23.

[40] Ibid., p. 11.

[41] Ibid.

[42] Ibid., p. 13.

(thetic–positional consciousness) is not possible. In such a situation, "it is agreed then that reflection must be united to that which is reflected-on by a bond of being that the reflective consciousness must be the consciousness reflected-on".[43] This reflected-on is pre-reflective (non-thetic, non-positional) consciousness.

The above observations regarding the unity between pre-reflective consciousness and reflective consciousness may be reassured by the following observation:

> The pre-reflective and the reflective cogitos are merely the two different phases of the one and the same consciousness. These are really the two successive stages – one of which necessitates the other. The pre-reflective phase is the pure subjectivity having no objectivity in it, but insofar as intentionality or projection is the essential feature of consciousness, it soon transforms itself into the reflective phase. In this reflective phase, consciousness is essentially "of" or about something; it reveals the object or Being in-itself. Consciousness, thus, here, is neither a container nor it is insulated; it is in the world.[44]

The Cogito in Phenomenology of Merleau-Ponty

The *cogito* is recognized by the proposition, "I think, I am". These two assertions are to be equated with each other; otherwise there would be no *cogito*. The meaning of the equivalence is explained in the following observation:

> It is not the "I am" which is pre-eminently contained in the "I think", not my existence which is brought down to the consciousness which I have of it, but conversely the I think which is re-integrated into the transcending process of the "I am": and consciousness into existence.[45]

---

[43] Sartre, J.-P., 1984, op. cit., p. 213.

[44] Roy, 2013, op. cit., p. 138.

[45] Merleau-Ponty, M., 2005, *Phenomenology of Perception*, p. 446.

It is further stated:

> I think, I am; but this is merely a verbal cogito, for I have grasped my thought and my existence only through the medium of language and the true formula of *cogito* should be "One thinks there one is."[46]

This clearly shows that the language too changes the meaning of the formula. There does not seem to be any place for ego in the proposed formula by Merleau-Ponty.

However, all thought of something is at the same self-consciousness, which is embodied in human being. If this fact is not acknowledged there would be no object. In this context, the following observation is worth stating:

> At the root of all our experiences and all our reflections, we find, then, a being which immediately recognizes itself, because it is its knowledge both of itself and of all things, and which knows its own existence, not by observation and as a given fact, nor by inference from any idea of itself, but through direct contact with that existence. Self-consciousness is the very being of mind in action. The act whereby I am conscious of something must itself be apprehended at the every moment at which it is carried out; otherwise, it would collapse.[47]

Having discussed various issues regarding Descartes' observation from things to thought, Merleau-Ponty has stated:

> Unless I learn within myself to recognize the junction of the *for-itself* and the *in-itself*, none of those mechanisms called other bodies will ever be able to come to life; unless I have an exterior, others have no interior. The plurality of consciousness is impossible if I have an absolute consciousness of myself. Behind the absolute of my thought, it is even impossible to conjecture a divine absolute. If it is perfect, the contact of my thought with itself seals me within myself, and prevents me from ever feeling that anything eludes my grasp: there is no

[46] Merleau-Ponty, M., 2005, op. cit., p. 466.

[47] Ibid., p. 432.

> opening, no aspiration towards an Other for this self of mine, which constructs the totality of being and its own presence in the world, which is defined in terms of "self-possession", and which never finds anything outside itself but what it has put there. This hermetically sealed self is no longer a finite self. There is ... a consciousness of the universe only through the previous consciousness of organization in the active sense of the word, and consequently, in the last analysis, only through an inner communion with the very working of godhead. It is ultimately with God that the cogito brings me into coincidence.[48]

It appears that consciousness is unique and universal according to Merleau-Ponty. In that it provides not only existential experience but it also reveals that the absolute transparency of thought makes destiny of human being as a thinking nature. However, we perceive a world only provided that before being facts of which we take cognizance that:

> World and that perception are thoughts of our own. What remains to be understood precisely is the way world comes to belong to the subject and the subject to himself, which is that *cogitatio* which makes experience possible: our hold on things and our states of consciousness. ... Perception and the perceived necessarily have the same existential modality, since perception is inseparable from the consciousness which it has, or rather is, of reaching the thing in itself.[49]

On the basis of above observation it may be said that according to Merleau-Ponty, perception and perceived have necessarily the same existential modality. There is no subject–object duality. This happens to be just opposite to Husserl's thought; under which distinction between the noesis and the noema is accepted. It is stated that "since every thought demands an object of thought, and this object has a relationship to the pure 'I' in the cognitive

---

[48] Merleau-Ponty, M., 2005, op. cit., p. 434.

[49] Ibid., pp. 435-36.

act, we find a remarkable polarity in every act; on the one side the 'I' pole and on the other 'object' as counter-pole".[50]

Since consciousness exists in me, it appears itself and transcends to the object. This involves a knowledge of itself, "its object, to will, and to know that one wills, to love and know one loves are one and the same act: love is consciousness of loving, will is consciousness of willing".[51] In such a situation, "everything is, then, truth within consciousness. There can never be illusion other than with regard to external object."[52]

While reducing consciousness in terms of its appearance with regard to some intangible reality, we are facing dilemma of an absolute consciousness on one hand and endless doubt on the other. If we reject the first solution, the cogito would be impossible? This objection brings us to the crucial point. The action is by definition: "The violent transition from what I have to what I am to have, from what I am to what I intend to be. I can accomplish the *cogito* and have assurance of genuinely willing, loving or believing provided that in the first place I actually do will, love or believe and thus accomplish my existence."[53]

Existence has been interpreted by Merleau-Ponty in a unique way. It always "carries forward its past, whether it to be by accepting or disclaiming it. We are, as Proust declared, parched on a pyramid of past life, and if we do not see this, it is because we are obsessed by objective thought."[54] This has been explained by Merleau-Ponty through acquisition. It is stated below:

> Acquisition must be accepted as an irreducible phenomenon. What we have experienced is, and remains permanently ours: and in old age a man is still in contact with his youth. Every

[50] Roy, K., 2013, op. cit., p. 144.

[51] Merleau-Ponty, M., 2005, op. cit., p. 439.

[52] Ibid.

[53] Ibid., pp. 444-45.

[54] Ibid., p. 457.

> present as it arises is driven into time like a wedge and stakes its claim to eternity. Eternity is not another order of time, but the atmosphere of time. It is true that a false thought, no less than a true one, possesses this sort of eternity: if I am mistaken at this moment, it is for ever true that I am mistaken. It would seem necessary, therefore, that there should be, in true thought, a different fertility, and that it should remain true not only as a past actually lived through, but also a perpetual present for ever carried forward in time's succession. This, however, does not secure any essential difference between truths of fact and truths of reason. For there is not one of my actions, nor one of my fallacious thoughts, once it is adhered to, which has not been directed towards a value or a truth, and which in consequence, does not retain its permanent relevance in the subsequent course of my life, not only as an indelible fact, but also as a necessary stage on the road to the more complete truths or values which I have since recognized. My truths have been built out of these errors, and carry them along in their eternity.[55]

In the context of above observation, it may be stated that whatever, we think or decide, according to Merleau-Ponty, "it is always against the background of what I have previously believed or done. ... We possess a truth, but this experience of truth would be absolute knowledge only if we could thematize every motive."[56]

However, the only way to think about thought is to think of something. This is essential to that thought not to take itself of an object. It is explained below:

> To think of thought is to adopt in relation to it an attitude that we have initially learned in relation to things: it is never to eliminate, but merely to push further back the opacity that thought presents to itself. Every halt in the forward movement of consciousness, every focus on the object, every appearance

[55] Merleau-Ponty, M., 2005, op. cit., pp. 457-58.

[56] Ibid., p. 460.

> of a "something" or of an idea presupposes a subject who has suspended self-questioning at least in that particular respect.[57]

The above observations clearly indicate that without subject (self-consciousness) it is rather difficult to think about thought.

The Transcendental Ego as Thinking Being

The transcendental ego is experienced as the ultimate core of consciousness, in the Western philosophy.[58] It is stated that the transcendental ego, "cannot be apprehended in the manner of an object – since it is a perennial subject – but it is nonetheless present in experience".[59] It is further stated that:

> The I is the transcendental ego, and the anxiety, joy, and body represent the empirical or psychological ego. The two egos are at opposite extremes of the intentional stream of consciousness. Our new triad therefore is *Transcendental Ego–Cogito–empirical ego*. The properties of the empirical ego (the *Cogitatum*) are not the same as those of the Transcendental Ego. Both egos, however, are clearly present in consciousness.[60] It may also be possible to appear as the pure Transcendental Ego.[61]

The transcendental ego is treated as the ultimate core of consciousness as mentioned above. Whereas according to Sartre, the transcendental I is death of consciousness.[62]

Transcendental Ego in Kant's Philosophy

According to Kant "the Ego is simple in thought".[63] This is explained below:

---

57 Merleau-Ponty, M., 2005, op. cit., pp. 460-61.

58 Koestenbaum, P., 1971, "Religion in the Tradiotion of Phenomenology", p. 185.

59 Ibid., p. 185.

60 Ibid., p. 186.

61 Ibid., p. 192.

62 Sartre, J.-P., 2012, op. cit., p. 7.

63 Kant, I., 1950, *The Critique of Pure Reason*, p. 239.

> The I or Ego of apperception and consequently in all thought, is singular or simple and cannot be resolved into a plurality of subjects and therefore indicates a logically simple subject – this is self-evident from the very conception of an Ego.[64]
>
> It may, further, be stated that the simple ego in thought is of itself important; "even although it presents us with no information about the constitution or subsistence of the subject".[65] Yet it is said that, "apperception in something real and the simplicity of its nature is given in the very fact of its possibility".[66]

It is, indeed, difficult to get clarity on important issues in Kant's *Critique of Pure Reason*. In this context the following observation is worth noting:

> Kant's rebuttals of the paralogisms, showing that the "I" that thinks cannot itself be thought by way of the understanding and its categories, need not detain us at length. It has a great deal in common with the Humean attack on Descartes; like Hume, Kant brings representation upon representation before the tribunal of the understanding and finds that, upon close examination, they dissipate. What must concern us, rather, is the question whether the posture of the *Critique*, as a whole, is tenable. If Kant is lecturing us that the soul, the "I think", and self-consciousness cannot be objects of any knowledge, what was he doing back in the Transcendental Deduction of Categories? Was he not, after all, showing us the way to talk about the "I", Self-consciousness and so on? Since that discussion did introduce us to an activity and a functioning of the soul, is Kant just shrinking back in the second half of his book, from drawing out the true implications of his own doctrine? Or was he right to reject a substantive metaphysics of the mind? It is over this question that we can trace the parting of

---

[64] Kant, I., 1950, op. cit., p. 238.

[65] Ibid., p. 244.

[66] Ibid.

> the ways among Kant's philosophical successors in Germany.[67]

Kant has also made distinction between thinking and knowing. In this context, it is stated that, "Kant claimed that we can think about things in themselves, but we cannot know them".[68] But it also ought to be recognized that, "thinking certainly lead to knowing and in fact the most important scientific gains of modernity are to be traced to thinking".[69]

Transcendental Ego in Husserl's Phenomenology

The transcendental ego, "for Husserl was consciousness as such, purged of all contingency by the method of *epoche*".[70] The *epoche*, the phenomenological reduction, is the bracketing of the natural attitude.[71] However, the transcendental ego happens to be the phenomenological basis and genesis of individual consciousness.[72]

The transcendental ego itself is, however, not "ontologically dependent upon anything else; and, therefore, the only real absolute is the transcendental ego, all else being ontologically dependent on it or relative to it".[73] This is further explained below:

> Only transcendental subjectivity has ontologically the meaning of Absolute Being, that it alone is non-relative, that is relative only to itself, whereas the real world indeed exists, but in respect to essence is relative to transcendental subjectivity, and in such a way that it can have its meaning

---

[67] Nicholson, G., 1962, *Illustrations of Being*, p. 35.

[68] Chatterjea, T. et al., 2014, *J.N. Mohanty Lectures on Kant's Critique of Pure Reason*, p. 248.

[69] Nicholson G., 1962, op. cit., p. 18.

[70] Roy, K., 2013, op. cit., p. 86.

[71] Sartre, J.-P., 2012, op. cit., p. 55.

[72] Roy, K., 2013, op. cit., p. 86.

[73] Medhidhammaporn, P., 1995, *Sartre's Existentialism and Early Buddhism*, p. 13.

> as existing reality only as the intentional meaning-product of transcendental subjectivity.[74]

The above observation shows that the ego is not a form-giving subject but it is a meaning-giving activity. In that it is the ground of experience. "It constitutes the meaning of the world through its conscious acts. The ego is actual because it lives in consciousness."[75]

Husserl in the *ideas* says that when he performs the phenomenological *epoche* (the phenomenological reduction), "the empirical ago and the whole world of the natural attitude are suspended. What remains as residue is the pure experience as act with its own proper essence. And act is found to be related to the transcendental ego."[76] It may be noted that without the reduction, "the apprehension of the ego is not possible. The reduction, therefore, turns out to be the necessary operation which renders pure consciousness accessible to us and subsequently the whole phenomenological region."[77]

What is equally important is that after phenomenological reduction, the appearance of the phenomenon of the transcendental ego, "discloses it to be closely related to the mystical experience of the inner self, the "Deeper Self", as Royce called it of the *Ātman* or *Puruṣa* as the Vedānta and Sāṁkhya forms of Hindu philosophy respectively have called it".[78]

As against the above observation, Sartre has denied the existence of transcendental ego. This is evident from the following observation:

> The phenomenological conception of consciousness renders

---

[74] Medhidhammaporn, P., 1995, op. cit., p. 13.

[75] Ibid.

[76] Ibid., p. 14.

[77] Ibid.

[78] Koestenbaum, P., 1971, op. cit., p. 185.

> the unifying and individualizing role of the I completely useless. It is, on the contrary, consciousness that renders the unity and personality of my I possible. The transcendental I thus has no *raison d'être*. Indeed, this superfluous I is actually a hindrance. If it existed, it would violently separate consciousness from itself, it would divide it, slicing through each consciousness like an opaque blade. The transcendental I is death of consciousness. The existence of consciousness, indeed, is an absolute, because consciousness is conscious of itself; in other words, the type of existence that consciousness has is that it is consciousness of itself.[79]

It may, further, be clarified here that there is no room for an I (ego) in unreflective consciousness.[80] This is also known as pre-reflective consciousness. The I only ever appears on the occasion of reflective act.[81] It is stated that "for Sartre does not merely claim that I is a product of reflective consciousness. Audaciously, he tried in addition to demonstrate its *absence* from *unreflective* consciousness."[82]

The transcendental ego, "is experienced as the source of consciousness whenever experiencing takes place, i.e whenever man is conscious. Anyone can disclose to himself the introspectively verifiable characteristics of the transcendental ego."[83] However, transcendental ego is experienced as distinct from the body and psychological states of the individual. I experience my anxiety, my joy and my body. "The I that does the experiencing is structurally different from that which it experiences; the I is the transcendental ego, and the anxiety,

[79] Sartre, J.-P., 2012, op. cit., p. 7.

[80] Ibid., p. 8.

[81] Ibid., p. 16.

[82] Ibid., p. xxi.

[83] Koestenbaum, P., 1971, op. cit., p. 185.

joy and body represent the empirical or psychological ego."[84] These two egos create a lot more problem in understanding the different states of ego. The other problem is that how the transcendental ego becomes the source of consciousness. If I am not conscious, where is the transcendental ego. In dreamless sleep, there is no ego, the moment when one awakes, I (ego) starts its operation. This seems to be the reason, for denying the existence of ego in pre-reflective consciousness by Sartre. But it also to be recognized that Sartre has accepted the role of ego in reflective consciousness. In fact, the ego becomes the object of consciousness rather than its source.

Pure Ego in Rāmānuja's Viśiṣṭādvaita of Indian Philosophy

The sleep is a most complex state. In that, one may experience pure consciousness. It is known only when one awakes from sleep and says that I have slept well or I could not sleep well. This seems to be reason for interpreting pure consciousness as witness consciousness in Advaita Vedānta. However, Śaṅkarācārya has taken deep sleep as the unity of subject and object. On waking up from sleep, one realizes that "I slept well". This was not acceptable to Rāmānuja, founder of the Viśiṣṭādvaita school of Vedānta. According to him, a person on waking from sleep says only that "I slept well" and has no consciousness of anything. Therefore, Rāmānuja denied the persistence of pure consciousness or witness consciousness in deep sleep.

According to Rāmānuja, the object of knowledge was absent in sleep, only "I" persisted in deep sleep. The soul remains in the state of self-consciousness, without any cognition at all in dreamless sleep. Thus, according to Rāmānuja, "self-consciousness is an essential and inseparable feature of consciousness. Self is a conscious subject which never loses its selfhood (*ahaṁ-pratyaya*). The *ahaṁ-pratyaya* is present even in

[84] Koestenbaum, P., 1971, op. cit., p. 186.

deep sleep though in a dim degree."[85] This shows that *ahaṁkāra* (ego) happens to be the subject of consciousness. In other words, consciousness is a reflection of *ahaṁkāra* (ego), which has been referred to as pure ego. This pure ego has been used by Rāmānuja in the place of pure consciousness of Śaṅkarācārya, experienced on waking from dreamless sleep. What is the most surprising is that on the one hand, Rāmānuja has advocated that it is the ego (*ahaṁkāra*) which controls the consciousness, on the other hand, consciousness is treated as eternal, because it is the attribute of *Ātman*, which is eternal.[86] The *Ātman* is treated as a substance and consciousness happens to be its attribute, therefore, it is also eternal according to Rāmānuja's philosophy.

Now the question arises, how is the substance related to its attribute? In this context, it is stated that "substance and its attributes are inseparably related by their very nature and hence there is no need to postulate as separate third entity to account for their relationship and as such there can be no room for the fallacy of infinite regress".[87] In the defence of inseparability, it has been further stated that "existence always implies qualification by way of attribute".[88] Yet, it has been observed that "Viśiṣṭādvaita has failed to give reasons and prove its claim that the attribute is inseparably related to the substance in relation of *apr̥thak-siddhi*".[89] *Apr̥thak* has meaning of inseparable. *Siddhi* in this system implies two things:

> *Sthiti* implies that an attribute can have no existence without the support of substance and *pratīti* implies that no attribute can be perceived except as related to a substance.[90]

---

[85] Saksena, S.K., 1971, *Nature of Consciousness in Indian Philosophy*, pp. 117-18.

[86] Ibid., p. 120.

[87] Rajagopal, L.V., 1993, *A Critique of Vedānta*, p. 146.

[88] Ibid., p. 148.

[89] Ibid., pp. 148-49.

[90] Ibid., p. 151.

Inseparability of attribute from its substance is justified on the analogy of knowledge relation, which clearly proves that "the subject–object relation is one that inseparably connects the subject with object".[91] In the same say, the very *svarūpa* of substance and attribute are inseparable.

The above knowledge relation does not seem to be appropriate because in this case there is *jñāna-tripuṭī* [triad of knower, knowing (means of knowledge) and known]. Without this triad, no experience will take place. In fact "it is only when the integrated state of consciousness, is broken up into the triplicity of knower, knowing and known that individual experience takes place".[92] However, for Rāmānuja, consciousness is associated mainly with knowing. This is evident from the following observation:

> To know is the very purpose of consciousness, the very existence of consciousness and even the very word "consciousness"; the word *cit* has emanated from the root *citi – citi-saṁjñāne* – that means to know. If one asks the question: What is consciousness?, it pre-supposes that one is conscious of something, otherwise one would not be able to pose the question. For Rāmānuja when thinking of something, *jñāna-tripuṭī* (the triad of knower, known and means of knowledge) comes in.[93]

The *jñāna-tripuṭī* (knower, known and knowing) is not different but fundamentally one in the Integral Vedānta as initiated by Sri Aurobindo. This approach is basically a transformation of the Advaita theory of consciousness. In that "in Reality, I, the knower, am the consciousness which knows: the knowledge is that consciousness, myself, operating; the known is also myself,

---

[91] Rajagopal, L.V., 1993, op. cit., p. 152.

[92] Taimni, I.K., 1998a, *The Secret of Self Realization*, p. 38.

[93] Laksmithathachar, M.A., 2009, "Study of Consciousness from the Point of View of Viśiṣṭādvaita Philosophy", p. 170.

a form or movement of the same consciousness".[94] Although such unification in consciousness may not be acceptable to Viśiṣṭādvaitins probably because Rāmānuja has made a distinction between the *Ātman* and consciousness, and in the place of pure consciousness he has brought in the pure ego as mentioned above.

The relationships among *jñāna-tripuṭī* components have been explained through the concepts of *svarūpa-jñāna* and *dharmabhūta-jñāna* of Viśiṣṭādvaita. The former treated as "I" consciousness shines for itself, the latter shines for the "I" consciousness.[95] This is similar to the Sāṁkhya system in which *Prakṛti* happens to be for the sake of *Puruṣa* and both (*Puruṣa* and *Prakṛti*) are treated as independent entities. However, *dharmabhūta-jñāna* is treated as the link between subject and object and it can also be the object of "I" consciousness.[96] A fallacy in this approach may be evident by the fact that *dharmabhūta-jñāna* even being the object of "I" consciousness, happens to be in its original state as all-pervasive like the Supreme Self. "As such, the *dharmabhūta-jñāna* is capable of understanding anything in this universe."[97] The object of "I" consciousness happens to be the *sarvajña* (omniscient) but not "I" consciousness, which replaces pure consciousness of Advaita Vedānta of Śaṅkara, who treated pure consciousness as *Brahman*, the Absolute Reality. This simply shows that Rāmānuja has not given serious thought in understanding pure consciousness and its implication, when he has replaced it with pure ego representing "I" consciousness in his philosophy of Viśiṣṭādvaita.

The following criticism of *apṛthak-siddhi* by M. Hiriyanna may be worth mentioning.

---

[94] Sri Aurobindo, 2001, *The Life Divine*, p. 148.

[95] Laksmithathachar, M.A., 2009, op. cit., p. 175.

[96] Ibid.

[97] Ibid.

> The notion of *apṛthak-siddhi* on which the conception is based is as imperfect as that of Nyāya-Vaiśeṣika-*samavāya* which it is intended to replace. The only difference is that while *samavāya* tries to unite what are supposed to be distinct, *apṛthak-siddhi* tries to separate what is supposed to be one. Both alike represent effort to seek what is not possible to have, viz. a half-way house between inclusion and exclusion.[98]

However, the following two observations regarding Rāmānuja's concept of "I" notion denoting the ego element in deep sleep, are also worth stating:

i. Sureśvara has argued that the Self or consciousness is present at all three levels of waking, dreaming and deep sleep. However, the "I" of ego-notion is present only at the first two levels. It is not present in the deep-sleep state. This proves that the "I" is not the Self. When the mind is present, then "I" is present. When the mind is absent, the "I" is absent.[99] This argument goes against Rāmānuja's proposition of the ego's presence in the deep-sleep state.

   The above argument of Sureśvara may be supported by another observation. It is stated that "the sleeper has first the experience of being without the experience that it is he *X* who is that being. He is not yet to himself an "I" (*Aham*). There is a vague sense of awareness without reference to conscious self. Then it comes to him, It is "I" (*X*) who went to sleep and am now awaking."[100]

   However, Śaṅkara's observation regarding pure consciousness may be supported quite emphatically on the basis of the concepts of pre-reflective consciousness and reflective consciousness as introduced by Sartre in his phenomenological analysis. The pre-reflective

---

98 Quoted by Rajagopal, L.V., 1971, op. cit., p. 153.

99 Grimes, J., 1992, *The Naiṣkarmyasiddhi of Sureśvarā, A Monograph*, pp. 98-99.

100 Woodroffe, J., 2001, *The World as Power*, pp. 209-10.

consciousness is non-egological, non-positional or non-thetic consciousness. Whereas the reflective consciousness happens to be positional or thetic consciousness. The ego arises at the reflective level according to Sartre. The pre-reflective consciousness is primary and reveal the reflective consciousness and not vice verse.[101] Further, the pre-reflective consciousness is immanently present in all acts of reflective consciousness and makes memory possible.[102] The pre-reflective consciousness of Sartre seems to be quite like the pure consciousness of Vedānta.

ii. The other argument is based on Kashmir Śaivism. It is stated that, " 'I' consciousness is of two kinds: one is pure and is Śiva, the light of consciousness reposing in itself. The other is a product of *māyā*. The pure ego rests on pure consciousness and the impure ego on outer objective forms."[103] This shows that "pure egoity is uncreated (*akr̥trima*) and free". The individual ego is a creation (*kr̥takatva*) imagined into existence (*kalpita*) by pure "I" consciousness.[104]

The above observations, however, seem to suggest that Rāmānuja does not seem to have given serious thought by replacing pure consciousness with that of pure ego, as mentioned earlier. Further, if he would have given serious thought even to pure ego, he would have never equated it with consciousness. Even, pure ego is capable of becoming *Brahman* of Advaita Vedānta. We are comparing the pure ego with *Brahman* mainly because it has been equated to Śiva being the Absolute Reality in Kashmir Śaivism.

These observations apart, it is equally important to state that Rāmānuja's concept of pure ego can be defended on the

---

[101] Srinivasan, G., 1994, *Insights into Inward Consciousness*, p. 59.

[102] Ibid., p. 60.

[103] Dyczkowski, M.S.G., 2005, *The Doetrine of Vibration*, p. 133.

[104] Ibid., p. 134.

basis of Husserl's doctrine of the transcendental ego in the phenomenological framework. It is stated that "the ego, writes Husserl, is himself existent for himself in continuous evidence; thus in himself, he is continuously constituting himself as existing".[105] According to Husserl, "when the ego is actually living in conscious act, that act is said to be an 'operated act' and the ego is the 'operative subject'. This is the most characteristic role of the ego as treated by Husserl in the ideas."[106]

We have stated both kinds of arguments: for and against Rāmānuja's concept of pure ego, which has replaced pure consciousness of Advaita Vedānta. What seems to be, however, the most important is the point of view adopted by a person. According to Advaita Vedānta, the causal substance alone is real, the appearances are mere illusion, having no existence of their own. This is known as Satkāraṇavāda theory that cause is the reality, which is the view of Śaṅkara. Whereas for Rāmānuja, the founder of Viśiṣṭādvaita school of Vedānta, both the substance and appearances are real. This theory is known as Satkāryavāda in which the effect is also real.[107]

Thinking Being in Kant's Philosophy

Kant has stated that, "I distinguish my existence, as that of a thinking being from that of other things external to me".[108] This is mainly because "all thinking beings are in themselves simple substances, as such, therefore, possess the inseparable attribute of personality and are conscious of their existence apart from and unconnected with matter".[109] However, thinking is defined in terms of consciousness as follows:

---

105 Quoted by Medhidhammaporn, P., 1995, op. cit., pp. 12-13.

106 Ibid., p. 13.

107 Swami Muni Narayana Prasad, 1999, *Praśna Upaniṣad*, p. 141.

108 Kant, I., 1950, op. cit., p. 239.

109 Kant, I., 1950, op. cit., p. 239.

> Consciousness is so constituted that, inasmuch as the thinking subject is at the same time its own object, it cannot divide itself – although it can divide its inhering determinations. For every object in relation to itself is absolute unity.[110]

It is, further, explained in the following observations:

> There is clearly a notion of consciousness which is such that a mere sensation is also a consciousness – a mode of consciousness, simply, having a sensation. We have to remember that *for Kant, consciousness is intellectual, conceptual thinking*. It has to do with thought, with understanding. He did not introduce the subject of consciousness in the chapter on Transcendental Aesthetics. The bare sensation is either an element of consciousness or anything of which I am conscious. There is no sensory consciousness. There is only intellectual consciousness. Consciousness is thinking. The sensation is pre-conceptual, but consciousness as Kant understands it, is consciousness of an object. And consciousness of an object is intellectual already, it is thought.[111]

The "I think" is quite important in the Kant's philosophy. This is mainly because it "must accompany all my representations, for otherwise something would be represented in me which could not be thought".[112] In this context, it is stated that, "there is unconscious process going on in which the manifold representations have been already synthesized. So, we only recognize this by thinking. Thinking simply recognizes what have already been achieved."[113]

The Buddhists have also similar views. The *ālaya-vijñāna* of Yogācāra Vijñānavāda of Buddhist's philosophy has four representations known as *vijñapti*s. These are stated below:

---

110 Kant, I., 1950, op. cit., p. 271.

111 Chatterjee, T. et al., 2014, op. cit., p. 163.

112 Kant, I., 1950, op. cit., p. 96.

113 Chatterjee, T. et al., 2014, op. cit., p. 127.

> There are four *vijñapti*s which are called *karma* (actions) from the point of view of agent (*kartṛ*). These are namely: (a) The *bhajana-vijñapti* (world as representation of consciousness), which is the appearance of the stable outer world. (b) The *āśraya-vijñapti* (substratum as a representation of consciousness), which is the appearance of the moving world – the material reality of the living being – the six senses (*āyatanas*) and their bases. (c) The *ahaṁ iti vijñapti* (self-awareness as a representation of consciousness). This is the introspective, continually operating thought "I am". (d) The *viṣaya-vijñapti* (objects as representation of consciousness), which is the appearance of shapes, sounds, etc.[114]

Thinking as Freedom in Hegel's Philosophy

According to Hegel, thinking is freedom. This is explained below:

> In thinking, I *am free*, because I am not in *other*, but remain simply and solely in communion with myself, and the object, which is for me the *essential* being, is in undivided unity my being-for-myself; and my activity in conceptual thinking is a movement within myself. It is essential, however, in thus characterizing this shape of self-consciousness to bear firmly in mind that it is *thinking* consciousness *in general*, that its object is an immediate unity of *being-in-itself* and *being-for-itself*. The selfsame consciousness that repels itself from itself becomes aware of itself as the element of *being-in-itself*; but at first it knows itself to be this element only as a universal mode of being in general, not as it exists objectively in the development and process of its manifold being.[115]

Thinking as Subject and Object

Consciousness has two aspects: the thinker and the thought. The thinker is the subject and the thought is the object. But both

---

114 Sparham, G., 1993, *Ocean of Eloquence*, p. 130.

115 Hegel, G.W.F., 1998, *Phenemenology of Spirit*, pp. 120-21.

subject and object are parts of consciousness. "To think" always means to think *something*. Therefore thinking always includes both the subject and the object of thought. So is the case with perceiving and knowing.[116]

Thought

Thought is the form of mental activity, which includes sensation, feeling and the whole universe so far as it is known.[117] The mental state itself causes that higher-order thought to occur.[118] According to Advaita Vedānta of Indian philosophy, thought is the apparent objectification of consciousness. This is explained below:

> The actual thought that results is always in terms of the senses, no matter how abstract that thought may be or by intuition it may have been arrived at ... Abstract thoughts and generalizations are, therefore, the objects of consciousness. As such they are quite distinct from introversion. An object of consciousness may be defined as whatever can recur in memory, for we remember only those things we have known.[119]

However, in the judgement, there is distinction of (a) and (b) as well as in their union. It may be stated that "without this distinction, the judgement is impossible. And for this logical distinction and union alike we need something which is neither (a) nor (b) but which comprehends acts upon both. This something we call the self."[120] This is a necessary condition of thought. In other words thought without the self cannot exist. The self becomes the thinker.

According to the sensational and physiological school, a

---

[116] Hanh, T.N., 2008, *Understanding of Our Mind*, p. 131. In this book the example has been explained through perceiving.

[117] Bowne, B.P., 1897, op. cit., p. 9.

[118] Rosenthal, D.M., 2005, *Counsciousness and Mind*, p. 25.

[119] Levy, J., 2004, *The Nature of Man According to the Vedānta*, p. 29.

[120] Bowne, B.P., 1898, op. cit., p. 22.

passive consciousness is possible, when particular units of feeling or impressions are united by association. This is supposed, "to give us the judgement as matter of course. On this view there is no unitary self which judges: but there are particular impressions grouped by association and this grouping is the judgement."[121]

This view, however, overlooks the objective side of the judgement and it can reach only a fictitious objectivity. This is explained below:

> The reality is always being only particular-associated impressions in some particular consciousness. In addition, the view has no inner consistency. To begin with, its particular states of consciousness which have no reference to self in them are fictions of abstraction, and no data of experience; real or possible.[122]

On the basis of above observations, it has been concluded that "*thought exists only in relation to a conscious and abiding subject. Apart from this relation, it is an unreal abstraction.*"[123] (emphasis added by italics). It is, further, reassured that "thought without a thinker and thought developing itself into a thinker – both of which notions are sheer fictions".[124]

The above observations indicate that without the thinker, it is difficult to explain the nature of thought. This will be all the more important in the case of thought process, because it is subjective depending on the thinker. Whereas thought becomes the object of thinker's self-consciousness. Since the consciousness of human being works through the mind and in that it becomes self-consciousness, which, while knowing others, knows itself. It may be categorically stated that there is no other entity in the entire universe which knows itself except the self-consciousness.

---

121 Bowne, B.P., 1898, op. cit., p. 23.

122 Ibid.

123 Ibid., p. 30.

124 Ibid., p. 304.

Therefore, the nature of thought and thought process cannot be examined without the self-conscious being.

Self (Self-Consciousness) and Knowledge

According to Sureśvara of the Advaita Vedānta, "When the self exists, the entire world exists. If the self is non-existent, all else will be non-existent."[125] This is known as the method of co-presence and co-absence (*anvaya-vyatireka*). It is, further explained:

> The self, which is of the nature of consciousness, is constant and necessary and therefore real, while the phenomena which contribute the world are inconstant, contingent, and therefore, non-real. If the self can be established, all else can be established. But if the self can not be established, nothing else be established.[126]

The self (i.e. *jīvātman*) has been interpreted as self-consciousness in the Advaita Vedānta. It is stated that pure consciousness (*Brahman*) is manifested human being as self-awareness that is direct and intuitive.[127]

According to Advaita Vedānta, any act of perception involves the *tripuṭī*, the cognizer, the cognized and the act of cognition. In this context, it is observed:

> From the cognizer (*cidābhāsa*), which is a reflection of consciousness residing in the intellect, arises a valid means of knowledge in the intellect, arises a valid means of knowledge (*pramāṇa*), which is a modification of the internal organ (*antaḥkaraṇa vr̥tti*). The consciousness upon reaching the object, assumes the form of that object, the modification is the transformation of the internal organ and connects the cognizer with the object cognized.[128]

---

[125] Grimes, J., 1992, op. cit., p. 18.

[126] Ibid.

[127] Swami Satprakashananda, 2001a, *Methods of Knowledge*, p. 91.

[128] Grimes, J., 1992, op. cit., p. 18.

> The *citābhāsa* is a reflection of consciousness in the internal organ; without the functioning of the mind or the internal organ no knowledge will arise.[129]

However, the *antaḥkaraṇa* going out to the object through the senses and assuming the form of object, is treated as the apparently absurd notion by Mukerji.[130]

Buddhists have also argued that "the existence of internal organ is a mere assumption which can neither be proved, nor is capable to account for the fact of several individual experiences".[131] As against this argument, the Vedāntin has argued that "without the assumption of internal organs actual individual cognition, in its positive aspects as well as its limitations, could not be accounted for".[132] This is explained below:

> As the internal organ, made up of these three parts, is of an exceedingly pure and transparent nature, Consciousness is manifested through it. Consciousness thus manifested indeed is one only, but is, according to the three several parts of the internal organ which manifest it, denoted by three different terms. That part of Consciousness which is particularized by the agent-part of the internal organ is called "knowing subject" (*pramātṛ*); that part which is particularized by the action-part is called "means of knowledge" (*pramāṇa*); and the part particularized by that part of the internal organ which serves for the manifestation of the object is called "(right) knowledge" (*pramiti*). In this way the "knowing subject", "the means of knowledge" and "knowledge" are clearly distinguished. In all these three, however, the form of the internal organ is the common factor; and as this form consists only in the relation subsisting between the knowing subject and the object known, it becomes possible for people to make use of such expressions

---

[129] Grimes, J., 1992, op. cit., p. 18.

[130] Mukerji, A.C., 1938, *The Nature of Self*, p. 166.

[131] Thibaut, G., 1994, *The Vivaraṇaprameya-Saṁgraha of Vidyāraṇya*, p. 146.

[132] Ibid., p. 147.

> as "this is known by me"– wherein all three appear as qualifying one another (this mutual qualification being made possible by the fact that the three have a factor common to them all). ... What we maintain rather is that Consciousness is the cause of perception insofar as it is manifested by the internal organ. Now there is a different internal organ for each man; how then can you say that our view implies a confusion of the experiences of all men?[133]

However, the existence of the internal organ has been justified by Śaṅkarācārya for the reason that if the internal is not admitted, there will be either the possibility of constant perception or non-perception.[134]

It is, however, observed that, "the really important point for a correct analysis of perception is furnished by the Advaita distinction between *antaḥkaraṇa* and *cit*, the unconscious changing principle and the conscious unchanging principle".[135] In this context the following observations are worth stating:

> There are two types of knowledge, the transitory and the permanent; of these, the latter is the pre-supposition of the former. If the perceptual knowledge were not distinct from the eternal knowledge of the self, Śaṅkara remarks, "the blind man could not see blue, yellow, etc. in his dreams".[136]
>
> Empirical knowledge (*laukikī-dṛṣṭiḥ*) is conditioned by mental modifications arising from the contact of the senses with sensibility; it appears and disappears. Eternal knowledge (*pāramārthikī-dṛṣṭiḥ*), on the contrary, does, not appear and disappear, as it is the very essence of the knower (*draṣṭuḥ svarūpatvāt*), much as heat and light form the essence of fire. In this sense again, eternal knowledge may also be called

[133] Thibaut, G., 1994, op. cit., pp. 144-45.

[134] Swami Gambhirananda, 2000, *Brahmasūtra-bhāṣya of Śrī Śaṅkarācārya*, verses ii-iii.32, p. 492.

[135] Mukerji, A.C., 1938, op. cit., p. 166.

[136] Ibid., p. 169.

the knowledge of the knower (*draskurdṛṣtiḥ*) as distinct from sense knowledge. There can be no distruction of the knower's knowledge, nor can it be an object of sense knowledge. The fleeting and fragmentary knowledge born out of the senses is something like a shadow (*pratichāyā*) of the "knower's knowledge", and consequently, the latter which is in fact the prevailing principle of the farmer cannot itself be revealed by sense knowledge.[137]

There could be no knowledge of a given object, such as the table or the chair, if we had not postulated the reality of a foundational type of knowledge which forms the background of the fragmentary knowledge that is produced piecemeal as the mind comes into relation with a particular aspect of the object such as, its colours. The foundational knowledge, therefore, does not itself come into existence or goes out of existence with the origin and disappearance of this particular knowledge, which, as put by Green, comes as waves. On the contrary, perception requires sensibility as well as consciousness neither of which, to put it again in the language of Green, admits of being reduced to or explained by the other.[138]

---

[137] Mukerji, A.C., 1938, op. cit., pp. 169-70.

[138] Ibid., p. 176.

1

Thinker as Self-Conscious Being

Introduction

THINKING always includes both: subject and object of thought. Yet the mind divides it in triplicity; thinker, thinking and thought, with a view to gain experience. If any aspect is missing in this triplicity, it creates duality which becomes rather difficult to reconcile it. This is evident from the observation based on thought and things. In this approach, two views have been expressed: (i) thought has been presented as an effect of things; and (ii) things have been viewed as produced by thought. "The former view has lost itself in the superficialities of sense thinking, and the latter has erred and strayed from the way from the confounding of the absolute and the human point of view."[1]

It has, however, been observed that the first view, i.e. things produce thought, leads to materialism. "Material origin of thoughts is no way surprising."[2] The materialism may be justified mainly because the matter serves as a medium of manifestation of both life and consciousness.[3] In the Indian context, the following observations are worth stating:

> Consciousness grows out of matter only when the latter becomes organic and develops the brain from within it as the crux of its organic systematization.[4] This may, further, be reassured by the fact that when the energy of the fundamental

[1] Bowne, B.P., 1897, *Theory of Thought and Knowledge*, p. 297.

[2] Ibid., p. 298.

[3] Singh, S.P., 2004, *Vedic Vision of Consciousness and Reality*, p. 17.

[4] Ibid.

> matter (*prakṛti*) gradually increases, it acquires the form of *caitanya* (consciousness).[5]

That apart, the most important fact is that thought is basically a creation of human being as thinker, who has self-consciousness. Thinker as thinking being and the "I" (ego) as thinker have already been mentioned in the Introduction. Here we are examining a self-conscious being. It may be mentioned that thinking being and self-conscious being are one and the same thing. Both are merely presenting human being who is responsible as thinker, thought and knowledge. In the knowledge episode human beings are examined in a dualistic way, i.e. thinker and thought, knower and known, and perceiver and perceived. It this context, it may be stated that thought cannot be thinker, known cannot be knower, perceived cannot be perceiver. This is mainly because thought, known and perceived are merely the objects of self-consciousness which is embodied in human beings according to the Vedānta school of Indian philosophy. However, self-consciousness and self-conscious being are one and the same thing. The main purpose for treating human being as a self-conscious being is to bring it in conformity with thinking being as mentioned in the Introduction.

Transcendental Unity of Self-consciousness

The transcendental unity of self-consciousness has been introduced by Kant, in the second edition of *The Critique of Pure Reason* which is evident from the following observation:

> As a self-consciousness that is devoid of material content, Kant describes this original unity as "pure" and original apperception (B132); as the condition of the possibility of empirical self-consciousness he also calls it transcendental apperception (A107) in the first edition, and in the second edition the transcendental unity of self-consciousness (B132) or more simply transcendental self-consciousness. The empirical

[5] Tilak, B.G., 2000, *Śrīmad Bhagavadgītā-Gītā Rahasya*, p. 218.

> subject which accompanies different representations, judging now this object and now that is in itself diverse. This subject lacks unity in its constant change. It only acquires the identity of the subject through a pre-empirical contribution that does not change, through that combining of representations in one consciousness whereby "I represent to myself the identity of the consciousness throughout these representations" (B133). This representation is a synthetic unity of self-consciousness insofar as it accomplishes such a combination, it is an original unity of self-consciousness.[6]

In the above observation, the transcendental unity of self-consciousness has been mixed up with the notions of subjective and objective. This is explained below:

> The empirical self-consciousness or what he calls empirical apperception or inner sense is subjective, but the transcendent unity of self-consciousness, which is also the synthetic unity of self-consciousness is called objective. It is called objective because of its transcendental role, intersubjective, sameness in all, and also in the sense of being responsible for the concept of object. We can note how the notions of "subjective" and "objective" are being mixed up in Kant.[7]

The subjective and the objective notions of transcendental unity of self-consciousness have been reconciled by Kant. Hoffe says:

> Kant concludes part proof II and draws the relevant conclusion (Section 26): "the categories are conditions of the possibility of experience, and are therefore valid a priori for all objects of experience" (B 161). The categories are thus capable of "prescribing, as it were, the law to nature" (B 159). Given the thoroughgoing correlation between subjectivity and objectivity, we cannot explain the transcendental structures of subjectivity without simultaneously grasping the pre-

---

[6] Hoffe, O., 2010, *Kant's Ctitique of Pure Reason*, p. 156.

[7] Chatterjea T. et al., 2014, *J.N. Mohanty Lectures on Kant's Critique of Pure Reason*, p. 185.

> empirical features of objectivity. Nor, for the same reason, can we understand the "deduction" without simultaneously considering the lawfulness of nature that is implicit in the categories, the pre-empirical presuppositions of the actual empirical laws of nature. It is only to be expected, therefore, that Kant returns to the question of the synthetic unity of apperception whom he finally completes the "deduction" in the chapter on "The System of All Principles of Pure Understanding". The transcendental "I think" is at once the unity of self-consciousness and the unity of nature, and thus both subjectivity and objectivity in one.[8]

It is, however, stated that, "unity of consciousness and unity of object are one and the same thing".[9] This has been shown by example as follows:

> If in counting, I forget that the units, which now hover before me, have been added to one another in succession. I should never know that a total is being produced through this successive addition of unit, to unit, and so would remain ignorant of the number. For the concept of number is nothing but the consciousness of this unity of synthesis.[10] This is the Kantian move. A number is generated by synthesis a priori synthesis, while counting we are not merely going from one to another, but we are adding the succeeding one to the preceding one. There are three things here. Unity = concept of unity = consciousness of synthesis.[11]

In the above unity three things are not different but they are one. It is known as the transcendental unity of self-consciousness. This unity is treated by Searle as a unified structure of consciousness which comes to us.[12]

---

[8] Hoffe, 2010, op. cit., p. 167.

[9] Chatterjea, T. et al., 2014, op. cit., p. 162.

[10] Ibid.

[11] Ibid.

[12] Searle, 2004, *Mind: A Brief Introduction*, p. 95.

VEDĀNTIC INTERPRETATION OF TRANSCENDENTAL UNITY OF SELF-CONSCIOUSNESS

Consciousness at transcendental level becomes an ontological or metaphysical principle as the Ultimate Reality.[13] It is further stated that, "knowledge of transcendental consciousness enables to face the mystery of death. The survival of consciousness after death is the greatest challenge to science and the greatest support to religion."[14]

However, the transcendental unity of self-consciousness seems to be like *Ātman* (Absolute Reality) of Indian philosophy. It is known, "as *astitva-jñāna* of *Brahman*, that is, the awareness that *Brahman* exists. It does not need any proof: It is self evident."[15] When pure consciousness (Absolute Reality) descends in human being, it becomes self-consciousness, which is referred to as witness self (*sākṣī*). It illumines the mental states: knowledge, ignorance, pain, etc. "The mental states are immediately cognized because of their presence to the witness self."[16]

Self-consciousness in Hegel's Philosophy

The transition from consciousness to self-consciousness is quite crucial for Hegel. This is mainly because, with self-consciousness we have entered into the native realm of truth, "the key concern of self-consciousness is with knowledge of the self that is mediated through the object, that is, a self-knowledge that comes through relationships with other objects (practical relationships) and other people (social relationships)".[17] This approach, according to Sartre, avoids solipism.[18] This will be

---

13 Swami Bhajananda, 2009, "Knowledge and Consciousness", p. 92.

14 Ibid., p. 99.

15 Ibid., p. 93.

16 Swami Satprakashananda, 2001a, *Methods of Knowledge*, p. 91.

17 Williamson, R.K., 1984, *Introduction to Hegel's Philosophy of Religion*, p. 104.

18 Sartre J.-P., 1984, *Being and Nothingness*, p. 321.

discussed later. However, the inclusion of the other has been justified by Hegel by the fact that in consciousness, the in-itself of the object and the being of the object for another become one and the same thing.[19] This in a way protects Hegel's idealism.

In the reflection of self-consciousness the perception of sensible world is involved. In this situation there is no involvement of other beings. This is explained:

> As self-consciousness, it is movement but since what it distinguishes from itself is *only itself as* itself, the difference, as anotherness is *immediately superseded* for it; the difference is *not*, and it (self-consciousness) is only the motionless tautology of: I am I; but since for it the difference does not have the form of *being*, it is not self-consciousness. Hence otherness is for it in the form of a *being*; or as a *distinct moment*; but there is also for consciousness the unity of itself with this difference as a *second distinct moment*. With that first moment; self-consciousness is in the form of *consciousness;* and the whole expanse of the sensuous world is preserved for it, but at the same time only as connected with the second moment; the unity of self-consciousness with itself; and hence the sensuous world is for it an enduring existence. ... The unity of self-consciousness with itself; this unity must become essential to self-consciousness, i.e. self-consciousness is desire in general. Consciousness as self-consciousness, henceforth has a double object; one is the immediate object; that of sense certainty and perception which however *for self-consciousness* has the character of a *negative;* and the second, viz. *itself,* which is the true essence; and is present in the first instance only as opposed to the first object. In this sphere, self-consciousness exhibits itself as the movement in which this anthesis is removed and the identity of itself with itself becomes explicit for it.[20]

However, notion of self-consciousness gets completed in three moments. These are stated below:

---

[19] Hegel G.W.F., 1998, *Phenomenology of Spirit,* p. 104.

[20] Ibid., p. 105.

i. The pure undifferentiated "I" is its first immediate object.
ii. This immediacy is itself an absolute mediation, it is only as a supersession of the independent object, in other words, it is desire. The satisfaction of desire is, it is true, the reflection of self-consciousness into itself, or the certainty that has become truth.
iii. But the truth of this certainty is really a double reflection, the duplication of self-consciousness. Consciousness has for its object one which, of its own self, posits its otherness or difference as a nothingness, and in so doing is independent. The differentiated, merely *living*, shape does indeed also superstate its independence in the process of life, but it ceases with its distinctive difference to be what is it. The object of self-consciousness, however, is equally independent in this negativity of itself; and thus it is *for itself* a genius, a universal fluid element in the peculiarity of its own separate being; it is a living self-consciousness.[21]

A self-consciousness exists for a self-consciousness. This is mainly because the unity of itself becomes explicit in its otherness. In this context it is observed that the I (ego) happens to be the object of desire, which is independent of the universal indestructible substance, the fluent self-identical essence.[22] This is, further, explained below:

> A self-consciousness, in being an object, is just as much "I" as object. With this, we already have before us the notion of *spirit*. What still lies ahead for consciousness is the experience of what spirit is – This absolute substance, which is the unity of the different independent self-consciousnesses which, in their opposition, enjoy perfect freedom and independence; "I" that is "We" and "We" That is "I". It is in self-consciousness,

---

21 Hegel, G.W.F., 1998, op. cit., p. 110. The reference covers all the three points mentioned in the text.

22 Ibid.

> in the notion of *spirit*, that consciousness first finds its turning point, where it leaves behind it the colourful show of the sensuous here-and-now and the night-like void of the super sensible beyond, and steps out into the spiritual daylight of the present.[23]

Lordship and Bondage

Self-consciousness lives outside of itself in an other self-consciousness in which it at once looses and also finds itself. However, "Each consciousness then acts itself as much as, it acts on the other, and what it does is as much done by the other to it, as by it to the other consciousness."[24] Each uses the other as the means by which it achieves self-consciousness. It is, further, observed that:

> Self-consciousness must be willing to sacrifice everything concrete for its own infinite self-respect and the similar respect of all others. A life and death struggle therefore ensures between the rival self-consciousness.[25]

> The self-consciousness of the Lord is essentially related to the being of the mere things he uses and uses up, and these he enjoys through the bondsman's self-consciousness. The bondsman prepares and arranges things for the enjoyment of the Lord. The self-consciousness of the Lord is likewise essentially related to the self-consciousness of the bondsman through the various punitive, constraining and rewarding instruments which keep the bondsman in thrall. The bondsman working on things does not completely overcome their thingness since they do not become what he wishes them to be, or not for himself. It is the Lord who reaps the enjoyment from the bondsman's labours.[26]

---

23 Hegel, G.W.F., 1998, op. cit., pp. 110-11.

24 Ibid., p. 520.

25 Ibid., p. 521.

26 Ibid., pp. 521-22.

The truth of independent self-consciousness is, therefore, to be found rather in the bondsman's self-consciousness than in the Lord's. Each is therefore the inverse of what it immediately and superficially is given as being.[27]

The bondsman has the further advantage that in working on the object he as it were preserves his labour, makes the outward thing his own and puts himself into it. Where as the Lord's dealings with the object end in vanishing enjoyments. The bondsman overcomes the otherness and mere existence of material thinghood more thoroughly than the Lord and so achieves a more genuine self-consciousness.[28]

Hegel thinks that the discipline of service and obedience is essential to self-consciousness; mere mastery of things alone would not yield it. Only the discipline of service enables the conscious being in master himself, i.e. his finite, contingent, natural self. Without this discipline formative ability would degenerate into a narrow cleverness placed at the service of personal self-will.[29]

Freedom of Self-consciousness

The freedom of self-consciousness takes place when it appeared as conscious manifestation in the history of spirit, which is called Stoicism.[30] "Its principle is that consciousness is a being that *thinks*, and that consciousness holds something to be essentially important or true and good only insofar as it *thinks* it to be such."[31] It is further observed that,

> While stoicism is the freedom which always comes directly out of bondage and returns into the pure universality of thought. As a universal form of the Worldspirit, stoicism could only

---

[27] Hegel, G.W.F., 1998, op. cit., p. 522.

[28] Ibid.,

[29] Ibid.

[30] Ibid., p. 121.

[31] Ibid.

> appear on the scene in a time of universal fear and bondage, but also a time of universal culture which had raised itself to the level of thought.[32]

However, the freedom of self-consciousness is indifferent to natural existence. In this context it is stated:

> Freedom in thought has only *pure thought* as its truth, a truth lacking the fullness of life. Hence freedom in thought too, is only the notion of freedom, not the living reality of freedom itself. For the essence of that freedom is at first only thinking in general, the form as such (of thought), which has turned away from the independence of things and returned into itself. But since individuality in its activity should show itself to be alive, or in its thinking should grasp the living world as a system of thought.[33]

Puruṣa (Self-conscious Human Being) in the Sāṁkhya–Yoga of Indian Philosophy

The *Puruṣa* is equated with the seer (i.e. *draṣṭā*), which in turn is nothing but pure consciousness. Although it is pure, it appears to see through the mind. It has been emphasized that the "*Puruṣa* according to the yogic philosophy is the Ultimate Reality hidden behind the phenomenal world in its subjective aspect."[34] However, it has been clearly stated that "not until the last vehicle has been transcended consciousness can be known in its purity. That is the *Puruṣa*, the real *draṣṭā*."[35] Similar observation has been made in the *Sāṁkhya-Kārikā* 19 of Īśvarakṛṣṇa, in which it is stated that the *Puruṣa* is pure witness, neutral spectator and non-agent.[36]

The *Puruṣa* is also defined negatively as eternal and

---

[32] Hegel G.W.F., 1998, op. cit., p. 121.

[33] Ibid., p. 122.

[34] Taimni, I.K., 1999, *The Sciences of Yoga*, pp. 185-86.

[35] Ibid., p. 187.

[36] Swami Virupakshananda (tr.), 2003, *Sāṁkhya-Kārikā of Īśvarakṛṣṇa*, p. 61.

indivisible "without variableness or shadow of turning" as resting ever in its own pure self-identity. It is deprived even of ideal activity and it becomes just the possibility of a pure consciousness.[37]

However, the *Puruṣa* can be inferred on various grounds referred to in the *Sāṁkhya-Kārikā* 17 of Īśvarakr̥ṣṇa. These grounds are:

1. *Saṁghāta-parārthātvāt* which means that all composite objects exist for the sake of someone other than themselves.
2. *Triguṅādi-viparyāyāt* that the *Puruṣa* is opposite to what is constituted by the three *guṇas*.
3. *Adhiṣṭhānāt* that the inanimate objects are in the need of being controlled by some conscious principle.
4. *Bhoktr̥bhāvāt* that there must be an experiencer-conscious principle.
5. *Kaivalyārtham* that man tries to attain the absolute freedom from the worldly affairs which are often resulting into sorrow, pain, etc.[38]

Having inferred the *Puruṣa* on the above grounds, it is stated that the *Puruṣa* or self may be known immediately in its reflection.[39] Since the *Puruṣa* is nothing but pure consciousness, it has to reflect mainly through the instrument of mind. As a result, the essential nature of pure consciousness (i.e. *Puruṣa*) cannot be known so long it identifies with the mind which happens to be the object of consciousness. But it is equally important that *Puruṣa* (self) cannot experience anything without the mind. This is evident from the following comment:

The self having been reflected in the mind (*buddhi*) and

[37] Radhakrishnan, S., 2002, *Indian Philosophy*, vol. 2, pp. 320-21.

[38] Swami Virupakshananda, 2003, op. cit., p. 55. This reference covers all the five points mentioned here.

[39] Bhattacharyya, K.C., 1983, *Studies in Philosophy*, p. 192.

> identified with it, appears to possess knowledge, pleasure, etc. which actually subsist in the mind. It means thereby that it is the reflection of self in the mind which appears to experience pleasure, pain, etc. while, in fact they are modes of mind only. ... The self appears to take on the characteristics of mind in which it has reflected. ... This is what is traditionally known as theory of single reflection.[40]

As against the theory of single reflection, Vijñānabhikṣu proposed double reflection. It is stated that "Just as there is a reflection of *buddhi* in the self, so there is a reflection of self in *buddhi* also, otherwise the self's experience would not be possible."[41] This double reflection seems to be self-contradictory in the sense that how it is possible to know the self, "if the self knows itself through the reflection, in itself, of the mental mode which assumes the form of the self".[42] In this context, Vijñānabhikṣu says: "There is no contradiction in the cognition of self by the self inasmuch as the self is essentially self-luminous and, hence it can be both, the illuminating agent and the illumined object, the knowing subject as well as the known object."[43] Vijñānabhikṣu further observes:

> Though there is no real difference in the nature of self, yet we may distinguish the self in its pure essence, as the original (*bimba*) from the reflection of the mental mode in the self, as an image of the self (*pratibimba*). Of these two aspects of the self, which is the knowing subject and which is the known object. Vijñānabhikṣu holds that the self as determined by the mental mode, which is modified into the form of the self as the knowing subject and the self in its pure essence free from all determinations, is known as object.[44]

---

[40] Ram, K., 1995, *Integral Non-Dualism*, p. 110.

[41] Sinha, J.N., 1958, *Indian Psychology*, vol. I, p. 235.

[42] Ibid.

[43] Ibid.

[44] Ibid.

Yet, the theory of double reflection of Vijñānabhikṣu has some basic problems. In the context, it is stated:

> The law of parsimony also favours the view of single reflection as the acts of perception, knowledge, etc. can be explained adequately with the help of this theory. In the Sāṁkhya philosophy, the effect in a sense is identical with the cause. In this case, the reflecting of the self is the effect of the original self. Therefore, the acts of perception, knowledge, etc. which appear to belong to the reflection can also be taken to belong to the original self.[45]

It may be pointed out that the double reflection theory of Vijñānabhikṣu has been amended by K.C. Bhattacharyya through the dual function of mind reflected in the self. Let us see how it works. In reflection, the mind plays dual functions: (i) the mind while reflecting the object, it gets modalized into substantial *vṛtti* similar to the object. The *vṛtti* of *buddhi* appears as the self-reflecting object. This has been referred to as the outward grades of objective substance and characterized as causal manifestation,[46] and (ii) while manifesting the object, the mind functions non-causally. In this case, the mind does not go into any substantial transformation as has been the case in the functioning *vṛtti*. This is known as the mental mode of subjective function of *bhāva*, without which no object can become an object of knowledge.[47] However, these two functions are illusorily referred to the self.[48]

This illusionary character has been assigned to the reflection of self in *buddhi-bhāva* mainly with a view to show that it is in conformity with the Sāṁkhya view that "the self is known as what mind is not as it is known in *viveka* (*bhāva* – the subjective

---

[45] Ram, K., 1995, op. cit., pp. 110-11.

[46] Bhattacharyya K.C., 1983, *Studies in Philosophy*, p. 158.

[47] Ram, K., 1995, op. cit., p. 123.

[48] Ibid., p. 124.

knowing function of the mind), which implies a mental mode of the form 'I am I'. It means that *bhāva* is a state of the mind superior to *vṛtti*, which happens to give rise to the former, the subjective function of the mind in which the self is known as what mind is not in the final stage of meditation."[49]

The above form of distinguishing a substantial function of mind from its non-substantial, non-causal function known as *bhāva* seems to have provided an improvement over Vijñānabhikṣu's theory of double reflection.

Self-Conscious Being in the Advaita Vedānta

It is stated: "The only direct cognition, in the strict sense, in pure consciousness manifests within each and every individual as the luminous self."[50] This has been again repeated by stating that "*Brahman* is manifest in every human being as self-awareness that is direct and intuitive."[51] This is explained below:

> This is immutable consciousness (*kūṭastha*) ever present as the witness self (*sākṣī*). It illumines the mental states: pleasure, pain, hope, fear, knowledge, ignorance, love, hate, memory, loss of memory and so forth. The mental states are immediately cognized because of their presence to witness self. It is the immediacy of self-awareness that makes an object immediately known. To be directly cognized, an object must be allied with luminous self. Knowledge is direct, i.e. perceptual, when the object is known directly. The immutable consciousness that the witness self is, being reflected in the mind and apparently limited by it, appears as the ego, the empirical self, which functions as the percipient (*pramātā*). So the percipient is inseparable from the witness self, its basis.[52]

The above description of immutable consciousness, self-

---

[49] Ram, K., 1995, op. cit., p. 125.

[50] Swami Satprakashananda, 2001, op. cit., p. 90.

[51] Ibid., p. 91.

[52] Ibid.

awareness (self-consciousness) refers to individual self (*jīvātman*). We are treating individual self as a self-conscious being.

However, there is a difference regarding the *jīva* (individual self) between the two post-Śaṅkara Advaita schools: the Vivaraṇa and the Bhāmatī. The former defines the *jīva* as a reflection of *Brahman* (i.e. pure consciousness), whereas the latter refers to *jīva* as *Brahman* limited by ignorance. The view of Vivaraṇa is known as *Pratibimbavāda*. It is also referred to as *cidābhāsa*, whereas the view of Bhāmatī is known as *Avacchedavāda* (theory of limitation). Both the views are stated below.

Vivaraṇa School of Vedānta

The individual self has been defined as the reflection of *Brahman* (pure consciousness) due to the organ of egoity acting as a limited adjunct (*upādhi*).[53] Further, a distinction is added by the fact that the individual self in dreamless sleep is particularized by nescience (ignorance) in general.

The following commentary on the *Vivaraṇaprameya Saṁgraha* XXXII is worth stating:

> The self – although in reality is nothing else, but pure consciousness and of an altogether non-objective character – insofar as reflected in the organ of Egoity superimposed upon it (the Self) becomes capable of relating itself to that sphere of thought and speech which is connoted by the word "I", and thus presenting itself to consciousness as fused with organ of Egoity – which is superimposed upon the Self in the "I", consciousness – itself is thought and spoken of, in a derived or metaphorical sense, as the object of this "I" consciousness. It is in this way that the superimposition of the "I" on the Self shows itself to be possible.[54]

---

[53] Thibaut, G., 1994, *The Vivaraṇapramēya Saṁgraha* of *Vidyāraṇya*, verse xxxi, p. 136.

[54] Ibid., xxxii, p. 140.

It may, however, be stated that consciousness as reflected in finite *ajñāna* (ignorance) and identified with mind is the empirical self, the ego, *jīva-caitanya*, the doer of actions and experiencer of their fruits (*kartā-bhoktā*). This functions as the cognizer (*pramātā*). Being subject to *ajñāna*, it ascribes to itself various psychical and physical conditions. It is also called *cidābhāsa* (the reflected self).[55]

Bhāmatī School of Vedānta

According to the Bhāmatī school, the self as pure consciousness is in conformity with scripture, traditional codes, epics and *Purāṇas*. It is by nature pure, conscious and liberated. The reality of self consists in its uncontradictable self-luminosity. The very nature of self happens to be as consciousness. The reality is not anything different from that.[56]

When the self as conscious gets united with the complex of gross and subtle bodies and the organs, it acquires the power to act and enjoy.

> Though self manifest, yet by intermixture with the objects like intellect, etc., it somehow becomes the object of the concept "I", the substrate of "I"ness and is (variously) designated *Jīva*, creature (*jantu*) or the knower of the field (*kṣetrajña*).[57]

The *jīva* is, however, not different from the self as consciousness. Yet, it is made by the concept "I" and for empirical usage it is treated as the agent and enjoyer. It has been further explained that "the *jīva* becomes an object if there is superimposition and he becomes an object".[58] This is mainly because the process of becoming is beginningless like the seed and the sprout. In this argument, there is no self-contradictory circularity involved because each subsequent superimposition takes for its object the

[55] Swami Satprakashananda, 2001, op. cit., p. 83.

[56] Sastri, S.S.S. and C.K. Raja, 1992, *Bhāmatī of Vācaspati*, p. 23.

[57] Ibid., p. 41.

[58] Ibid.

previous superimposition and its impressions they have left.[59] It may, however, be stated that *jīva* is not an object, as non-different from the self as consciousness. Yet, it becomes an object because of its conditioned form.[60] In the context of *jīva* as an object of the ego notion, the following observation may be worth noting:

> The Bhāmatī explains the ego-notion as figurative, using the form "somehow". The effect of this is to weaken the force of the words in Śrī Śaṅkara's commentary. "But it (the self) is not altogether a non-object, since it is the object of ego-notion". This passage in Śrī Śaṅkara's commentary is an answer to the objection "How could an object be superimposed on something that is not an object?" One should only say of the Self, he replies, that it is not the object of the notion "you": it is not right to say that it is not an object in any sense whatever. For here the words of the commentary accept that the self is the object of notion "I". Note also that the opponent is not here made to raise the difficulty of how the Self could be a knowing subject having the notion of "I" for its object – nor is anything said by the exponent of the finally accepted view to dispel this difficulty.[61]

However, the inner self appears to be delimited by the mind and other organs. This works as both an object and a subject at the same time. As a result, the *jīva* performs the action and enjoys its experiences. This is supported by twofold ignorance as the effect and cause, the substratum of the ego sense.[62]

Relation between the Absolute and the Individual Self

According to Vācaspati Miśra, relation between the Absolute and individual self is stated below:

59 Sastri, S.S.S. and C.K. Raja, 1992, op. cit., p. 41.

60 Ibid.

61 Alston, A.J., 1997, *The Method of the Vedānta of Swami Satchidanandendra*, p. 591.

62 Sastri, S.S.S. and C.K. Raja, 1992, op. cit., p. 59.

> The universal consciousness, which is the object (*viṣaya*) of nescience, is *Īśvara*, and the same consciousness, which is the abode (*āśraya*) of nescience is an empirical self. He admits many nesciences, which abide in many *jīva*s. Many individual souls are the abodes of many individual nesciences (*tulā-vidyā*). But one *Īśvara* is the object of all nesciences. The world appearances differ in different individual souls because of their different nesciences. An individual soul itself is conditioned or limited by its nescience is the material cause of its world appearance.[63]

This limitation (*avaccheda*) concept of the individual soul may be supported by Madhusūdana Sarasvatī's approach in defining the *jīva*. He has adopted a twofold approach:

1. Image consciousness (*bimba-caitanya*) concealed by ignorance is *Īśvara* and consciousness as counter-image (*pratibimba*) in ignorance is *jīva*, or
2. pure consciousness not concealed (*anupahita*) by ignorance is *Īśvara* and the consciousness concealed by ignorance is *jīva*.[64]

Jīva being delimited by the internal organ, it becomes a knower of limited objects which come into contact with the internal organ through the eyes, etc. As a result, *jīva* becomes the experiencer of many things.[65]

However, there is difference between Madhusūdana Sarasvatī and Vācaspati: The former believes in *Ekajīvavāda* (one soul in all human beings), whereas the latter has proposed *Anekajīvavāda* (many individual souls). In order to justify one soul in all human beings, it is stated:

> Since all the respective differences can be explained on the

---

[63] Sinha, J., 1971, *A History of Indian Philosophy*, vol III, p. 221.

[64] Timalsina, S., 2006, *Seeing and Appearance*, pp. 127-28.

[65] Swami, Gambhirananda, 2007, *Bhagavad-Gītā* of Madhusudane Sarasvati p. 509.

> basis of differences themselves of internal organs, which are the repositories of happiness, sorrow, etc., therefore, there is no valid proof of the multiplicity of the self, which is changeless and illuminator of all, because it permeates everything through its nature as Existence and Self-effulgence.[66]

It may, however, be mentioned that the individual self (i.e. *jīvātman*) is also known as the witness self. In this conext, the witness consciousness explained is as follows.

Witness Consciousness

It has been observed that the witnessing consciousness does not perform any action and hence it is not an enjoyer or a sufferer. In that, it is mainly a disinterested onlooker.[67] This witnessing approach has been adopted mainly to show that, "witnessing consciousness witnesses not merely what the individual does in his waking state but also dream state and also the dreamless sleep. The consciousness that is aware of the 'blank' of dreamless, cannot be ordinary experience of objects. Witnessing consciousness which cannot go to sleep, is there to 'know' the state of sleep."[68]

The above observations resemble the deep-sleep experience of the Advaita Vedānta. In the deep sleep, pure consciousness persists, as a result when one wakes up from sleep one immediately remembers that, "I slept well and I do know anything". This shows that remembering of the sleep experience becomes possible mainly because of the persistence of pure consciousness in deep sleep.

It may, however, be stated that the *ālaya-vijñāna* of Yogācāra has been referred to as the soul in disguise and compared with the *Ātman* of the Advaita Vedānta. There are substantial

---

66 Swami, Gambhirananda, 2007, op. cit., p. 87.

67 Bhattacharyya, S. 2004, "Phenomenology and Indian Philosophy", p. 70.

68 Ibid., p. 71.

differences between the two. Yet, on point of ego there is an agreement. It has been observed that the *ālaya* represents a stage where the sense of ego has not arisen.

> The closest parallel to this conception in the Brāhmanical systems is that of the *sakṣī* in Advaita Vedānta. The *sākṣī* is pure consciousness as covered by indeterminate ignorance (*avidyāvacchinna*) and is sharply distinguished from the empirical subject (*pramātā*). Consciousness has not yet been individualized by mind (*antaḥkaraṇa*).[69]

Pure consciousness has been used as witness consciousness in the Advaita Vedānta. This happens to be the knower of three states of consciousness: deep sleep, dream and waking. However, there is no difference between the *Ātman* and *sākṣī* (witness) according to Śaṅkarācārya. It may be stated that later on a distinction between the two has been made.

Dharmarāja Adhvarīndra in the *Vedānta-Paribhāṣā* has made a distinction between the *Ātman* and *sākṣī*. Pure consciousness (eternal consciousness) is referred to as the *Ātman*. When it is limited by the mind (*antaḥkaraṇa*), it becomes, the *jīva* (individual self). But when pure consciousness has the mind as its limiting adjunct (*upādhi*), it becomes the *sākṣī* (witness consciousness). In the case of *jīva*, the mind is a qualifying attribute (*viśeṣaṇa*). Whereas in the case of *sākṣī*, the mind is a limiting adjunct (*upādhi*).[70]

However, the Vedānta has recognized two orders of Reality: the transcendental and the empirical; the former is the Absolute and the latter is the relative. It may be noted that from the empirical plane being the experience of duality, the absolute reality of non-dual may be difficult to know. Yet, it is not beyond experience, as is evident from the following observation:

---

[69] Chatterjee, A.K., 1999, *The Yogācāra Idealism*, p. 97.

[70] Swami Madhavananda, 2000, *Vedānta Paribhāṣā of Dharmarāja Adhvarīndra*, pp. 37-38.

> Being the Reality and the source of all phenomena, it is not an entity beyond experience. It is the inner self (*pratyak-ātman*) of all, the eternal Subject. It is self-cognized within phenomena; that is, it is intuitively cognized, directly and immediately, as the Pure Witness Self (*sākṣī*) within by all beings. It is the Ground and Source of all objective experience, internal or external, on the phenomenal plane, just as one is aware of one's eyes without seeing them, for they enable one to see all things. This is the noumenal point of view. All phenomena are revealed by, and get their validity from the Self, which is Pure Witness Subject in all.[71]

The pure witness subject is nothing but pure consciousness which one may get by abstracting from empirical consciousness all the limitations like mind and matter. In that, it becomes mindless and bodiless (i.e. removing involvement of consciousness in material things) consciousness.[72] This pure consciousness is treated as the Absolute Reality, which in turn is referred to as the *Brahman* or the *Ātman* in Advaita Vedānta. It may be explained by taking the instance of an individual human being who never exists a moment without thinking about his plan of work in the mind to actualize it. In fact, every human being searches constantly "for the new avenues of self-expression, so that one can actualize for oneself the self content of happiness. By extension of the farthest limit, what is true for the individual is also true for the Absolute Reality."[73]

The existence of consciousness lies in the never-ending functional states of its manifestation. In every functional state, it attains a new form. It takes numerous forms. In fact, it is stated:

> There is no actual state in which consciousness is functionless. Unmanifest consciousness, as reality behind all the functional states, is only a verticalized version, or an abstraction. When

---

71 Swami Mukhyananda, 2006, *Sri Shankaracharya*, pp. 49-50.

72 Woodroffe, J., 2001, *The World as Power*, p. 303.

73 Swami Muni Narayana Prasad, 2009a, *The Taittirīya Upaniṣad*, p. 137.

the same is seen horizontally it appears as the manifest world. What is called creation here is only the process by which the vertical or abstract Reality becomes horizontalized and attains a manifest form. It is nothing other than the unfoldment of the endless creative urge inherent in the Self or Consciousness.[74]

[74] Swami Muni Narayana Prasad, 2009a, op. cit., p. 138.

2

Nature and Process of Thought

Introduction

THOUGHT, being the form of mental activity, is directly related to human thinking.[1]

> Thought includes everything which can exist for us. Sensations, feelings, the whole universe, indeed, so far as it is known belong to thought. From this point of view, thought has no antithesis, but is all-inclusive.[2]

It has also been assured that "thought exists only in relation to a conscious and abiding subject. Apart from this relation, it is an unreal abstraction."[3] It is further stated that "consciousness is the absolute condition of all thought; it seems as if a discussion of consciousness were a necessary preliminary to the theory of thought. This seeming, however, is misleading."[4] This is mainly because of the following reason:

> Since consciousness is an accompaniment of all mental states, it is easy to think that it is a distinct element by itself. This is logical illusion. The spatial figures also in which we speak of consciousness lead to the fancy that consciousness is something which contains other mental states, or which furnishes the stage for their operations. But in fact consciousness is so simple, homogeneous mental state, antecedent to objects, or apart from objects; it arises only in connection with particular

---

[1] Bowne, B.P., 1897, *The Theory of Thought and Knowledge*, p. 8.

[2] Ibid., p. 9.

[3] Ibid., p. 30.

[4] Ibid., p. 19.

> objects and in nothing by itself. When consciousness is empty of object there is nothing left.[5]

The consciousness as nothingness does seem to the lack of reality. This is evident from the following observation:

> consciousness has nothing substantial, it is pure "appearance" in the sense that it exists only to the degree to which it appears. But it is precisely because consciousness is pure appearance, because it is total emptiness (since the entire world is outside it) – it is because of this identity of appearance and existence within it that, it can be conscious as the absolute.[6]

It may, further, be stated that consciousness is completely empty, but is, "fully transparent, just as a mirror, having no content of its own, reflects the objects that come before it, so also consciousness being itself Nothingness, reveals the other objects and is confronted with them".[7] However, the consciousness as nothingness is treated by Sartre as freedom. This is stated below:

> Freedom is precisely the nothingness which is *made-to-be* at the heart of man and which forces human reality to make itself instead of *to be*. As we have seen, for human reality to be is to choose oneself; nothing comes to it either from the outside or from within which it can *receive or accept*. Without any help whatever, it is entirely abandoned to the intolerable necessity of making itself be – down to the slightest detail. Thus, freedom not a being; it is *the being* of man – i.e. his nothingness of being.[8]

It is stated that the unity of the mental subject is the main condition ,of thought. This may be the unity and identity of the thinking self.[9] As mentioned in the Introduction that

---

[5] Bowne, B.P., 1897, op. cit., p. 19.

[6] Sartre, J.-P., 1984, *Being and Nothingness*, p. 17.

[7] Roy, K., 2013, *Subjectivity in Science*, p. 124.

[8] Sartre, J.-P., 1984, op. cit., pp. 568-69.

[9] Bowne, B.P., 1897, op. cit., p. 20.

thinking self includes both subject and object of thought. In that, thinking itself becomes unity. In this context it may be stated that the feelings are experienced, "as the part of a single, unified, conscious field. Consciousness of the normal non-pathological kind comes to us with a unified structure. Kant called this unity of the conscious field the transcendental unity of apperception."[10] This transcendental apperception is known as the transcendental unity of self-consciousness.[11] It may be noted that self-consciousness happens to be *jīvātman* (self) according to Vedānta school of Indian philosophy.

However, the most important is the distinction between what is in sense and what is in thought. "Physical objects live and move and have their being mainly in a world of rational conceptions, which can be entered only for thought."[12] This thought is objectively valid. Whereas, "we see a special order of mental activity which works over sense data into rational forms. From this point of view, thought might be defined as process whereby the mind works over the raw material of the sensibility into the forms of intelligence."[13] This mental activity is known as thought process[14] which happens to be the subjective aspect of thought.

Nature of Thought in Advaita Vedānta

According to Vedānta, thought is the apparent objectification of consciousness.[15] "I think means, I am conscious of thoughts."[16] This shows that thought occurs in human experience. Each

---

10 Searle, J.R., 2004, *Mind: A Brief Introduction*, p. 95.

11 Hoffe, O., 2010, *Kant's Critique of Pure Reason*, p. 156.

12 Bowne, B.P., 1897, op. cit., p. 11.

13 Ibid.

14 Ibid., p. 17.

15 Levy, J., 2004, *The Nature of Man According to the Vedanta*, p. 29.

16 Ibid., p. 71.

thought constitutes an object of consciousness.

It is, however, observed that thought being mental activity, it is treated as a concrete thought. Whereas thought by the causal body of Vedānta is known as an abstract thought.[17] The concrete thought is explained below:

> When a man thinks of a concrete object – a book, house, landscape, etc. – he builds a tiny image of the object in the matter of his mental body. This image floats in the upper part of that body, usually in front of the face of the man, and at about the level of the eyes. It remains there as long as the man is contemplating the object, and usually for a little time afterwards, the length of life depending upon the intensity and the clearness of the thought. The form is quite objective and can be seen by another person possessed of mental sight. If a man thinks of another person he creates a tiny portrait in just the same way.[18]

The abstract thought deals with relation of things having forms and qualities. This is evident from the following observation:

> Wherever we have things with forms and qualities to consider and these things are related to one another in some definite manner, there comes in abstract thought to define the relations between them. All scientific generalizations and laws, all philosophical systems, all principles are concerned with defining the relations of things or ideas to one another and come within the domain of abstract thought. The concrete and abstract are thus inseparable although they are entirely different in nature. They are intertwined in the field of the intellect as the warp and woof in a fabric.[19]

However, according to Bhagavan Ramana Maharshi, the mind is nothing other than the I thought. The mind and the ego are one and the same. In fact, the mind is nothing but only thought.

---

[17] Taimni, I.K., 1998b, *Self-Culture in the Light of the Ancient Wisdom*, p. 110.

[18] Powell, A.E., 2000b, *The Astral Body*, p. 45.

[19] Taimni, I.K., 1998b, op. cit., p. 111.

This is explained below:

(i) Arranging thoughts in the order of value, the I-thought is the all-important thought. Personality-idea or thought is also the root or the stem of all other thoughts, since each idea or thought arised only someone's thought and is not known to exist independently of the ego. The ego therefore exhibits thought activity.[20]

(ii) This "I" thought is not pure. You are now identifying yourself with the wrong "I", which is the "I" thought. This "I" thought rises and sinks. Whereas the true significance of "I" is beyond both. See to whom the trouble is. It is the "I"-thought, hold it. Then the other thought vanishes.[21]

The Postulates of Empirical Thought in Kant's Philosophy

The postulates of empirical thought, corresponding to the categories of modalities, are stated as follows:

1. That which agrees with the formal conditions of experience (according to perception and conceptions) is possible.
2. That which connects with the material conditions of experience (sensations) is *actual*.
3. That of which the connection with the actual is determined according to universal conditions of experience is *necessary* (exists necessarily).[22]

These principles described as only, explanations of the conceptions of possibility, actuality, and necessity as employed in experience; are really treated as principles by which we decide what is possible, what is actual, and what is necessary. The three conceptions involved do not, according to Kant, enlarge our knowledge of the nature of objects, but only

[20] Ramana Maharshi, 1999, *Absolute Consciousness*, pp. 162-63.

[21] Ibid., p. 163.

[22] Prichard, H.A., 1909, *Kant's Theory of Knowledge*, p. 308. This reference covers the three points of empirical thought.

> express their relation to the faculty of knowledge, i.e. they only concern our ability to apprehend an object whose nature is already determined for us otherwise as at least possible, or as real, or as even necessary.[23]

However, in order to understand the above principles and the proof of them, one must have certain preliminary considerations. These are stated below:

1. The very problem of distinguishing the possible, the actual and the necessary presupposes the existence of distinctions which may prove open to question. It presupposes that something may be possible without being actual and again that something may be actual without being necessary.[24]
2. Kant's mode of approaching the problem assumes that we can begin with a conception of an object, e.g. of a man with six toes, and then ask whether the object of it is possible, whether if possible, it is also actual and whether, if actual, it is also necessary. In other words, it assumes the possibility of separating what is conceived from what is possible, and therefore a fortiori from what is actual and from what is necessary.[25]
3. Kant in speaking of a conception is thinking to use Locke's phraseology, not of a simple conception, such as that of equality or of redness, but a "complex" conception, such as that a centaur or of a triangle in the sense of a three-sided three-angled figure. It is the apprehension of a complex of elements.[26]
4. What is said to be possible, real, or necessary is not the

---

[23] Prichard, H.A., 1909, op. cit., p. 308.

[24] Ibid., p. 309.

[25] Ibid.

[26] Ibid., p. 310.

conception but the corresponding object.[27]

5. Kant distinguishes objective real and fictitious conceptions in two ways. He speaks of establishing the objective reality of a conception as consisting in establishing the possibility of a corresponding object, implying therefore that a fictitious conception is a conception of which the corresponding object is not known to be possible. Again, he describes as fictitious new conceptions of substances, powers and interactions, which we might form from the material offered to us by perception without borrowing from experience itself.[28]

It is now possible to state more precisely that the postulates of empirical thought are applied to the three epistemic levels.

> The postulates add to the concept of a thing (of something real) of which they otherwise say nothing, the cognitive faculty from which it springs and in which it has its seat (B. 286). They indicate the manner in which the concept of things is connected with the faculty of knowledge in general (B. 287).[29]

The postulates are briefly stated as follows:

i. With respect to possibility the criterion of non-contradiction is not sufficient. As far as the governing perspective of empirical employment is concerned, it is not enough to know that something can be thought without formal contradiction. For we must also be able to construct the relevant object such as a geometrical figure (B. 267b). The object must, therefore, satisfy not merely the formal conditions of thought, but also those of sensible intuition. If this, and only this, doubtful condition is fulfilled, then we know we have to do with (empirically or really)

---

27 Prichard, H.A., 1909, op. cit., p. 310

28 Ibid.

29 Hoffe, O., 2010, op. cit., p. 221.

possible objects.[30]

ii. It is only sensation or perception which discloses actuality, which teaches us that something is really present. Significant natural phenomena such as magnetism, electricity or gravitation cannot of course themselves be directly perceived. But from the perception of attracted iron filings we can infer the existence of a magnetic matter pervading all bodies (B. 273).[31]

iii. If the connection of our perceptions is determined in accordance with universal conditions of experience (B. 266), then the connection in question must be regarded as necessary. Kant does not claim that the contingent relations of the actual world or the laws of nature which underlie them are necessary. The third postulate has nothing to do with a formal, logical or semantic modality, with an absolute necessity according to which something must be the case in all possible conceivable worlds. With respect to the empirical employment of the understanding, we are again solely connected with the epistemological and methodological necessity that is expressed in two a priori laws of nature, "nothing happens through blind chance" and "no necessity in nature is blind, but always a conditioned and therefore intelligible necessity" (B. 280).[32]

It has been further observed:

> Thought is the act of referring a given intuition to an object. If the mode of this intuition is unknown to us, the object is merely transcendental and the conception of the understanding is employed only transcendentally, that is, to produce unity in the thought of a manifold in general. Now a pure category in which all conditions of sensuous intuition

---

[30] Hoffe, O., 2010, op. cit., p. 221.

[31] Ibid., pp. 221-22.

[32] Ibid., p. 222.

> as the only intuition we possess – are abstracted, does not determine an object, but merely expresses the thought of an object in general, according to different modes. Now, to employ a conception, the function of judgement is required, by which an object is subsumed under the conception, consequently at least the formal condition, under which something can be given in intuition.[33]

It may, however, be stated that the subjectivity and the objectivity of thought are inseparable. This is stated below:

> Kant's insight that the subjectivity of thought (and that of intuition as well) is indispensable to objectivity namely the unity of subjectivity and objectivity overcomes Cartesian dualism with its two worlds of subjective thought (*res cogitans*) and objective, spatially extended things (*res extensae*).[34]

Thought in Sir William Hamilton's Philosophy

According to Hamilton, there are two faculties: Sense or external perception and self-consciousness or internal perception. Through self-consciousness we apprehend what occurs in the internal world or world of thought.[35] It is stated:

> If I try to conceive myself existent without a thought – without some form of consciousness – I am unable. This or that thought may not be perhaps necessary; but of some thought it is necessary that I should be conscious, otherwise I can no longer conceive myself to be. A suspension of thought is thus a suspension of my intellectual existence: I am, therefore, essentially a thinking – a conscious being; and my true character is that of an intelligence – an intelligence served by organs. ... But this thought, this consciousness, is possible only in, and through, the consciousness of Self. The Self, the I, is recognized in every act of intelligence, as the subject to which that act belongs. It is I that perceive I that Imagine. I

---

33 Kant, I., 1950, *The Critique of Pure Reason*, p. 185.

34 Hoffe, O., 2010, op. cit., p. 161.

35 Bart, W.H., 1995, *Philosphy of Knowledge*, vol. I, p. 53.

> that remember.[36]

However, identifying being with thought does seem to be appropriate for the obvious reason that thought becomes the object of self-consciousness of human being, as mentioned above. This may be reassured by the observation of Thomous Reid. It is stated:

> I am not thought, I am not action, I am not feeling: I am something, "that thinks, and acts and feels". The self or I is permanent, and has the same relation to all the succeeding thoughts, acts, and feelings which I call mine.[37]

Laws of Thought

The supreme law of thought is called the principle of contradiction or more correctly the principle of non-contradiction.[38] In this context, it may be noted that according to Kant, "my thought contains no self-contradiction".[39] This shows that the law of contradiction does not apply to thought. It is, however, stated:

> Existence is the highest category or condition of thought. ... All thought we are conscious of an act or modification of self, we are conscious of only as subjective existent. All thought, therefore, implies the thought of existence; and this is the varitable exposition of the enthymeme of Descartes – *cogito, ergo sum*. I cannot think that I think, without thinking that I exist – I cannot be conscious, without being conscious that I am. Let existence, then, be laid down as necessary form of thought, As a secondary or subjective condition of thought, I postulate that of Time. This likewise cannot be denied me. ... Existence and Time being categories of all thought.[40]

---

[36] Bart, W.H., 1995, op. cit., p. 166.

[37] Bowne, B.P., 1897, op. cit., p. 27.

[38] Bart, W.H., 1995, op. cit., vol. II, p. 368.

[39] Kant, I., 1950, op. cit., p. 168.

[40] Bart, W.H., 1995, op. cit., vol. II, pp. 398-99.

Now the question is: is there a need to postulate Existence and Time as conditions for thought. According to Vedānta, the entire universe including existence of Time and Space are embodied in human beings because they are self-consciousness. All the conditions of thought and thought in itself become the object of self-consciousness of human being. In fact, thought arises mainly due to response of memory which is also embodied mainly in human being. That apart, the other fact is that Hegel has also denied the laws of thought.[41]

Hegel's Denial of Laws of Thought

The laws of thought are denied by Hegel on the following grounds:

i. Laws of thought have no meaning apart from the reality with which thought is necessarily concerned; laws of thought are laws of "thinking", and thinking is both form and content.[42]

ii. Observation gives each law an absolute being of its own, as if it were detached from the unity of self-consciousness, whereas this unity is the fundamental principle of each and all the laws, which only exist in and by a single process of that unity. Hence a type of logic, confined to "observing" laws of thought, is necessarily untrue.[43]

Thought and Being in Hegel's Philosophy

According to Hegel, Being and thought are identical. This is explained below:

> In general, in virtue of the principle that as expressed it before, substance is implicity and in itself subject, all content makes its reflection into itself in its own special way. The subsistence

---

41 Bowne, B.P., 1897, op. cit., p. 31.

42 Hegel, G.W.F., 2002, *The Phenomenology of Mind*, vol. I, p. 195.

43 Ibid.

> or substance of anything that exists is its self-identity; for its want of identity, or oneness with itself, would be its dissolution. But self-identity is pure abstraction; and this is just thinking. When I say Quality, I state simple determinateness; by means of its quality one existence is distinguished from another or is an "existence"; it is for itself, something on its own account, or subsists with itself because of this simple characteristic. But by doing so it is essentially Thought; Here we find contained the principle that Being is Thought; here is exercised that insight which usually tends to deviate from the ordinary non-conceptual way of speaking of the identity of thought and being.[44]

This identity of thought and being does not seem to be appropriate mainly because thought happens to be the object of self-consciousness, which is embodied in human beings as mentioned above. In this context, Sartre's observation is worth quoting. He has stated that "if we are to refute solipsism, then my relation to the Other is first and fundamentally a relation of being to being, not of knowledge to knowledge".[45] This means that it does not seem to be logical to establish the identity between thought and Being.

Higher Order Thought

According to Rosenthal, "we are conscious of those states by having thoughts about them. And, because these thoughts are about other mental states, we can call them higher order thoughts (HOTs)."[46] It has been, further, explained in the following observations:

1. HOT would be conscious only when one has a third order thought about it, and we can assume that such third order

[44] Hegel, G.W.F., 2002, op. cit., p. xlvi.

[45] Sartre, J.-P., 1984, op. cit., p. 329.

[46] Rosenthal, 2005, *Consciousness and Mind*, p. 4.

thoughts are rare.[47]

2. The HOT hypothesis explains awareness of the self not perceptually, but by appeal to our having thoughts about the self. ... HOTs are seldom conscious, but when they are, we have a reflective, introspective awareness of the self. HOTs make us conscious not only of our mental states, but also of the self that is in those states.[48]
3. The mental state itself causes that higher order thought to occur.[49]
4. Although discussions of consciousness often make metaphorical appeal to the so-called inner sense, no such sense actually exists.[50]
5. Higher order thought ... allows a ready distinction between a mental state's being introspectively and non-introspectively conscious. Mental states are introspectively conscious if the relevant higher-order thought is itself a conscious thought.[51]
6. The HOT model explains the difference between mental phenomena that are conscious and those which are not. On their own, thoughts, perceptions and feelings are not conscious. Their sometimes being conscious consists in their being accompanied in those cases by suitable HOTs about them. By "suitable", I mean that whenever the HOT is conscious, it seems spontaneous, and therefore, unmediated. Those HOTs make us conscious of our conscious thoughts, feelings and perceptions, though

---

47 Rosenthal, 2005, op. cit., p. 8.

48 Ibid., p. 16.

49 Ibid., p. 25.

50 Ibid., p. 43.

51 Ibid., p. 130.

typically the HOTs are not themselves conscious.[52]

7. The only other way we are conscious of things is having thoughts about them as being present. So, that must be how we are aware of conscious states: a state is conscious if one has a HOT about that state. We seem to be conscious of our conscious states in a direct unmediated way. We can capture that intuitive immediacy by stipulating that HOTs seem to one to rely on no inference of which one is conscious. We are seldom aware of any such HOTs. But we can explain that by supposing that is rare that HOTs are accompanied by third order thoughts, and hence rare that HOTs are, themselves, conscious.[53]
8. The atomistic character of this model, however, may seem to prevent it from being able to explain our sense of the unity of consciousness. If each conscious state owes its consciousness to a distinct HOT, how could we come to have a sense of such unity? Why would all our conscious states seem belong to a single, unified self?[54]
9. In the case of unity, Rosenthal has discussed Kant's concept of transcendental unity of self-consciousness (B. 132). In this context, it is observed that it is unclear how any such transcendental posit could explain the appearance of conscious mental unity, since that appearance is itself an empirical occurrence.[55]
10. Kant's observation about the dispersed character of empirical consciousness suggests that no empirical account can help to explain such actual unity.[56]

---

52 Rosenthal, 2005, op. cit., p. 273.

53 Ibid., p. 297.

54 Ibid., pp. 297-98.

55 Ibid., p. 298.

56 Ibid.

11. The HOT model suffices to explain such unity … we can regard the thought as in effect characterizing that referent as the individual who thinks that very thought. Each first-person thought thus disposes us to have another thought that identifies the self as the thinker of that first-person thought. … Every HOT characterizes the self it refers to solely as the bearer of target states and, in effect, as the thinker of the HOT itself. Nothing in that characterization implies that this bearer is the same from one HOT to the next. But there is also nothing to distinguish one bearer from another. And our seeming to be aware in a direct and unmediated way of the self each HOT refers to tilt things towards apparent unity. Since we seem to be directly aware of the self in each case, it seems subjectively as thought there is a single self to which all one's HOT refer, a single bearer for all conscious states. … This helps explain why our sense of unity seems to go hand in hand with our ability to engage in introspective consciousness. … Introspective consciousness results in a sense of one's conscious states as all unified in a single conscious subject. … One cannot find a self when one seeks it perceptually. The HOT model, by contrast, provides an informative explanation of the way we do seem to be introspectively conscious of the self.[57]

Critical Assessment

It is, indeed, difficult to understand how HOT can explain the introspective consciousness? This is mainly because thought happens to be the object of self consciousness of human being. This has been already mentioned briefly in the Introduction. Here we are presenting the complete version as follows:

> The actual thought that results is always in terms of the senses, no matter how abstract that thought may be or by what intuition it may have been arrived at. As an example, man is

[57] Rosenthal, 2005, op. cit., pp. 299-301.

> used in the title of this book to denote the characteristics of the human state. But no sooner is the word apprehended than some kind of visual representation appears, however, vaguely, before the mind's eye. Similarly, all abstract notions, whether they refer to qualities, numbers, relations or concepts, require the support of some object of sensory perception, even if it be only a symbol such as cipher or a sound. Abstract thoughts and generalizations are, therefore, the objects of consciousness. As such they are quite distinct from introversion.[58]

The above observations may be reassured in the sense that thought is the objective side of consciousness, whereas the self of human being is known as self-consciousness which happens to be the subjective side of consciousness. Therefore, it may be said that even HOT cannot appropriately explain introspective consciousness.

According to Sartre, consciousness can be the source of consciousness.[59] If this view is accepted, introspective consciousness can be explained either by access consciousness or self-consciousness.

Thought Process and Atom

According to Rosenthal, HOTs have also the atomistic character. Its implication is quite important for both: thought process and the atom. This is explained below:

> When an atom makes a transition, or a "jump" from one stationery state to another, the actual process cannot be visualized or imagined. There is no intermediate stages. We cannot breakdown into its components. The entire process of transition from one state to another is a non-visualizable, unanalyzable, unity. It is indivisible. Its parts cannot even be imagined. It is a "quantum jump" as we call it. The interesting thing is that there is an analogous situation for thought

[58] Levy, J., 2004, op. cit., p. 29.

[59] Sartre, J.-P., 2012, *The Transcendence of the Ego*, p. 15.

processes. As we "think" – in any sequence of thoughts – there is always, a sudden, discontinuous jump from one thought to the next. We are not aware at all of any intermediate stages. If we were so aware, no thinking would be possible. There would be an almost infinite sequence of "sub-thoughts" between two thoughts, like an infinity of points between the two ends of a line. *Quantum jumps for thought appear to be as much a necessity for the conscious self as these are for the atom.*[60]

Vaiśeṣika's Atomic Theory of Indian Philosophy

In the Vaiśeṣika's atomic theory, atoms are imperceptible. "Each kind of atom has got distinct individuality. The atoms of Kaṇāda are primarily at rest. They are distinguished from souls. Both atoms and souls are co-eternal."[61] This atomic theory according to Radhakrishnan, has been formulated, "on purely metaphysical grounds and tried through it to simplify the world to thought".[62]

The Atomic Theory

In the development of a thing from the atomic up to the highest organic state, there are four states: (i) atoms, (ii) molecules, (iii) inorganic compounds, and (iv) organic compounds. In this context, the following observations are worth noting:

> At the outset we must understand that this question is not purely mechanical but chemical, biological, psychological and ethical as well, for at every step in the life of an atom a new factor comes into play. At first it is purely mechanical or dynamical, viz. vibration. Then comes the influence of heat which at once destroys the primary qualities of the atom and develops secondary qualities. By this heat one is to understand physical heat – the action of the Tej atom.

[60] Kothari, D.S., 2002, "Atom and Self", p. 298.

[61] Panda, N.C., 2008, *Māyā in Physics*, p. 7.

[62] Radhakrishnan, S., 2002, *Indian Philosophy*, vol. II, p. 194.

Table 2.1: The Process of Eleven Moments

Stage	*Moment*	*Changes Occurred*
Chemical action: gradually	1st moment	Atomic change starting with the disintegration of the binary molecule.
increasing the heat of Tej atom	2nd moment	Loosening of the molecular cohesion in a compound substance.
	3rd moment	Dissolution of the molecule.
	4th moment	Disappearance of molecular qualities, e.g. colour, etc. (Molecular colour, for instance, after the decomposition of the molecule cannot produce any photographic action; similarly the molecular sap cannot stimulate our nerve of taste or touch.)
Beginning of atomic action	5th moment	The production of another quality. The atom is now in its original naked state, hence its original quality manifests itself.
	6th moment	Arrest of atomic reaction. Here the atomic action has reached, so to speak, its lowest ebb.
	7th moment	Now comes the guidance of conscious soul or spirit. After resting for a period of an infinitesimal fraction of a moment atomic activity resumes its course.
Spiritual guidance	8th moment	Its character changes; the result of the contact of spirit with matter is mind and life, which now for the first time comes into line. In the case of man germ and sperm-cell come into line with mind and soul. In the case of vegetable seed a crude sensitiveness is developed together with the power of assimilating all the nutritive elements derived from the soil, the air and the light. In the case of inorganic substances a kind of energy arises which not only keeps all the particles together, but also accumulates fresh particles of a similar nature and thus the substance grows in

Cont.

Stage	*Moment*	*Changes Occurred*
		volume or in height. The entering of this factor displaces the atoms. The whole group feels the pulsation of life, seeks more space, moves about, and thus becomes separated from its old surroundings. Along with the separation it is conjoined with a new position. It links itself to a new substance and in this way binary molecule is again produced.
	9th moment	Manifestation of atomic quality in the new binary molecules. The properties of the atoms now reappear under a new form in the developed compound substance. The physiology, for instance, with its nervous system and sensorium has now been formed. The senses, which are developed from the atoms, now respond to the stimuli of heat, light, taste, smell and touch. A stable compound substance has now been formed. Our expectation is that after developing this fully matured form the process will stop. As a matter of fact atomic forces, life, mind and soul now stand in proper relation to each other – but other forces are at work, of which may be mentioned (a) the past moral history of the soul, (b) cosmic disturbances, (c) disharmony between the inner series of mind, life and body. Hence a 10th stage may arise.
Cosmic action	10th moment	Immediately *after* the cessation of former process a new force may follow or come into play, or, *before* the completion of the 9th stage a new force may arise and change the direction or modify the grouping.
	11th moment	New division in the component whole may be caused leading to the formation of several new, independent parts.

Source: Sri Ānanda Ācārya, 1985, *Tattvajñānam or the Quest of Cosmic Consciousness*, 1985, pp. 52-54.

> When the atom passes the stage of pure chemical action it comes under the influence of life – in other words what was atom becomes an organic substance informed with life. This "life" then comes under the direction of mind, and mind, again develops according to moral law. But life and mind do not grow out of atom; it is the influence of the conscious soul that brings life and mind in line with the molecular aggregate.[63]

The Eleven Moments Theory

Thus, we see that "at each step there is a change in the very nature of the substance, a change which we may say amounts to metamorphosis. This process is so rapid that we can only follow it with our mind. The stages we have noticed here can be understood on the analogy of the growth of the germ-plasm under the influence of body–heart or of a seed under the influence of solar heat. In the language of Vaiśeṣika doctors this process is called 'the process of eleven moments'."[64] It is given in the following statement.

> One thing should be noticed here, viz. the self-renewing power of the substance at every moment. It is the nature of all activity to renew itself at every moment.[65]

Functions of Different Atoms

The functions of different atoms as mentioned in Table 2.1 are explained briefly below:

> This explanation, which is called Eleven Moments Theory, help us to picture how intimately the chemical, physical, nervous and ethical properties displayed by things are bound up with the activity of their constituent atoms. We understand how the inherent instability of binary molecules prevents things from being permanent; they transform under heat and

[63] Sri Ananda Acharya, 1985, *Tattvajñānam*, p. 51.

[64] Ibid., pp. 51-52.

[65] Ibid., p. 54.

> revert to a less and less unstable state. In this act of change a ray is shot out from the atom; it loses its structure and its parts; the succeeding atom is of a totally different complexion from its predecessor.[66]

Thought Process in Buddhist Philosophy

As mentioned earlier that thought process is subjecture. This has been explained quite meticulously in the Theravāda school of Buddhist philosophy. One moment of matter is equivalent to seventeen moments of mind. This is a description of the short duration of the material life faculty.[67] It is further observed that "the lifespan of a *citta* is termed in the *Abhidhamma,* a mind-moment (*cittakkhaṇa*). This is a temporal unit of such brief duration that, according to commentators, in the time that it takes for lightning to flash or the eyes to blink billions of mind-moments can elapse."[68] However, out of seventeen moments of mind, first three moments are known as *bhavaṅga* – mind which becomes the source of thought.

The *bhavaṅga citta* is the theory of life-constituent mind propounded by Theravāda Buddhist philosophy. It is meant "the cause, reason, indispensable condition, of our being regarded subjectively as continuous; the *sine qua* of our existence, that without which one cannot subsist or exist".[69] In *bhavaṅga* state, the mind is vacant, as has been the case of dreamless sleep. This state is known as *vithi-mutta* (thoughtless or thought free). Such existence is termed *bhavaṅga* (being). However, thought and being are not identical in the Buddhist philosophy. This is explained as follows:

> Being, which is *vithi-mutta,* is opposed to thought, which *vithi-citta.* Though there is thus a contrariety, yet there is

66 Sri Ananda Acharya, 1985, op. cit., p. 54.

67 Collins, S., 1982, *Selfless Persons*, pp. 241-42.

68 Bhikkhu Bodhi, B., 1999, *A Comprehensive Manual of Abhidhamma*, p. 156.

69 Aung, S.Z., 1979, *Compendium of Philosphy*, pp. 265-66.

> a similarity between the two, in that both are subjective.[70] However, "*Bhavaṅga* denotes a functional state (or moment) of subconsciousness. As such it is the subconsciousness state of mind – below the threshold of consciousness – by which we conceive continuous subjective existence as possible."[71] It may, therefore, be inferred that the consciousness does not stop during dreamless sleep. The state of subconsciousness flows on without interruption. The continuity of *bhavaṅga citta* is arrested when "an active cognitive process ensures for the purpose of cognizing the object".[72]

When an object is presented through sense-doors to consciousness, *vithi citta* (processed consciousness) arrested "a series of discrete cognitive events leads one to the other in a regular and uniform order. This order is called *citta niyām,* the fixed order of consciousness."[73] In order to have complete perception of the objects, consciousness has to pass through seventeen moments of mind. It may be stated that one moment of matter seems to have seventeen moments of mind. These seventeen conscious moments are given below:

1. *Atīta bhavaṅga* (past subconsciousness)
2. *Bhavaṅga calana* (disturbance of subconsciousness)
3. *Bhavaṅga upaccheda* (subconsciousness – cut-off)
4. *Pañca-dvārāvajjana* (advertence through the five sense doors)
5. *Pañca-viññāṇa* (consciousness through one of the five senses)
6. *Sampaṭicchana* (reception)
7. *Santīraṇa* (examination)

---

[70] Aung, S.Z., 1979, op. cit., p. 9.

[71] Ibid., p. 266.

[72] Bhikkhu Bodhi, 1999, op. cit., p. 123.

[73] Ibid., p. 151.

8. *Voṭṭhapana* (determining)

9-15. *Javana* (impulsions)

16-17. *Tadrammaṇa* (registering)

The above series has been divided in the following four categories:

i. Moments starting from one to three represent the initial entry of perceptual object into the subject's awareness.[74]

ii. Moments four to eight represent a gradually increasing attention to object in which its particular nature and qualities are recognized.[75]

iii. Moments nine to fifteen represent the full cognition of the object.[76]

iv. Moments sixteen to seventeen represent a registering of the perception as whole. These two moments are the transition from perception of the short memory progressing further to storage in the long-term memory.[77]

The lifespan of a *citta* is termed in the *Abhidhamma* – a mind-moment (*cittakkhaṇa*). This is evident from the following observation:

> This is a temporal unit of such brief duration that, according to the commentators, in the time that it takes for lightning to flash or the eyes to blink, billions of mind moments can elapse. Nevertheless, though seemingly infinitesimal, each mind moment in turn consists of three sub-moments – arising (*uppāda*), presence (*thiti*), and dissolution (*bhaṅga*). Within, the breadth of a mind moment, a *citta* arises, performs its momentary function, and then dissolves, conditioning the next *citta* in immediate succession. Thus, through the sequence

---

[74] Collins, S., 1982, op. cit., p. 242.

[75] Ibid.

[76] Ibid.

[77] Ibid., p. 243.

> of mind moments, the flow of consciousness continues uninterrupted like the waters in a stream.[78]

However, Ācārya Ānanda (author of the *Mūla-Ṭīkā* to the *Abhidhamma-piṭaka*) has rejected the sub-moment of presence in relation to mental phenomena on the basis of Citta-Yamaka chapter of the *Yamaka,* which speaks only of the arising moment and dissolution moment of consciousness, but not of a presence moment. This was not accepted by Ācārya Anurudha, author of a comprehensive manual of *Abhidhamma* on which the above observation is based. In this context, the following observation of Ledi Sayadaw is worth stating:

> Ledi Sayadaw regards the moment of presence as the midpoint between the two phases of arising and falling (*udaya-vaya*), just as, when a stone is thrown upwards, a moment is needed before it starts falling downwards.[79]

It is further stated:

> Many commentators take the presence moment to be implied by the Buddha's statement: there are three conditioned characteristics of the conditioned; arising, passing away, and the alternation of that which stands (A-3:47/:152). Here the presence moment is identified with the alternation of that which stands (*thitassa aññathatta*).[80]

Bhavaṅga Citta and Transcendental Ego

Out of above seventeen moments, the first moment is known as subconsciousness (process-freed consciousness) and remaining the sixteen moments are processed consciousness.

> "This processed consciousness appears to have subconsciousness or *bhavaṅga* as its origin. *Bhavaṅga* is that from which all thought processes emerge when necessary conditions are present. And

[78] Bhikkhu Bodhi, 1999, op. cit., p. 156.

[79] Ibid.

[80] Ibid.

> for this reason, Buddhaghoṣa regards subconsciousness as the condition of active consciousness."[81]

In this sense subconsciousness is compared with the transcendental ego, which according to Husserl:

> "... is the origin of conscious acts. Thus, subconsciousness may be viewed as a functional substitute for the transcendental ego as well as the substantial self (*Ātman*) in Buddhist thought."[82]

However, the Buddhist would not accept the view that subconsciousness is a self in disguise. The self or ego is not liable to change, but subconsciousness changes every moment.[83]

Order of Thought (Citta-Niyāma) in Buddhist Philosophy

This is explained as:

> There are two elements in every consciousness. The Constant and Variable. *Vithi* is, figuratively speaking, the road along with the mind travels by marked, well-defined, permanent stages (*thanā*'s). The fixity and constancy of these stages give rise to the Order of Thought (*citta-niyāma*), which corresponds to Mansel's Form of Consciousness. The form of consciousness, the constant element, is opposed to the matter of consciousness which, as supplied in this or that experience, constitutes the variable element; but it must be borne in mind that is Buddhism, both subject and object are variable at every moment. With Mansel, who holds that the subject is the constant element, there is only one form. But in Buddhism there are several forms of consciousness, each of which will be designated as a process of thought, whenever it takes place as fact.[84]
>
> We have said that time is the *sine qua non* of the succession of mental states. To every separate state of consciousness

[81] Medhidhammaporn, P., 1995, *Sartre's Existentialism and Early Buddhism*, p. 143.

[82] Ibid.

[83] Ibid.

[84] Aung, S.Z., 1979, op. cit., p. 25.

(*cittuppāda*), which takes part in a process of thought as a functional state, either in the subjective form of the stream of being, which we have described as free from process (*vithi-mutta*), or in the objecture form of a conscious act of mind or thought, which we shall describe a process consciousness (*vithi-cittā*), there are three phases – genesis (*uppāda*), development (*thiti*) and dissolution (*bhaṅga*). Each of these phases occupies an infinitesimal duration of time – an instant (*khaṇa*) – so that to every separate state of consciousness, there are three instants, in which successively it becomes, exists, and disappears. These three instants – nascent, static, and ceosant (or arrested) – together form the mental moment (*citta kkhaṇa*), the period occupied by any single state of consciousness, or any separate act of mind or thought. And it pleases commentators to say that there are more than one billion of such thought moments in the time that would be occupied by that shortest flash of lightning.[85]

Vedāntic Interpretation of Constant and Variable's Aspects of Every Consciousness

In the above observations, the constant and the variable aspects of every consciousness seem to have been treated as two different entities. This is because the constant aspect is treated just as opposite to the variable aspect of every consciousness. Such interpretation does not seem to be appropriate; for it creates duality in consciousness, whereas the fact is that consciousness itself is unity, but its functions are many. It ought to be recognized that different functions of consciousness are merely the manifestations of consciousness of itself. In this pathway of manifestations or reflections, the functions of consciousness and consciousness itself are merely two different phases of the one and the same consciousness.

In the earlier interpretation the concept of *vitta-mutta* is

[85] Aung, S.Z., 1979, op. cit., pp. 25-26.

treated as constant. If this concept is taken into thought episode, it becomes the pre-thought stage. When this *vitta-mutta* reflects, it becomes the *vitta-citta,* resulting into the operational aspect of thought. It may be noted that in this approach the *vitta-mutta* and the *vitta-citta* are not different but both are merely the two successive stages: One necessitates the other. In other words, both are one and the same thing. This is mainly because the latter, i.e. *vitta-citta,* is nothing but merely the manifestation of the former, i.e. *vitta-mutta.*

3

Thought, Memory and Time

Introduction

THOUGHT is response to the memory according to the Vedānta philosophy.[1] In the Nyāya dualist tradition, memory requires the contact between the self and the inner sense. This happens to be the causal condition of all cognitions. "So when memory is said to arise from the disposition alone, what is meant is that memory is not dependent on anything, but disposition as specific (*viśeṣa*) causal condition."[2] In fact, memory is treated as reproductive cognition or productive experience (*anubhava*).[3]

According to the Buddhist philosophy, memory indicates "a habitual and cultivated sense of awareness of what is going on within the body and mind".[4] This may be compared with the Vaiśeṣika conception of memory. It is the presence of residual impressions (*saṁskāra*).[5] In fact, the continuity of human beings takes place through *karma* (action) and its *saṁskāra* (disposition). The former leaves its impression in the mind, which is referred to as *saṁskāra.* This is the Vedāntic interpretation.

Thought and time are also discussed in this chapter. This is mainly because the source of thought is consciousness, which

---

[1] Levy, J., 2004, *The Nature of Man According to the Vedānta,* p. 72.

[2] Chakrabarti, K.K., 2001, *Classical Indian Philosophy of Mind,* p. 35.

[3] Ibid.

[4] Haldar, A., 2001, *Some Psychological Aspects of Early Buddhist Philosophy Based on Abhidharmakoṣa of Vasubandhu,* p. 86.

[5] Kapani, L., 2013, *The Philosophical Concept of Saṁskāras,* p. 77.

itself is temporal in the manifestation for knowing the certain things. The temporality of consciousness will be explained later.

Saṁskāra (Disposition) and Consciousness

In the dependent origination (*pratītyasamutpāda*), *saṁskāra* is the second link, which happens to be the cause of consciousness. In this context, it is observed:

> The thoughts and impressions of former lives become crystallized or remain in a miniature form within the inner personality of the dying man. We may ask what sort of consciousness the baby has while in the mother's womb, before it becomes self-conscious? Now we can imagine that a child becomes self-conscious sometime after it is born, but what is the form of consciousness in the foetus and in the new-born baby – between the period of its entrance into mother's womb and drawing of self-consciousness? It can not be asserted that the mind of the foetus was a mere blank, a vacuum, for then, in the absence of mind, there would be nothing to preserve the body and guide the formative process in such a way to cause it to resemble that of a human being. Hence it must be concluded that the mind of the foetus was in a subconscious state in which all the accumulated forces of the past lives were busy in the darkness of the sub-world, building up the future man. *Saṁskāra* is this life process developing into self-consciousness. If there were no *saṁskāra*, there would not arise self-consciousness. Thus *saṁskāra* is the unconditional antecedent of consciousness.[6]

It may, however, be further stated:

> I can remember only what I have known. I remember not only my thoughts. I remember also my having thought. It follows that I, as thinker or individual, am the object of consciousness, but as the knower of this and of all other objects, it follows that I am consciousness itself.[7]

---

[6] Ānanda Ācārya, Sri, 1985, *Tattvajñānam*, pp. 299-300.

[7] Levy, J., 2004, op. cit., p. 78.

This shows that the thinker happens to be an object of self-consciousness.

Memory and Consciousness

According to Sir William Hamilton, without memory our mental states cannot be compared or distinguished from each other and referred to self. This is explained below:

> The notion of the ego or self arises from the recognized permanence and identity of the thinking subject in contrast to the recognized succession and variety of its modifications. But this recognition is possible only through memory. The notion of self is, therefore, the result of memory. But the notion of self is involved in consciousness, so consequently is memory![8]

However, memory is immediate knowledge of the past. But in philosophical propriety, "it is not a knowledge of the past at all, but a knowledge of the present and a belief of the past. But in whatever terms we may choose to designate the contents of memory, it is manifest that these contents are all within the sphere of consciousness."[9] It may also be stated that "the hypothesis which postulates consciousness without memory, violates the fundamental laws of our intellectual being".[10]

According to Vedānta, the relationship between memory and consciousness is explained as follows:

> Since the objects of consciousness appear discontinuously; and since, moreover, the conscious subject, made objective in the form of the claiming I-thought, also appears discontinuously, the consciousness that illuminates them seems to be discontinuous too. When non-dual consciousness seems in this way to be conditioned by time, it seems to assume the form of a faculty of remembering that gives cohesion to what would otherwise be a state of total flux unimaginable

8 Bart, W.H., 1995, *Philosophy of Knowledge*, vol. I, p. 205.

9 Ibid., p. 221.

10 Ibid., p. 369.

> and impossible because it could not be known by a knower who by his having no continuity, must perforce change at every perception: he could not even know himself. *Memory and the consciousness of individual existence are therefore synonymous.*[11] (Emphasis added by italics.)

Memory in Buddhist Philosophy

Memory has been captured by Diṅnāga through the self-cognition theory by asserting that a state of consciousness must have two appearances: object appearance and cognition appearance. This is explained below:

> If this twofold appearance of a cognitive state is not admitted then it would be difficult to explain, according to Diṅnāga, the recollection of a past cognitive state. Recollection is caused by the memory impression of a previous experience. But we see that we collect not only the object of previous experience but also our previous experience itself. Unless this twofold appearance was present in our previous experience, we could not have recollection of the two in this manner. Diṅnāga argued that this proves further that each cognition is self-cognized. For, unless a cognition is self-cognized, it can never be recollected. The Naiyāyikas hold that a cognition is not self-cognized, but cognized by another piece of cognition. According to Diṅnāga, this theory leads to an infinite regress because to make recollection possible the second piece of cognition must be cognized by a third piece of cognition and so on ad infinitum. Thus, Diṅnāga established that there is a self-cognition aspect in each state of consciousness, where both the apprehensible and apprehension are revealed.[12]

Memory in the Vaiśeṣika's philosophy

For the Vaiśeṣika's, memory is dealt in two ways: (i) a particular

---

[11] Levy, J., 2004, op. cit., p. 79.

[12] Matilal, B.K., 1997, *Logic, Language and Reality*, p. 243.

conjunction between *ātman* and *manas*, and (ii) residual impressions. Both are explained below:

> Memory takes place through the contact (*saṁyoga*) *between ātman* (soul) and *manas* (mind).[13] This is the non-combinative cause or contingguity such as reflection or mediation or reinterpretation.[14]
>
> The efficient cause of memory is residual impressions (*saṁskāra*s) and experience. This forms the real contact of memory. "Memory is that knowledge which is produced by *saṁskāra*s only, deposited in the *ātman* by a direct or new experience (*anubhava*) in the past".[15]

The observation that *saṁskāra*s are deposited in the *ātman* does not seem to be correct. This is mainly because *ātman* being pure consciousness nothing can be deposited in it. One may experience *ātman* by purification of his self-consciousness, which is the most difficult task. The fact, however, is that *saṁskāra*s get deposited in *jīvātman* of human being, who has mind.

Memory in the Nayāya Philosophy

Memory plays as important role in cognition of the Nyāya philosophy. Gautama has provided a larger number of causes of memory. These causes, as commented by Vātsyāyana, are stated below:

i. Attention (*praṇidhāna*), the fixing of the mind, with a desire to recollect something.
ii. Association (*nibandha*) or connection of different experiences that suggest of one another. It also may include the fixing of things in the plexus of the body through *yoga*.[16]

---

[13] Kapani, L., 2013, op. cit., p. 76.

[14] Safaya, R., 1976, *Indian Psychology*, p. 176.

[15] Kapani, L., 2013, op. cit., p. 77.

[16] Safaya, R., 1976, op. cit., p. 157; *Nyāya Bhāṣya* III.2.44. The explanation is based on Vātsyāyana's commentary.

iii. Repetition (*abhyāsa*), securing persistence for the previous impressions.

iv. Sign (*liṅga*) which leads the mind to the thing signified, e.g. recollecting fire after seeing sun.

v. Characteristic mark (*lakṣaṇa*) that recalls the class to which the object belongs.

vi. Similarity (*sādṛṣya*) that associates the ideas of similar objects. Likeness of a picture of a lady may remind us of a particular lady.

vii. Possession (*parigraha*), suggesting the owner of the thing owned. The servant reminds us of the master.

viii. The relationship between refuge and refugee (*āśraya–āśrita sambandha*). The pupil reminds us of the teacher and vice versa.

ix. Immediate sequence or contiguity (*anantaryya*). The preceding act reminds us of the succeeding.

x. Separation (*viyoga*), which reminds us of which is separated.

xi. Identity of function or co-profession (*ekākaryya*). One teacher reminds us of another teacher.

xii. Enmity (*virodha*) of two rivals, one reminds us of another. Rāvaṇa reminds us to Rāma.

xiii. Excess (*atiśaya*), which reminds us of tḥat which has produced the excess or superiority.

xiv. Acquistion (*prāpti*), which frequently reminds us of its source.

xv. Intervention (*vyavadhāna*) or cover: The sheath recalls the sword.

xvi. Pleasure and pain (*sukha–duḥkha*).

xvii. Desire and aversion (*icchā–dveṣa*).

xviii. Fear (*bhaya*).

xix. Need (*arthitva*), reminding one of what a person needs, in terms of food and clothing.

xx. Action (*kriyā*) which suggests the agent. The chariot maker is recalled by the chariot.

xxi. Affection (*rāga*). One frequently remembers the person one loves.

xxii. Merit (*dharma*). It reminds one of the merits attained in the previous birth, and it enables one to retain what one reads and hears.

xxiii. Demerit (*adharma*). It reminds a person the causes of suffering in the past.[17]

The recollections are not possible simultaneously. All these several causes are not cognized at the same time.

The Concept of Saṁskāra of Sāṁkhya–Yoga

Saṁskāra is defined as follows:

> *Saṁskāra* is a subconscious or subliminal (*sūkṣmarūpa*) continuation of what was once a conscious activity (*vyāpāra*), whether cognitive, affective or conative. A conscious activity when gone through does not absolutely end there. It simply passes into a potential and hidden (*avyakta* and *sūkṣma*) condition below the threshold of consciousness. It goes on ad infinitum more and more below the level of the ordinary consciousness. This for pragmatic reasons lights up only between certain limits. Stimuli and brain excitements of certain degrees of intensity only evoke response. But the activities do not leave when pragmatic consciousness fails to notice them. They go on. ... Thus, the course of any activity (*vyāpāra*) in mental life displays itself when above the threshold of consciousness as conscious activity and when it sinks below the threshold it is called *saṁskāra* or tendency or potential due

[17] These twenty-three causes are taken from Safaya, R., 1976, op. cit., pp. 157-58.

to unconscious mental operations.[18]

In *Sāṁkhya-Kārikā* 52 it is stated:

> Without the (subjective) dispositions, there would be no (objective) evolution of the *tanmātras*; and without the objective, there would be no subjective. Therefore, there proceeds a twofold evolution, known as the objective and the subjective.[19]

This shows that in the subjective evolution, the dispositions (*vāsanās*) are inherent; and it influences the perception in the phenomenal world. This has been clarified in the commentary of *Yogasūtras* IV.6 of Patañjali. It states:

> The "natural mind" is the product of evolutionary growth and is the repository of the *saṁskāra*s of all the experiences which it has throughout during the course of successive lives. These *saṁskāra*s in their totality are referred to as *karmāśaya* the vehicle of *karmas*.[20]

It is thus evident that the concepts of *saṁskāra* and *vṛtti* are introduced in perception by Patañjali, the author of *Yogasūtras*. *Vṛtti* is derived from the root *vṛt* which means to exist. This is explained below:

> So *vṛtti* is a way of existing. In considering the ways in which a thing exists, we may consider its modifications, states, activities or its functions. All these connotations are present in the meaning of *vṛtti* but in the present context, this word is best translated by the words modifications or functionings. ... Since *citta* has a functional existence and comes into being only when consciousness is affected by matter, the word functionings perhaps expresses to the maximum degree the significance of *vṛtti* in the present context.[21]

---

[18] Woodroffe, J., 2001, *The World as Power*, p. 105.

[19] Swami Virupakshananda, 2003, *Sāṁkhyakārikā of Īśvarakṛṣṇa*, pp. 107-08.

[20] Taimni, I.K., 1999, *The Science of Yoga*, p. 391.

[21] Ibid., p. 8.

Vṛttis are fivefold: right knowledge (*pramāṇa*), wrong knowledge (*viparyaya*), fancy (*vikalpa*), sleep (*nidrā*) and memory (*smṛti*). Right knowledge and wrong knowledge are those images which are formed by the direct contact through the sense organs with the objects, whereas *vikalpa* and *smṛti* comprise all those images which are formed without any direct contact with the objects. However, in the dream state, there is no control over such images, but is mostly influenced by the desires present in the subconscious mind.[22]

It may, however, be stated that the moment consciousness comes in contact with matter, it starts exerting human life. Thereafter *saṁskāra*s (dispositions) begin to form. As evolution progresses, dispositions become more complicated due to desires and actions. These actions leave some kind of impression, which restricts us in some way later. "Our desires produce potential energy which draws us irresistibly to the environment or conditions in which they can be satisfied."[23] Our thoughts also produce *saṁskāras*.[24]

In fact, the doctrine of *saṁskāra* is directly related to the law of *karma*. This may be seen from the following observation:

> The subconscious impressions can be traced to the residual *karma* of the past lives which accompanies *jīva* from birth to birth in two forms: (1) the individual tendencies, propensities, interests and urges called *vāsanā*, and (2) the merit and demerit of the past actions. These accompany the soul after death, remain in seed form and bear fruit in the coming life in accordance with the law of *karma*. The *vāsanā* propels him to act in a particular direction, and merit and demerit (*dharma–adharma*) fructify at proper occasions causing pleasant or unpleasant incidents of life. The seat of the *Saṁskāras* according

---

22 Taimni, I.K., 1999, op. cit., p. 14.

23 Ibid., p. 394.

24 Ibid., p. 395.

to Yoga is *karmāśaya*.[25]

However, there seems to be cyclic causation between *saṁskāra* and *vṛtti*. The former causes the latter, which in turn leaves some impressions to be accumulated in the previous *saṁskāras*.[26]

In the *vṛtti* theory, the mind gets modified according to the impression created by the object. In such a situation, the mind at times obscures consciousness.[27] Therefore, it may not be possible, "to obtain a true impression of the object as long as the mind itself is not free from its *vṛtti*s. The impression created will depend upon the condition of the receiving mind and as all minds are in different conditions because they have followed different paths in their evolution, they must get different impressions from the same object."[28] It may be noted that mind becomes one with object only in *samādhi* when all the *vṛtti*s are suppressed.

According to Sāṁkhya, "a *saṁskāra* is tendency, while a *vṛtti* is action: both are *vyāpāra* (energizing) of *antaḥkaraṇa*".[29] There is no denying the fact that "an external world actually existing outside along with its objects, but all this comes to be known to us in the forms *antaḥkaraṇa* takes by projecting itself on the same via the senses".[30]

In the above-mentioned *Sāṁkhya-Kārikā* 52, there is a defect of mutual dependence. This problem has been solved by Vācaspati Miśra in the following commentary:

> Experience is not possible without the vehicles of experience in the form of sense organs: and the creation of internal

---

[25] Safaya, R., 1976, op. cit., pp. 276-77.

[26] Ibid., p. 277.

[27] Taimni, I.K., 1999, op. cit., p. 395.

[28] Ibid., p. 411.

[29] Woodroffe, J., 2001, op. cit., p. 121.

[30] Singh, S.P., 2004, *Vedic Vision of Consciousness and Reality*, p. 75.

organs in turn is not possible without the dispositions such as virtue and the rest. Nor discriminating wisdom, which brings about the emancipation, is possible without both of these evolutions. Thus is established the appropriateness of both forms of evolution (viz. subjective evolution proceeding from the *buddhi* and the objective evolution proceeding from the *tanmātras*). The defect of *mutual dependence* (*anyonyāśraya doṣa*) does not affect this theory, because the creation being eternal, it would be like the analogy of the seed and the sprout (*bījāṅkura-nyāya*, which is a maxim involving an eternal series of seed and sprout. As the seed produces the sprout, so the latter in turn reproduces the former. Each, therefore, is a cause and effect.) The production of subjective and objective evolutions even at the very beginning of the present cycle (*kalpa*) is due to the subliminal impressions left behind by the corresponding subjective and objective evolutions in the earlier cycle: thus, this theory of the emanations of the evolutions is quite appropriate and is accepted by all.[31]

Advaita Vedānta Theory of Saṁskāra (Disposition)

According to Vedānta, each cognition lasts as long as the corresponding mental mode lasts. "When the mode disappears it leaves an impression (*saṁskāra*) on the mind. The memory of cognition is due to this. A cognitive mode does not require any other cognitive mode for its manifestation, so it is said to be self-manifest."[32] In fact, the cumulative effect of *saṁskāras* determines an individual's course of life here and hereafter, indicating thereby the continuity of human beings. It may be stated that the subtle impressions (*saṁskāras*) left "by *karma* on the mind of doer that cling to him whatever he may be, here or beyond, and fructify in due course. As a man sows, so does he reap".[33]

While commenting on the basis of *Chāndogya Upaniṣad*

---

[31] Swami Virupakshananda, 2003, op. cit., pp. 108-09.

[32] Swami Satprakashananda, 2001a, *Methods of Knowledge*, p. 94.

[33] Ibid., p. 210.

V.10.5, it is stated: "In the case of tendencies, there is no total destruction of results of work, and hence there is the possibility for residual results. Since this is so, therefore, it is logical that transmigration becomes possible owing to the results remaining as residues after the enjoyment of (other) results of actions."[34] This shows that human beings perpetuate their rebirth in *saṁsāra* (empirical world) because of the residue of kārmic forces which reside in *antaḥkaraṇa* (mind) as *saṁskāra.* However, the former experience has been explained on the basis of the commentary on *Bṛhadāraṇyaka Upaniṣad* IV.4.2. This passage shows that how every organ gets unified with the subtle body of the dying man. "When the vital force departs, all the organs follow. Then the self has particular consciousness and goes to the body which is related to that consciousness. It is followed by knowledge, work and past experience."[35] The commentary on this verse, summarized below, is worth noting:

> As a matter of fact, everybody has at that moment a consciousness which consists of impressions in the form of particular modifications of his mind (regarding the next life). ... It has been stated that departing self, loaded with materials, goes making noises like a cart. (This load consists of) the impressions of experiences regarding the results of past actions. These impressions take part in initiating fresh actions as also in bringing past actions to fruition; hence they too accompany. Without these impressions no action can be done, nor any results of past actions be achieved, for the organs are not skilful in unpractised work. But when the organs are promoted to work by the impressions of past experience, they can easily attain skill even without practice in this life. It is frequently observed that some are clever in certain kinds of work, such as painting, from their very birth, even without practice in this life, while others are unskilful even in some very easy tasks. ... Hence,

---

[34] Swami Gambhirananda, 2003, *Chāndogya Upaniṣad* V.10.5, p. 366.

[35] Swami Madhavananda, 1997, *The Bṛhadāraṇyaka Upaniṣad with Commentary of Śaṅkarācārya* IV.IV.3, p. 489.

> these three – knowledge, work and past experience – are the food on the way to the next world, corresponding to the load of the carter. Since these three are the means of attaining another body and enjoying (the results of one's past work), therefore one should cultivate only the good forms of them, so that one may have a desirable body and desirable enjoyments. This is the purport of the whole passage. ... Therefore, the impressions called past experience, under the control of person's knowledge and work, stretch out, like a leech, from the body, retaining their seat in the heart, as in the dream state, and build another body in accordance with his past work; they leave their seat, the old body, when a new body is made.[36]

The Epistemology of Recollection (Smṛti)

According to Mahādevānanda, a follower of Śaṅkara, founder of the Advaita Vedānta, recollection is produced by a residual impression (*saṁskāra*) alone. True recollection accords with a real object perceived in the past.[37] However, the Vedānta adds the identity of the self also for the purpose of recollection. This is explained below:

> Recollection presupposes the identity of the self, that perceived an object in the past, that retained its residual impression, that revives the impression, and that remembers it as present. Recollection is produced by a residual impression (*saṁskāra*) of a past perception. All schools of Indian philosophers are unanimous in this view. The past perception, the residual impression, and the present recollection abide in the same substratum. Then only recollection can be adequately accounted for.[38]

However, the internal organ (*antaḥkaraṇa*) has four aspects: *manas*, *buddhi*, *citta* and ego. It is *citta*, which works as storehouse of residual impression. This is explained below.

---

[36] Swami Madhavananda, 1997, op. cit., IV.IV.2, pp. 491-93.

[37] Sinha, J.N., 2008, *Indian Psychology*, vol. III, p. 170.

[38] Ibid., p. 172.

CITTA

Citta is treated as the modification of the inner organ which remembers.[39] It is the storehouse of all the past impressions, tendencies, instincts, hereditary, traits and *saṁskāras* (impressions).[40] In the commentary on *Muṇḍaka Upaniṣad* III.1.9, it is, however, stated that "reflecting mind (*citta*) thus has *cetanā* behind it, energizing it to reflect and this *cetanā* in its turn is inter-woven by the fivefold *prāṇas*. The reflecting faculty left behind *citta* becomes as purified *cetanā*."[41] The *cetanā* is consciousness.

Memory in Sir William Hamilton Bart's Philosophy

Memory is treated as the conservative faculty by Bart. But, "without a power of acquisition, a power conservation could not be exerted; and without the latter, the former would be frustrated, for we should lose as fast we acquired."[42] However, the fact is that, "memory principally and properly denotes the power of the mind possesses of retaining hold of the knowledge it has required, is generally admitted by philosophers".[43]

It is observed that the knowledge which we acquired is retained in and by the mind. This in a way establishes the fact of memory.[44] The knowledge that we have acquired by perception and self-consciousness does continue to endure in the mind until it gets annihilated by other causes. This is explained below:

> This would in fact be the case, where the mind merely is passive in the impression it receives: for it is a universal law of nature, that every effect endures as long as it is not modified

[39] Swami Nikhilananda, 1997, *Vedānta Sara of Sadānanda*, verse 68, p. 46.

[40] Safaya, 1976, op. cit., p. 223.

[41] Swami Muni Narayana Prasad, 1998, *Muṇḍaka Upaniṣad*, p. 108.

[42] Bart, W.H., 1995, op. cit., vol. II, p. 205.

[43] Ibid., pp. 206-07.

[44] Ibid., p. 210.

> or opposed by any other effect. But the mental activity, the act of knowledge, of which I now speak, is more than this: it is an energy of the self-active power of a subject one and indivisible; consequently a part of the ego must be detached or annihilated, if a cognition once existent be again extinguished. Hence it is, that the problem most difficult of solution is not, how a mental activity endures, but how it ever vanishes ... our internal activities in a ceaseless vicissitude of manifestation and disappearance. This apparent contradiction, therefore, demands a solution.[45]

The solution to the above problem has been provided in "the theory of obscure or latent modifications (that is, mental activities, real but beyond the sphere of consciousness)".[46] However, "the disappearance of internal energies from the view of internal perception does not warrant the conclusion that they no longer exist for we are not always conscious of all the mental energies, whose existence cannot be disallowed".[47] In this context, the following observation is worth stating:

> We take note of our memory only in its influence on our consciousness: and, in general; do not consider that the immense proportion of our intellectual possessions consists of our delitescent cognitions. All the cognitions which we possess or have possessed, still remain to us – the whole complement of all our knowledge still lies in our memory; but as new acquisitions are continually pressing in upon the old, and continually taking place along with them among the modifications of the ego, the old cognitions, unless from time to time refreshed and brought forward, are driven back, and become gradually fainter and more obscure. This obscuration, is not, however, to be conceived as an obliteration, and as a total annihilation.[48]

---

45 Bart, W.H., 1995, op. cit., vol. 2, pp. 211-12.

46 Ibid., p. 212.

47 Ibid., pp. 212-13.

48 Ibid., p. 213.

It may, however, be noted that all mental activities, all acts of knowledge which persist, we never lose them but become obscure. "The obscure cognition may exist simply out of consciousness, so that it can be recalled by a common act of reminiscence."[49]

Pratyabhijñā (Recognition) School of Kashmir Śaivism

In Pratyabhijñā, recognition is defined as:

> Recognition, however, must not be identified either with memory (*smṛti*) or with perceptual cognition (*pratyakṣa-jñāna*). It is, rather, the combination of both. Memory is given rise due to the activation of the subliminal impressions (*saṁskāras*). Although through perception an object may be cognized as well as perceived, but it is never recognized. In the event of recognition what happens is that the mental impression goes invariably along with the direct perception of the object. The uniqueness of recognition lies in the fact that the object that is being cognized is easily identified with the object that has previously been known. Thus, recognition is characterized by an intuitive awareness with regard to the identity of the substance that persists through its two states.[50]

Thought and Time

Thought is temporal because its source consciousness is also temporal according to Sartre. Further, thought operates within time and space. This is evident from the observation that, "one conscious being viewing itself in extension, subjectively as Time, objectively as Space".[51] This in a way indicates that time and space become one because both are embodied in human being according to the Advaita Vedānta school of philosophy.

---

[49] Bart, W.H., 1995, op. cit., vol. II, p. 215.

[50] Pandit, M.L., 2012, *The Philosophical and Practical Aspects of Kāśmīra Śaivism*, p. 78.

[51] Aurobindo, Sri, 2001, *The Life Divine*, p. 144.

Thought as Existence

Thought is treated as existence of human being by Bart. This is explained below:

> Existence is the highest category or condition of thought. … No thought is possible except under this category. All that we perceive or imagine as different from us, we perceive or imagine as objectively existent. All that we are conscious of as an act or modification of self, we are conscious of only as subjectively existent. All thought, therefore, implies the thought of existence; and this is the veritable exposition of the enthymeme of Descartes – *cogito ergo sum*. I cannot think that: I think without thinking that: I exist – I cannot be conscious, without being conscious that I am. Let existence then be laid down as a necessary form of thought.[52]

Thought as Time

Time is postulated as the second category or subjective condition of thought. It is stated:

> This likewise cannot be denied me. It is the necessary condition of every conscious act: thought is only realized to us in succession, and succession is only conceived by us under the concept of time. Existence and existence in time is thus an elementary form of our intelligence.[53]

The above observation may be supported by the following statement:

> Time is primarily a law of thought. Whereby the mind relates events under the form of antecedence and sequence, and thus makes the temporal experience possible. Given the temporal experience, we may by abstraction get the idea of time; but the temporal experience itself is possible only through a peculiar relating of thought.[54]

---

[52] Bart, W.H., 1995, op. cit., vol. II, pp. 398-99.

[53] Ibid., p. 399.

[54] Bowne, B.P., 1897, *Theory of Thought and Knowledge*, p. 66.

Objective Time

Objective time is explained through the past event. This is stated below.

> I am thinking of the past event through my present thought. That is, my present idea or content is intentionally directed to something which is not itself present existentially in my mind. The past event occurred apart from my present thought, this is quite obvious. On the other hand, the event has no meaning for *me*, until it is a content of my consciousness. It is not of course necessary for the existence of the event that I should think about it; that is, my mind or my judgement does not constitute an element in the life of the event itself, it is not sustained by *my* judgement. Yet, it has a meaning for me only inso far as it is actualized in my experience.[55]

Thought as Space

When we think about any events objectively it becomes space. However, according to Kant, space is the form of all phenomena of the external sense is the subjective condition of sensibility.[56] This shows that space is perceived by outer sense. Whereas time is a form of inner sense. Both space and time exist in us (human beings have representation of space and time). This is the reason for treating time and space as one. Time and space are percieved simultaniously.

TEMPORALITY OF CONSCIOUSNESS

According to Sartre, consciousness is temporal.[57] This shows that "temporality is a dimension of human consciousness. He thinks that the being of human reality is itself time".[58] Sartre has

---

[55] Mukerji, A.C., 1957, *Self, Thought and Reality*, p. 104.

[56] Kant, I., 1950, *The Critique of Pure Reatson*, p. 47.

[57] Sartre, J.-P., 1984, *Being and Nothingness*, p. 29.

[58] Bhadra, M.M., 2004, *A Critical Survey of Phenomenology and Existentialism*, p. 362.

defined temporality as follows:

> Subjective process whereby the for-itself continuously lives its project of nihilating the in-itself. Through temporality the for-itself sets up its own measure for the duration and self-identity of things. Time is not in things but flows over them. The for-itself as what it has been (Past), is a flight (Present) toward what it projects to be (Future).[59]

It has been further explained:

> The for-itself endures in the form of a non-thetic consciousness (of) enduring. But I can feel the time which flows; and apprehend myself as a unity of succession. In this case I am conscious of enduring. This consciousness is thetic and strongly resembles a knowledge just as duration which is temporalized under my regard is roughly like an object of knowledge.[60]

It may be noted that without pre-reflective (non-thetic, non-positional) consciousness, the reflective (thetic-positional) consciousness is not possible. In such a situation, "it is agreed then that reflection must be united to that which is reflected-on by a bond of being that the reflective consciousness must be the consciousness reflected-on".[61] This reflected-on is pre-reflective (non-thetic, non-positional) consciousness. However, "the reflected-on, itself, is its past and its future".[62]

Consciousness, Thought and Time

The whole process of thinking is consciousness. In that, thought is consciousness, thought is time. Therefore, "consciousness is treated as the result of time".[63] However, Krishnamurti has

---

[59] Sartre, J.-P., 1984, op. cit., p. 807.

[60] Ibid., p. 211.

[61] Ibid., p. 213.

[62] Ibid., p. 219.

[63] Krishnamurti, 2007, *Choiceless Awareness*, p. 71.

further observed:

i. The thinker and thought are one; without thought, there is no thinker. And when there is no thinker and only thought, then there is an awareness of thinking without thought, and thought comes to an end.[64]

ii. The thought being transient, mutable, can be altered, but thinker who creates thought can be permanent. He is the permanent entity, whereas the thought is changeable, it can be changed according to circumstances, according to environmental influence, but he the thinker remains. He is the thought and if thought ceases he is not, surely, although all our books say differently.[65]

Krishnamurti himself has contradicted his own statement. He has stated that thinker who creates thought and he (thinker) can be permanent. Later on he has made thinker as thought, showing thereby that without the thought there is no thinker. Whereas thinker is permanent and has self-consciousness, when it manifests thought becomes its object. Now the question is that thinker can survive without thought in some circumstances like meditation, whereas thought has no existence at all without thinker. Further, in thinking both thinker and thought are involved.

As regards the observation that consciousness is the result of time does not seem to be conceptually correct. This is mainly because time being an "arrow" moving always onwards, it does not know itself. How then it would create consciousness? It is consciousness which makes the time into past, present and future. In fact, the time happens to be the object of self-consciousness which is embodied in human being.

---

[64] Krishnamurti, J., 2007, op. cit., p. 81.

[65] Krishnamurti, J., 1997, *Reflections on the Self*, p. 174.

4

Thought as the Source of Nature and Quantum Physics

Introduction

THIS chapter attempts to discuss two main issues: (i) thought as the source of nature,[1] and (ii) modern physics' has tendency to undermine the principle of causation.[2] In the quantum theory, causality has been replaced by what is called the principle of indeterminacy.[3]

Thought as the source of nature does not seem to be appropriate in the sense that it becomes the object of self-consciousness, which is embodied in human being known as *jīvātman* (self) according to the Advaita Vedānta school of Indian philosophy. An inference may, therefore, be drawn that it is the self-consciousness rather than thought, which becomes the source of nature. It may be mentioned here that self-consciousness while knowing the objective world, it knows itself. There is no other entity which knows itself.

However, the main feature of the implicate order of quantum physics is that it has extended to the field of consciousness, so as "to comprehend both cosmos and consciousness as a single-unbroken totality of movement".[4] The implicate order in a way to represent ourselves, as the order present to the senses. This

---

[1] Mukerji, A.C., 1957, *Self, Thought and Reality*, p. 214.

[2] Ibid., p. 224

[3] Ibid., p. 225.

[4] Bohm, D., 2012, *Wholeness and the Implicate Order*, p. 219.

is stated below.

> The fact that this order is actually more or less the one appearing to our senses. ... This can be done only when we bring consciousness into our universe of discourse and show that matter in general and consciousness in particular, at least in a certain sense, have this implicate (manifest) order in common.[5]

It also ought to be recognized that matter itself is causality, which is explained as:

> For matter is absolutely nothing but causality. ... Its being is its acting; it is not possible to conceive for it any other being. Only as something acting does it fill space and time; its action on the immediate object (which is itself matter) conditions the perception in which alone it exists. The consequence of the action of every material object on another is known only insofar as the latter now acts on the immediate object in a way different from that in which it acted previously; it consists in this alone. Thus cause and effect are the whole essence and nature of matter. ... Its whole being and essence consist only in the orderly and regular change produced by one part of it in another; consequently, its being and essence are entirely relative.[6]

The Quantum Theory of Physics

It is observed that "the quantum theory is, at present, the most basic way available in physics for understanding the fundamental and universal laws relating to matter and its movement".[7] The world view in which the universe is regarded as a continuous field, but according to the quantum theory the field is discontinuous. This is equally applicable to "particle-like, and that it is as undermined in its actual behaviour as is

---

[5] Bohm D., 2012, op. cit., p. 236.

[6] Cross, S., 2014, *Schopenhauer's Encounter with Indian Thought*, p. 63.

[7] Bohm, D., 2012, op. cit., p. xv.

required in the particle view of relation as whole".[8]

According to the quantum theory, the "movement is in general discontinuous in the sense that action is constituted of *indivisible quanta* (implying also that an electron, for example, can go from one state to another, without passing through any states in between)".[9] However the electron is never separated from a certain quantum field which fundamentally affects it and exhibits certain novel features. "This quantum field satisfies Schrodinger's equation, just as the electromagnetic field satisfies Maxell's equation. It, too, is therefore causality determined."[10] In the causal interpretation, "the electron moves under own energy but the formation is the *form* of the quantum wave directs the energy of electron".[11] This is further, explained below:

i. The electron travels toward a screen containing two slits. Clearly, it can go through only one slit on the other. But the quantum wave can pass through both. On the outgoing side of the slit system, the quantum waves interfere to provide a highly complex quantum potential which does not generally fall off with the distance from the slits. ... In the deep valleys and broad plateaus, the quantum potential changes rapidly. In these regions, there is a strong force on the particle which is deflected, even though there is no classical fares operating. The movement of the electron is, therefore, modified to produce the scattering pattern. In this case the wave-like properties do not arise in any essential duality of the quantum particle but from the complex effects of the potential.[12]

ii. The explanation of the quantum properties of the electron

[8] Bohm, D., 2012, op. cit., p. xv.

[9] Ibid., p. 222.

[10] Bohm, D. and F.D. Peat, 1987, *Science, Order, and Creativity*, p. 88.

[11] Ibid., p. 90.

[12] Ibid., pp. 90-93.

given above emphasized how the *form* of the quantum potential can dominate behaviour. In other words, information contained within quantum potential will determine the outcome of a quantum process.[13]

iii. Consider a radio wave, whose form carries a signal – the voice of an announcer, for example. The energy of the sound that is heard from the radio does not, in fact, come from this wave but from the batteries or power plug. This latter energy is essentially "unformed", but take up its form from the information within the radio wave. This information is *potentially* active everywhere but only *actually* active when its form enters into the electrical energy of the radio.[14]

iv. The analogy with the causal interpretation is clear. The quantum wave carries "information" and is, therefore, *potentially* active everywhere, but it is *actually* active only when and where this energy enters into the energy of the particle. But this implies that an electron, or any other elementary particle, has a complex and subtle inner structure that is at least comparable with that of a radio. Clearly this notion goes against the whole tradition of modern physics, which assumes that as matter is analysed into smaller and smaller parts, its behaviour grows more elementary. By contrast, the casual interpretation suggests that nature may be more subtle and strange than was previously thought.[15]

In quantum theory, however, it is not possible to speak of the particle's trajectory "when we say that the particle is also wave. What we mean is that the wave pattern as a whole is a manifestation of the particle. The picture of travelling waves is

---

[13] Bohm, D. and F.D. Peat, 1987, op. cit., p. 93.

[14] Ibid.

[15] Ibid.

thus totally different from that of travelling particles."[16]

It may further be stated that in quantum theory the atomic phenomena can be described in terms of probabilities. Therefore, it can never be said that atomic particle exists at a certain place nor can it be said that it does not exist. "Being a probability pattern, the particle has tendencies to exist in various places and thus manifests a strange kind of physical reality between existence and non-existence. We cannot, therefore, describe the state of the particle in terms of fixed opposite concepts."[17]

The duality of the particle has been resolved through the probability waves in the sense that the pair of opposites is transcended by the atomic reality.[18] Yet, it is most difficult to accept this transcendental theory of quantum physics.[19] This duality has, however, been reconciled in another way. It is stated:

> A photon, or an electron, has a dual aspect, a wave aspect and a particle aspect. Two aspects are complementary. The one aspect excludes the other aspect. That is why the two aspects are not contradictory. A contradiction between them could arise only if the two aspects could be observed at the same time. But this never happens; and we have compelling theoretical arguments that this could not happen. *The wave and the particle aspects are complementary and not contradictory.*[20] (emphasis added by italics)

It has been further explained that "at the root of the wave-particle duality is the principle of absolute indistinguishability, absolute identity of particles of the same kind. All electrons in the universe are absolutely identical, absolutely indistinguishable

---

[16] Capra, F., 1989, *The Tao of Physics*, p. 165.

[17] Ibid., p. 166.

[18] Ibid.

[19] Ibid., p. 167.

[20] Kothari, D.S., 2002, "Atom and Self", p. 311.

from one another."[21]

In the total wave function, the identity of individual electron is completely lost. There is no separate individuality of electron in the total wave function. This is explained below:

The Concept of One in Many and Many in One

> *The electrons have submerged themselves, as it were in one 'brotherhood' of electrons*. The Many have become One ... when we speak of the total-wave-function or the field, and the many identical particles incorporated in the wave function. It is not sort of an aggregate, a sum of the Many. In an aggregate, the Oneness is no more than an euphemism for the Many that are still visible, may be dimly in the aggregate. The concept of Oneness in quantum mechanics is a totally, fundamentally, new concept. It has no analogy, no parallel, whatever in classical physics or in everyday experience. Common sense fails to be of any aid. The One is an abstract space, the Many in physical space. The two aspects are complementary[22] (emphasis added by italics).

The above concept of One in Many and Many in One, in the case of electron may be supported by the *Avataṁsakasūtra* of Vijñānavāda school of Buddhist philosophy. Although the Sūtra has not been incorporated in the teaching of Vijñānavāda,[23] its teachings of interbeing and interpenetration are very important for unlocking the door of reality and get rid of our notions concerning the world.[24] The main teaching of the *Avataṁsakasūtra* is stated as follows:

> *The one is in the all, and the all is in the one* (emphasis is added by *italics*). One thing contains everything else. In the everything is the one. In our own age, atomic physicists who have looked

[21] Kothari, D.S., 2002, op. cit., p. 313.

[22] Ibid., p. 314.

[23] Hanh, T., 2008, *Understanding Our Mind*, p. 81.

[24] Ibid., p. 83.

> deeply into the molecular world have had to abandon concepts of inside and outside, self and other. They know that one atom is made up of all other atoms. One electron is made up of all other electrons. In a molecule or an atom, we can see the presence of all other molecules and atoms. One atom contains the whole universe. *In one person everything in the universe is present*[25] (emphasis added by italics).

The *Bṛhadāraṇyaka Upaniṣad,* too supports the concept of One in Many and Many in One. It says: "Being an organic product of *Ātman,* everything in the world has got essentially to be of the same nature as *Ātman* with its dual capacity of forming the centre and the periphery of the everything."[26] This is illustrated by means of fifteen examples taken from physical elements, luminaries and certain human values, organizations and creations[27]. "*Ātman* is the controller of all both from inside and outside as are the centre and periphery of the wheel serving as the controller of the spokes."[28] The example of earth is described as follows:

> *As the essence of all and all as the essence of the earth.* This fantastic relativity of things happens to be visualized by the sage particularly in view of the earth and every product of it having envisioned as an abode of one and the same *Ātman.* It is interesting here to note the point of difference in the concept of relativity as mooted out by the Upaniṣad in this instance and as formulated by Albert Einstein. While Einstein's theory of relativity makes out the relativity of things with reference to spatio-temporal measurements, the Upaniṣadic sage goes back to the *Ātman* as the root of everything including time and space. In his view, the earth's capacity to form the essence of everything born on this earth as well as the capacity of

---

25 Hanh, T., 2008, op. cit., pp. 162-63.

26 Singh, S.P., 2004, *Vedic Vision of Consciousness and Reality,* p. 254.

27 Ibid.

28 Ibid., p. 255.

> everything born on this earth to form the essence of the earth, arises from the fact that the earth as well as each one of its products has got embodied in it one and the same *Ātman*[29] (emphasis added by italics).

Similar type of explanation has been given for the other examples such as water, air, sun and moon, as mentioned above.

According to Advaita Vedānta, the self is *caitanya* (consciousness) itself and it shines in its own light: it is called *svayam-prakāśa* (self-shining). This consciousness is not a contingent product of an interaction between the subject and the object.[30] One can, however, experience self-shining or pure consciousness in dreamless sleep in which the dualism of the "I" and "not I" (*aham* and *idam*) vanishes altogether.[31] But it would not be correct to state that in such a state, consciousness ceases to be, because the consciousness according to Vedānta is permanent and eternal.[32] Further, in dreamless sleep, one experiences that "I have slept well", indicating thereby the actual existence of some pleasant experience – a blissful consciousness.[33]

This dreamless consciousness is interpreted as *nirvikalpaka jñāna*. When this consciousness gets differentiated, it becomes *savikalpaka jñāna*.[34] It is thus evident that *one* undifferentiated consciousness (i.e. pure consciousness in dreamless sleep) becomes *Many* as differentiating consciousness (i.e. *savikalpaka jñāna*) in manifestation.

It may be stated that One in Many and Many in One are possible "because the self is consciousness. Consciousness can assume many forms without endangering its non-duality. Even

---

29 Singh, S.P., 2004, op. cit., p. 254.

30 Datta, D.M., 1998, *The Six Ways of Knowing*, p. 42.

31 Ibid., p. 44.

32 Thibaut, G., 1944, *The Vivaraṇaprameya Saṁgraha of Vidyāraṇya*, p. 121.

33 Datta, D.M., 1998, op. cit., p. 44.

34 Ibid.

while being aware of the many, consciousness itself does not cease to be one. Everything is rooted in consciousness. And even after the myriad possible objects are eliminated, consciousness will still remain."[35]

It is important to recognize that in quantum physics, consciousness has a significant role which has no counterpart in classical physics.[36] In this context, it is stated that "to understand the implicate order, Bohm has found it necessary to regard consciousness as an essential feature of the holomovement and to take it accounted explicitly in his theory".[37]

Matter: Wholeness and Implicate Order

Bohm's contribution in developing a new theory of the relation between consciousness and matter in a scientific manner is the most exciting.[38] However, it has been observed that "in a discussion of the 'wave function of the universe', the implicate and generative order of the whole is involved. Out of this whole emerge sub-wholes (including observers), which themselves can be organized into wider contexts, and these in turn are further organized until the total universe is encompassed in this way."[39]

An attempt has recently been made to examine the Bohm's contribution in establishing the relationship between consciousness and matter in a logical framework. This is evident from the following observation:

> Matter as a whole can be understood in terms of the notion that the implicate order is the immediate and primary actuality (while the explicate order can be derived as a particular, distinguished case of the implicate order). ... If

[35] Grimes, J., 1992, *The Naiṣkarmyasiddhi of Sureśvara*, pp. 107-08.

[36] Kothari, D.S., 2002, op. cit., p. 315.

[37] Capra, F., 1989, op. cit., p. 353.

[38] Ibid., p. 352.

[39] Bohm, D. and F.D. Peat, 1987, op. cit., p. 196.

matter and consciousness could in this way be understood together, in terms of the same general notion of order, the way would be opened to comprehending their relationship on the basis of some common ground. Thus, we could come to the germ of a new notion of unbroken wholeness, in which consciousness is no longer to be fundamentally separated from the matter. David Bohm points out that if all actions are in the form of discreet quanta, the interactions between entities (e.g. electrons) constitute a single structure of indivisible links, so that the entire universe has to be thought of as an unbroken whole. ... Eventually, Bohm points out that matter and consciousness are manifestations of "implicate order", which enfolds all that which is. We may remark that this is strikingly similar to the Vedāntic notion, in the light of which a contradiction between mind and body is resolved.[40]

What Is Order

Order has been defined by Bohm in a very broad sense. "Whatever we do presupposes some kind of order."[41] However, order may be experienced in a number of different ways. For instance, "there is the order of number, of points on a line, of space and time, of the movement of a particle through space, and of the functioning of a machine. But order need not be only mechanical or restricted to inanimate systems."[42]

Notions of order depend upon one's ability to perceive similarities and differences in reflections. In fact, the perception begins through the gathering of differences and similarities of the object. For instance, in the case of vision, we gather first, "differences as primary data of vision, which are then used to build of similarities. The order of vision proceeds through the perception of differences and the creation of similarities of these

---

[40] Joshi, M.M., 2006, "Life, Mind and Consciousness", pp. 25-26.

[41] Bohm, D. and F.D. Peat, 1987, op. cit., p. 111.

[42] Ibid.

differences."[43] Similar is the case with the thought process, when we think about some objects, some broad images regarding those objects are formed and then categories are formed through a mental perception of their differences from some general background.

It may be stated: "order is neither subjective nor objective, for when a new context is revealed, then a different notion of order will appear."[44] The concept of order is, however, by itself quite general. "But one of its most fundamental and deepest meanings is that it lies at the root of structure, which is a key issue, not only in science but in life as whole."[45]

Quantum Field Theory and Implicate Order

In the quantum field theory, the implicate order and the causal interpretation are quite simple. It is stated that "instead of taking a particle as the fundamental reality, start with the field. ... The field is continuous and by itself would spread out from any source. However, because the super-quantum potential is non-linear and non-local, it is able under certain conditions, to provide a subtle kind of immediate connection between distant regions of the field."[46]

In the causal interpretation of field theory, there are two implicate orders in a specified relationship.[47] The first implicate order is the field itself. The second implicate order is explained as follows:

> The second implicate order is then obtained by considering the super quantum wave function. This is related to the whole field as the original quantum wave function is related to the

[43] Bohm, D. and F.D. Peat, 1987, op. cit., p. 112.

[44] Ibid., p. 125.

[45] Ibid., p. 141.

[46] Ibid., p. 182.

[47] Ibid.

particle. A more detailed treatment shows that the super quantum wave function also moves in kind of implicate order which is, however, far subtler and more complex than is the first implicate order. This then comprises the second implicate order.[48]

Implicate Order and Generative Order

The relationship between the implicate order and the generative order is very close. The former is the particular case of the latter. However, the implicate forms are generated in an order of unfoldment. In this process, the whole happens to be quite relevant to each part.[49] "If there are higher implicate orders, then a similar generative order will prevail through out all the levels. Ultimately, it is, of course, the holomovement and what may lie beyond, from which all is generated."[50]

The implicate order and the explicate or generative order have been explained by a Buddhist monk and scholar Hanh with a lot more clarity in capturing their subtleties. His explanation is given below:

> The British nuclear physicist David Bohm proposed the terms "Explicate order" and "implicate order" to describe what Buddhist teachings call ordinary and ultimate reality. In the explicate order, everything exists outside of everything else. The elephant exists outside of the rose, the table exists outside of the forest, you exist outside of me, and so on. The explicate order is what we see when we don't look into things very deeply. But, as Bohm discovered, when we look more deeply into the nature of each so-called elementary particle, we see that one particle is made of all other particles. The notions we use in our daily life can no longer be applied in the domain of the infinitely small. In one particle, you can identify the existence of all other particles. Looking deeply into the nature

[48] Bohm, D. and F.D. Peat, 1987, op. cit., pp. 182-83.

[49] Ibid., p. 184.

[50] Ibid.

of a particle reveals to us the implicate order, where everything is inside of everything else.[51]

However, Bohm's concept of implicate order has been compared with the Sāṁkhya–Yoga philosophy. This is stated in the following statements:

> A Bohmian deterministic interpretation which argues for a non-local implicate order that is determinative of the manifest explicate order. Clearly, Sāṁkhya–Yoga is most compatible with a Bohmian interpretation that would argue for an all pervasive (non-local) physicalist (*mūlaprakṛti*) or *citta* that is an unmanifest (*avyakta*) yet determinative implicate order that is constantly supporting or generating the explicate order or in other words the "manifest" (*vyakta*) world of ordinary awareness.[52]

In the context of awareness, the contribution of the Sāṁkhya–Yoga philosophy is something unique. In that, the following observation is the most important:

> In addition to the physicalist intentionalities of awareness (*citta*) which are at the base of both the implicate and explicate orders of the physical world, there is a non-intentional pure contentless consciousness (*Puruṣa*) that provides the warrant not only for quantum observership but for communal communication and the system of life itself. It is essential witness (*sākṣin*) whose simple all-pervasive presence allows everything to be, and like the hologram it is present in its entirety in every self-awareness (hence *Puruṣa bahutva*).[53]

Consciousness and Implicate Order

We have dealt above mainly the material process in terms of the implicate order. "But the consciousness happens to be

---

[51] Hanh, T., 2008, op. cit., p. 82.

[52] Larson, G.J., 2003, "The Anthropic Principle: Life, Cosmos and Consciousness", p. 186.

[53] Ibid., p. 187.

much more of the implicate order than that of matter."[54] It may be stated that the consciousness has been captured by Bohm through the thought process, which is definitely in the implicate order. "The very word implicate, meaning enfolded, suggests that one thought enfolds another and that a train of thought is actually a process of enfoldment of a succession of implications."[55] However, consciousness is organized through a generative order, which is more or less similar to the totality of the generative and implicate order that organizes matter.[56]

In order to know that how consciousness and matter are related, there are two possibilities: (i) "to regard them as two generative and implicate orders, like separate but parallel streams that interrelate in some way,[57] and (ii) to treat them only as one order, whose ground includes the holomovement and may go beyond."[58]

Consciousness and Matter

There are two opposite views regarding consciousness: (i) held by many neuroscientists that "consciousness is an epiphenomenon of the brain"; and (ii) the opposite view is that "consciousness is a pure disembodied spirit in some kind of interaction with matter".[59] However, Bohm has evolved an alternative view, which is stated below.

> Based on the notion that reality is inexhaustible and whatever we say a thing is, it is something more and also something different. Hence, for example, if we say that consciousness is a material process, this may well be fairly accurate up to a point. But it is also more. Its ground is the infinite depths of

---

[54] Bohm, D. and F.D. Peat, 1987, op. cit., p. 185.

[55] Ibid.

[56] Ibid., p. 186.

[57] Ibid.

[58] Ibid.

[59] Ibid., p. 210.

> the implicate and generative orders, going from the relatively manifest on to ever greater subtlety.[60]

Now let us see how consciousness and matter are interconnected in the quantum field theory of physics.

Interconnection between Consciousness and Matter

It has been shown earlier that existence of an electron particle as well as electron wave are complementary in the quantum field theory of physics. This paves the way for an essential link between consciousness and the primary field. It may be noted that "the fundamental realities of the primary field and consciousness are inseparable aspects of the same underlying process".[61] It has been observed:

> David Bohm has named this underlying process the *implicate order*. Basil Hiley suggests: "Mind and matter are but different projections from this deeper implicate order, where such a division does not exist." He also emphasizes that "the implicate order is not some woolly metaphysical construction, it is a precise description of the underlying process," which is supported by credible mathematical analysis.[62]

However, it has been further explained:

> In pre-space, the potentialities of consciousness and the primary field are united through mutual participation on a universal scale. Put another way, the essence of the implicate order is the one *source* that enfolds both the primary field (the common source of at least everything physical) and consciousness. Based on this thesis, it would be logical to infer that *the one source of the world's great spiritual traditions is grounded in the scientific reality*.[63]

---

60 Bohm, D. and F.D. Peat, 1987, op. cit., p. 210.

61 Bhaumik, M., 2005, *Code Name God*, p. 176.

62 Ibid.

63 Ibid., p. 177.

The net energy of the universe happens to be zero. Therefore, the universe must have also started from the value of zero. In this context, it has been observed that "the late visionary physicist David Bohm did not stop at zero. He conceived of something transcending zero and named it the implicate order which consists of the concurrent existence of all potentialities in the multidimensional pre-space. ... He suggests that material reality and consciousness are projections from this implicate order."[64]

Bohm has also evolved the concept of "holomovement" with a view to capture dynamic phenomenon of which all forms of the material universe flow. "The aim of his approach is to study the order enfolded in this holomovement not by dealing with the structure of objects, but rather with the structure of movement, thus taking into account both the unity and the dynamic nature of the universe. According to Bohm, space and time emerge as forms flowing out of the holomovement: they too are infolded in its order."[65]

That apart, the other fact is that "the universal interconnectedness of things and events, however, seems to be a fundamental feature of the atomic reality which does not depend on a particular interpretation of the mathematical theory".[66] This is explained by David Bohm as follows:

> One is led to a new notion of unbroken wholeness which denies the celestial idea of analysability of the world into separately and independently existing parts. ... We have reversed the usual classical notion that the independent elementary parts of the world are the fundamental reality, and that the various systems are merely particular contingent forms and arrangements of these parts. Rather, we say that inseparable quantum interconnectedness of the whole universe is the fundamental reality and that relatively independently

---

[64] Bhaumik, M., 2005, op. cit., pp. 196-97.

[65] Capra, F., 1989, op. cit., p. 353.

[66] Ibid., p. 149.

> behaving parts are merely particular and contingent forms within the whole.[67]

Observer in Quantum Physics

It is stated that "quantum physics does not recognize an objective world independent of the subject who observes. The observer in the act of observation, influences the thing observed and substantially alters it. We cannot observe anything in Nature without influencing and altering it."[68]

In quantum physics, the observer in a real sense, the part of the experiment. However, "the Copenhagen interpretation puts much emphasis on the consciousness of the observer".[69] In this context, it is pointed out that "Einstein was a better critic of the Copenhagen interpretation of Niels Bohr".[70]

Einstein did not accept the notion of quantum theory. He assumed that:

> The physical world exists independently of the human observer. Heisenberg criticized this notion of Einstein and called it "dogmatic" or "metaphysical" realism. He said: Quantum theory does not allow a completely objective description of Nature.[71]

The Copenhagen interpretation of quantum mechanics has accepted the physical world as an idea of the observer, but it does not consider the physical world as non-material. The physical world is perceived: "But we cannot be sure that our description conforms to the suchness of the world."[72]

It may, however, be reassuringly to be told that:

---

[67] Capra, F., 1989, op. cit., pp. 149-50.

[68] Panda, N.C., 2008, *Māya in Physics*, p. 96.

[69] Ibid., p. 97.

[70] Ibid., pp. 97-98.

[71] Ibid., p. 98.

[72] Ibid., p. 99.

> In atomic physics, the scientist cannot play the role of a detached objective observer, but becomes involved in the world he observes to the extent that he influences the properties of the observed objects. John Wheeler sees this involvement of the observer as the most important feature of quantum theory and he has, therefore, suggested replacing the word "observer"by the word participator.[73]

This has been explained by Wheeler himself as:

> Nothing is more important about the quantum principle than this, that it destroys the concept of the world as "sitting out there"; with the observer safely separated from it by a 20 centimeter slab of plate glass. Even to observe so miniscule an object as an electron, he must shatter the glass. He must reach in. He must install his chosen measuring equipment. It is up to him to decide whether he shall measure position or momentum. To install the equipment to measure the one prevents and excludes his installing the equipment to measure the other. Moreover, the measurement changes the state of the electron. The universe will never afterwards be the same. To describe what has happened, one has to cross out that old word "observer" and put in its place the new word "participator". In some strange sense the universe is a participator's universe.[74]

Emerging Implications

The main highlights emerging from the above observations of the quantum theory of physics are stated below:

i. The concept of causality does not seem to be undermined in the quantum physics. It is rather explained in different ways.

ii. Consciousness is treated as an essential feature of the holomovement in the quantum theory. This has become

---

[73] Capra, F., 1989, op. cit., p. 153.

[74] Ibid.

the important force as compared to the implicate order emerging from the matter. It may, however, be stated that Einstein by bringing the observer in the General Theory of Relativity has revolutionized the concept of space and time and put an end to the idea of absolute time which is advocated by Aristotle and Newton. Time and space have become relative concept. This is mainly because of the observer, which happens to be a self-conscious human being.

iii. Self-consciousness of human being has become the source of nature in the sense that the physical world is known by self-consciousness. This may be supported by the following observation based on the Indian philosophy of Vedic Vision of Consciousness and reality.

iv. All these transmutations that matter has undergone during the last one to two centuries are obviously a work of human consciousness. It is consciousness which broke the tangible chunk of matter into ordinarily invisible atoms, and the latter into absolutely invisible particles. Again, it is consciousness which saw particles as sheer quanta of energy constantly in a state of flux and unpredictable in regard to its position and velocity. Had the scientists' consciousness not been involved in this act of transformation, matter must still have remained only in chunks, both big and small.[75]

---

[75] Singh, S.P., 2004, op. cit., p. 2.

5

Kant's Theory of Knowledge

Introduction

THE main sources of knowledge happen to be perception and self-consciousness. Perception operates at two levels: (i) external perception dealing with external world; and (ii) internal perception mainly concerned with inner sense. These two kinds of perception in a way depend upon self-consciousness in the sense that if one is not conscious, nothing will be perceived. The other fact is that the possibility of all kinds of knowledge exists within the time and space. Therefore, this chapter attempts to deal with Immanuel Kant's theory of perception, time and space.

Perception and Consciousness

According to Kant, there are two main sources of knowledge. In the first source object is given to us. This is known as the faculty of receiving representations (receptivity of impressions). The second one is the power of cognizing by means of the representations received in the first source. This is referred to as spontaneity in the production of conceptions. Both are either pure or empirical. "They are empirical, when sensation (which presupposes the actual presence of the object) is contained in them; and pure when no sensation is mixed with the representation."[1]

Perception is treated by Kant as empirical consciousness. This is explained below:

Perception is empirical consciousness, that is to say, a

[1] Kant, I., 1950, *The Critique of Pure Reason*, p. 64.

> consciousness which contains an element of sensation. Phenomena as objects of perception are not pure, that is, merely formal intuitions, like space and time, for they cannot be perceived in themselves. They contain, then, over and above the intuition, the materials for an object (through which is represented something existing in space or time) that is to say, they contain the real of sensation; as representation merely subjective, which gives us merely the consciousness that the subject is affected, and which we refer to some external object. Now, a gradual transition from empirical consciousness to pure consciousness is possible, inasmuch as the real in this consciousness entirely vanishes, and there remains a merely formal consciousness (*a priori*) of the manifold in time and space.[2]

The above observations seem to be quite cumbersome in the sense that it is rather difficult to pinpoint two faculties of knowledge. Further, the statement that consciousness contains an element of sensation does not seem to be correct. This is mainly because consciousness does not contain anything. Everything exists outside consciousness. That is why Sartre has treated consciousness as nothingness. The other fact is that Kant has evolved the concept of transcendental unity of self-consciousness. Through this concept, it is quite easy to establish the unity between space and time. Yet Kant has treated space and time separately. Whereas the science, Yogācāra Vijñānavāda of Buddhist philosophy and Vedānta have treated time and space as one.[3] The Integral Vedānta of Sri Aurobindo has established the unity between time and space as mentioned earlier.

It may, however, be stated that in the self-consciousness, the knower, knowledge and the known are not different entities, but they become one and the same thing. In fact, "our mentality makes a distinction between these three because without

---

[2] Kant, I., 1950, op. cit., p. 136.

[3] Misra, V.N., 2017, *Saṁsāra and Nirvāṇa*, see chapter 2, "Space and Time", pp. 94-133.

distinction, it cannot proceed; losing its proper means and fundamental law of action, it becomes motionless and inactive".[4] But in reality, the knower, knowledge and the known become one in self-consciousness of human being. This has already been discussed in the Introduction.

Sensibility

The main function of sensibility is to receive an object. Except sensibility, there is no other way to receive an object. This means that "the mind's capacity to receive an object and sensibility is in identical terms. There is absolutely no difference between the two."[5] When sensibility receives an object, it must be in order to be there, it works in two forms, i.e. the forms of space and time. Now the question arises: What does Kant mean by space and time and how both to be forms of sensibility?

According to Kant, space is the way in which sensibility receives an object as outside us. When we receive an object as arranged, it is called spatial relation. This relation is referred to as the relations of the side by side, above, behind and so on.[6] On this basis, an inference has been drawn that the objects are received in the form of space.

The objects are also received by mind or sensibility in time, which is referred to as inner sense. This means that "we receive an object as arranged in what is called temporal relation, namely the relation before and after".[7] In other words, we receive an object in the form of time.

Understanding

The main function of understanding is to operate upon an object which has been received by sensibility. However, according

---

[4] Aurobindo, Sri, 2001, *The Life Divine*, p. 148.

[5] Gupta, R.K., 1986, *Exercises in Conceptual Understanding*, p. 6.

[6] Ibid.

[7] Ibid.

to Kant, "not only can an object, as received exist, without understanding, but understanding can also exist without its function of operation upon the object in question".[8] When we want to obtain synthetic a priori propositions, then understanding starts its function on an object received by sensibility.

Interaction

It may, however, be recognized that without interaction between sensibility and understanding knowledge of any kind is not possible. This is explained as:

> Without sensibility no object would be given to us and without understanding no object would be thought. Thoughts without content are empty, perceptions without conceptions are blind. Hence it is as necessary for the mind to make its conceptions sensuous (i.e. to add to them objects in perception) as to make its perceptions intelligible (i.e. to bring them under conceptions). Neither of these powers or faculties can exchange its function. The understanding cannot perceive and senses cannot think. Only by their union can knowledge arise.[9]

Perception

According to Kant, "Objects are given in perception".[10] However, the general view is that the mind being conceived as having to confirm to objects. But according to Kant, objects are to be conceived as having to confirm to the mind. But if we consider Kant's real position, "we see that these views are only verbally contrary, since the word objects refers to something different in each case".[11] Since, objects must approach the mind with a view to know them, one has to assume that "the mind lays down the conditions for the objects to become objects for knowledge.

---

[8] Gupta, R.K., 1986, op. cit, p. 7.

[9] Prichand, H.A., 1909, *Kant's Theory of Knowledge*, p. 28.

[10] Ibid., p. 22.

[11] Ibid., p. 15.

Unless objects conform to these preconditions they will not be objects for human knowing."[12] Now let us see how objects are defined by Kant.

Object

> *The Kantian object is the possibility of identification and re-identification.* We must be able to say that there is the same thing as that. It must be something which endures in time so that we can return to it again.[13]

In the Transcendental Aesthetic, the object has been defined in a different way. This may be clear from the following observations:

> Of course I am seeing a table. Kant believes that the table as an object goes far beyond what is merely given to me. My belief that I am seeing the table, a physical object, is really the conclusion that I arrive at. But where I begin the premises, not logical premises, but the data with which I begin are data such as sensation. So there is a gap between the sensory representations; tactual, visual and different representations and the conclusion I arrive at is that here is a physical object. There is a gap between the evidence and the conclusion. As a physical object the table is not merely now. It has a duration. It is an enduring object. It will outlast my present perception. I walk out of this room and the table would continue to be there. So the belief that this is a physical object contains more than what my sensory experience provides me with. That I think is the very fundamental Kantian idea. In the very conception of an object, there is much more than sensory evidence. ... My present experience of this table is limited in time. But the claim that this is an object implies. I am predicting about the future course of experience and am remembering the past course. We are not simply describing what is now. What is wrong in saying that I see this table in front of me? I see a physical

---

[12] Masih, Y., 2002, *A Critical History of Western Philosophy*, p. 333.

[13] Chatterjea, T. et. al., 2014, *J.N. Mohanty Lectures on Kant's Critique of Pure Reason*, p. 142.

> object. It is true that I see a physical object. Kant would agree with it. We do perceive physical objects. But the concept of physical object means for more than what can be given in my experience. ... Kant's point is even when I perceive an object, the object is the result of synthesis, because that belongs to the very conception of an object.[14]

However, the theory of perception is based upon our physical organs. It assumes that the reality is to be apprehended in space and time. It asserts that by "the action of the bodies upon physical organs our sensibility is affected and that thereby sensations are originated in us".[15]

Sensation

According to Kant, "matter is that which corresponds its sensation; and form is the principle of ordering of those sensations".[16] At another place it is stated that "perception is due to the operation of things outside the mind, which act upon our sensibility and thereby produce sensations".[17] In the light of these observations how one can understand the Kantian thesis that:

> Sensations which are modifications of my mind, purely subjective states, are ordered in space and time? I can understand that sensations are ordered in time, because my series of sensations would be succeeding in time, but how can sensation be localized in space out there? If sensation is a purely subjective state, and if it does not have any intentional object, that is a serious problem. Sometimes Kant says: *sensation is something in my conceptual consciousness, in my experience and sometimes he says it is the real what corresponds to the real in intuition, in perception, in space.* There is a category admitted by Kant, which is the category of reality, and he says

---

[14] Chatterjea, T. et. al., 2014, op. cit., pp. 152-53.

[15] Prichard, H.A., 1909, op. cit., p. 31.

[16] Chatterjea T. et al., 2014, op. cit., p. 50.

[17] Prichard, H.A., 1909, op. cit., p. 30.

> what corresponds to reality in my experience is sensation. That means only when I have a sensation I know something is real. The schema of the concept of reality are time filled with sensation. So sensation for him is always connected with the sense of reality.[18]

It is further stated by Kant that "in all appearances, the real that is an object of sensation has intensive magnitude, that is degree". (p. 201 A 166 B 207).[19] This is explained below:

> The real is an object of sensation. Intensive magnitude means that sensation by itself has no extensive magnitude. Sensation has no spatial dimension. But sensations vary only intensively, they may be more or less intense. Because of this Kant held the view that space is not sensed. There is no sensation corresponding to space, no sensation of spatiality. Since sensation by itself is only intensive or qualitative, it can have more or less degree of intensity. ... Sensations are a posteriori, they are received. But that in which sensations are ordered must be there already in the human mind *a priori*, viz. space and time. Kant writes, "I term all representations *pure* (in the transcendental sense) in which there is nothing that belongs to sensation" (p. 66, B 35).[20]

Now let us see how the external perception takes place. This is stated below.

External Perception

It is stated that:

1. Now how can there exist in the mind an external perception which precedes the objects themselves, and in which the conception of them can be determined a priori? Obviously not otherwise than insofar as it has its seat in the subject only, as the formal nature of the subject

---

[18] Chatterjea, T. et al., 2014, op. cit., p. 50.

[19] Ibid.

[20] Ibid., pp. 50-51.

to be affected by objects and thereby to *obtain immediate representation*, i.e. perception of them, and consequently only as the form of the external sense in general.[21]

2. Space is not something which we conceive but something which we perceive. From their a priori character, i.e. from the consciousness of necessity involved, it is concluded that perception of space must be a priori a new sense, that of taking place before the perception of objects in it. From the fact that we perceive space before we perceive objects in it, and thereby are able to anticipate the spatial relations, which condition these objects, it is concluded that space is only a characteristic of our perceiving nature, and consequently that space is a property not of things in themselves, but only of things as perceived by us.[22]
3. The question is *How is it possible to perceive anything a priori?* A perception is such a representation as would immediately depend upon the presence of the object. Hence it seems impossible originally to perceive a priori because perception would in that case have to take place without an object to which it might refer, present either formerly or at the moment, and accordingly could not be a perception. ... How can perception of the object precede the object itself? Kant here finds himself face-to-face with the difficulty created by the preceding section. Perception, as such, involves the actual presence of an object; yet the pure perception of space involved by geometry – which, as pure, in the perception of empty space, and which, as the perception of empty space, is a priori in the sense of temporally prior to the perception of actual objects – presupposes that an object is not actually present.[23]

---

[21] Prichard, H.A., 1909, op. cit., pp. 49-50.

[22] Ibid., p. 50.

[23] Ibid., p. 54.

4. Kant unquestionably identifies, a form of perception with an actual perception. It is at once an actual perception and a capacity of perceiving. This is evident from the words "It is possible only in one way for my perception to precede the actuality of the object. ... viz. *if it contains nothing but the form of the sensibility.*"[24]
5. The conclusion that space is only the form of sensibility can be connected with the a priori character of geometrical judgements without presupposing the existence of a perception of empty space, his position will be rendered more plausible.[25]

Space and Time

The *aesthetic* deals with the a priori knowledge relating to sensibility. This knowledge is concerned with space and time according to Kant.[26]

SPACE

Space has been defined by Kant as follows:

> Space is a necessary *a priori* representation; which underlies all our intuitions. We can never represent to ourselves the absence of space, though we can quite well think it as empty of objects. It must therefore be regarded as the condition of the possibility of appearances, and not as determination dependent upon them. It is an *a priori* representation, which necessarily underlines outer appearances (p. 68, A24, B-39). We can never represent to ourselves the absence of space, though we can quite well think it as empty of objects. It implies that our representation of space is independent of the representation of objects.[27]

---

[24] Prichard, H.A., 1909, op. cit., p. 56.

[25] Ibid., p. 60.

[26] Ibid., p. 36.

[27] Chatterjea, T. et. al., 2014, op. cit., p. 64.

Kant's further argument is that "space is one that there are not many spaces which are not parts of one space".[28] However, it has been argued that "space is one, parts of space are its limitations, parts are only thought of as in the whole. Hence, space is intuition."[29]

It is, however, observed that:

> Everywhere Kant assumes that to be *a priori* means to be already in the mind. Is that analytically true? Kant holds that the *a priori* is subjective in origin. It must already be in the human mind. Is this sentence – The *a priori* is subjective in origin, an analytic truth or a synthetic truth? Kant seems to treat it as an analytical truth. If it is *a priori*, it must be found prior to any perception of an object, and so must be found in us. To me, the sentence, however, seems to be synthetic. Because the concept of *a priori only means that its truth is justified, independent of sensory evidence.*[30]

That apart, the fact, however, remains that according to Kant, "our spatial perceptions are not foreign to us, but manifestations of our general perceiving nature; and this view finds expression in the assertion that space is a form of perception or of sensibility".[31] In this context the following observation is worth noting.

> Unfortunately, however, Kant frequently speaks of this form of perception as if it were the same thing as the actual perception of empty space. In other words, he implies that such a perception is possible, and confuses it with a potentiality, i.e. the power of perceiving that which is spatial. The confusion is possible because it can be said with some plausibility that a perception of empty space – if its possibility be allowed – does not inform us about actual thing, but only informs us

---

[28] Chatterjea, T. et. al., 2014, op. cit., p. 67.

[29] Ibid., p. 68.

[30] Ibid., p. 72.

[31] Prichard, H.A., 1909, op. cit., p. 37.

> what must be true of things, if there proves to be any; such a perception, therefore, can be thought of a possibility of knowledge rather than as actual knowledge.[32]

It is also observed that "Kant was led to think of space and time as the only forms of perception".[33] This does not seem to be appropriate because in space external objects are involved. Whereas in time, the internal states of mind like thinking and perceiving are perceived. Therefore, it would be more appropriate to state that in space, perception happens to external one. Whereas in time, internal perception is involved.

Time and Inner Sense

METAPHYSICAL EXPOSITION OF THE CONCEPTION

It is stated that:

1. Time is not an empirical conception. For neither coexistence nor succession would be perceived by us, if the representation of time did not exist as a foundation a priori. Without this presupposition we could not represent to ourselves that things exist together at one and the same time; or at different times, i.e. contemporaneously, or is succession.[34]
2. Time is a necessary representation, lying at the foundation of all our intuition. With regard to phenomena in general, we cannot think away time from them, and represent them to ourselves as out of and unconnected with time, but we can quite well represent to ourselves time void of phenomena. Time is therefore given a priori. In it alone is all reality of phenomena possible. These may all be annihilated in thought, but time itself; as the universal

---

[32] Prichard, H.A., 1909, op. cit., p. 37.

[33] Ibid., p. 40.

[34] Kant, I., 1950, op. cit., p. 49.

condition of their possibility cannot be so annulled.[35]

3. Time has only one dimension. Different times are not coexistent, but successive (as different spaces are not successive but coexistent). These principles cannot be derived from experience.[36]
4. Time is not a discursive or as it called, general conception but pure form of serious intuition.[37]
5. That infinity of time signifies nothing more than every determined quantity of time is possible only through limitations of one time lying at the foundation.[38]

The third point mentioned above is treated by Kant as transcendental. In this context it is stated that "the conception of change and with it the conception of motion; as change of place is possible only through and in the representation of time; that if this representation were not an intuition (internal) *a priori*, no conception of whatever kind, could render comprehensible the possibility of change".[39]

Concluding Observations

It is observed that:

(a) Time is not something which subsists of itself, or which inheres in things as an objective determination, and therefore remains, when abstraction is made of the subjective condition of the intuition of things. For in the former case, it would be something real, yet without presenting to any power of perception any real object. In the latter case as an order of determination inherent is

---

[35] Kant, I., 1950, op. cit., pp. 49-50.

[36] Ibid., p. 50.

[37] Ibid.

[38] Ibid.

[39] Ibid.

things themselves.[40]

(b) Time is nothing else than the form of the internal sense, i.e. of the intuitions of the self and of our internal state. For time cannot be any determination of outward phenomena. It has to do neither with shape nor position, on the contrary it determines the relation of representations in our internal sense.[41]

(c) Time is a condition a priori of all phenomena whatsoever – the immediate condition of all internal, and thereby the mediate condition of all external phenomena.[42]

It may be noted that if we take objects as they are in themselves, then time is nothing. The empty time also cannot be perceived. It is further stated that:

> The empirical reality of time, that is, its objective validity in reference to all objects which can ever be presented to our senses. And as our intuition is always sensuous, no object ever can be presented to us in experience, which does not come under the conditions of time. On the other hand, we deny to time all claim to absolute reality.[43]

ELUCIDATION

> Now, changes are only possible in time, and therefore time must be something real, But there is no difficulty in answering this. I grant the whole argument. Time, no doubt, is something real, that is, it is the real form of our internal intuition. It therefore has subjective reality, in reference to our internal experience, that is, I have really the representation of time and of my determination therein. Time, therefore, is not to be regarded as an object, but as the mode of representation of myself as an object. But if I could intuit myself, or be intuited by

---

[40] Kant, I., 1950, op. cit., p. 51.

[41] Ibid..

[42] Ibid., p. 52.

[43] Ibid.

> another being, without this condition of sensibility, then those very determinations which we now represent to ourselves as changes, would present to us a knowledge in which the representation of time, and consequently of change, would not appear. The empirical reality of time, therefore, remains, as the condition of all our experience. But absolute reality, according to what has been said above, cannot be granted it. Time is nothing but the form of our internal intuition.[44]
>
> Time itself does not change, but only something which is in time. To acquire the conception of change, therefore, the perception of some existing object and of the succession of its determination is one word, experience is necessary.[45]

According to Kant, time is experienced at two levels: original and derived. The original time experience is the form of inner sense. Whereas, "the derived time is also experienced as a form in which things happen in space".[46] It may be stated that time happens to be the form of both senses, indicating thereby time gets *a priority* over space. This is because, "space has a limited role, but time encompasses space within itself because even the things that we perceive in space are also in time".[47]

However, imagination is the faculty dealing with time. In this context, the following observation is worth stating:

> In imagination, we remember the past which is gone and anticipate the future, which is not yet. The function of imagination is always to keep the time which is escaping us under our grip. Without imagination, we cannot know anything. A process which is caught up in the flow of time requires imagination to still have a control of it. If we were being which is not caught up in time that is to say whose experiences are not ordered in time we would not need

[44] Kant, I., 1950, op. cit., p. 53.

[45] Ibid., pp. 55-56.

[46] Chatterjea, T. et al., 2014, op. cit., p. 59.

[47] Ibid., pp. 59-60.

imagination.[48]

Further, time is an irreversible, one-dimensional flow. This is explained thus:

> The idea that time's flow is irreversible and my consciousness always is at a moment (point) that is always a now. I am always in a now. The past is gone on this picture. But then how do I have the sense of the past? For, I would be confined in the solipsism of the now. How does the past at all arise in me? One might say by memory. That is a true answer. But on this picture, the memory is not there, the memory is again in another now. That means the fact of remembering does not help to escape from the solipsism of the now. So one can never get rid of this now and have a conception of the past and the future.[49]

Priority of Time over Space

So far we have discussed time and space as one. Even, "the inner sense and the outer sense go together with regard to their certainty. They are on the same level. Both are equally certain. Even then, one must concede that for Kant inner sense has priority. But that was not with regard to certainty. There is a priority because space is the form only of outer sense and time is the form of both outer and inner."[50] In this context, it is quite important to know how one experiences time. This is explained below:

> I experience myself in time, and time is the form of my internal self-experience. No experience of myself is of reality, but only of appearances. I appear to myself, I do not know myself really as I am, any more than I know how really things are. In both cases, through inner sense I only intuit appearances. As an appearance, I am in time although as a thing in itself, I am not

---

[48] Chatterjea, T. et al., 2014, op. cit., p. 60.

[49] Ibid., pp. 74-75.

[50] Ibid., p. 87.

in time. I do not know myself. Kant held, "Time is in me and I am in time". The container is at the same time the contained. I contain time, but time also contains me. This shows that I can think of myself in different ways. I can think of everything in two different ways: as appearance and as the thing in itself. When I think of myself as appearance then I am in time, but if think of myself as I am in reality then I am not in time, time is rather the form of my sensibility.[51]

[51] Chatterjea et al., 2014, op. cit., pp. 85-86.

6

Knowledge and Consciousness in Advaita Vedānta

Introduction

THERE are two kinds of knowledge mentioned in the *Muṇḍaka Upaniṣad*. These are *parā-vidyā* and *aparā-vidyā*. Both are interpreted in different ways. Śaṅkarācārya has interpreted *parā-vidyā* as the higher knowledge and *aparā-vidyā* as the lower knowledge.[1] There is the higher knowledge by which one attains imperishable, whereas the lower knowledge is treated as ignorance.[2] On the other hand, according to Swami Muni Narayana Prasad, *parā* is the transcendental and *aparā* happens to be the immanent.[3] Consciousness "while in transcendence it remained in its pure form, in immanence it assumed all possible forms the world consists of".[4] It also ought to be recognized that knowledge will not take place without consciousness. This seems to be the reason that knowledge and consciousness are treated as intergral parts in Advaita Vedānta of Indian philosophy.

In the case of human being, "self-consciousness is essentially a case of knowledge. It makes present to us our own Self. It is not a construction, it is not an illusion and, therefore, it is direct knowledge."[5] Further, according to Udayana, "no prior experience is involved in one's being merely directly aware of

---

1 Swami Gambhirananda, 2007, *Muṇḍaka Upaniṣad*, p. 9.

2 Ibid., p. 10.

3 Swami Muni Narayana Prasad, 1998, *Muṇḍaka Upaniṣad*, p. 14.

4 Singh, S.P., 2004, *Vedic Vision of Consciousness and Reality*, p. 402.

5 Stcherbatsky, T., 1996, *Buddhist Logic*, vol. II, p. 30.

oneself. Such self-awareness is always an immediate and original experience."[6] It may be stated that without self-consciousness (i.e. self-cognition) recollection of events is not possible. These observations suggest that self-consciousness (i.e. *jīvātman*) of human being becomes the centre of the universe. This self-consciousness is treated as foundational consciousness, on which perceptual knowledge is based according to Advaita Vedānta.

Self-consciousness and Knowledge

The most important aspect of the foundational consciousness is that it is treated as knowledge, according to Vedānta. It is explained below:

> There can be no objects of knowledge without knowledge. None can prove something that is not known, and the attempt to prove it would be as absurd as to maintain that there is no eye, though the form is apprehended. The objects may change their essence, but consciousness cannot be said to change inasmuch as it witnesses all objects irrespective of the place where they may happen to be; the fact of being known is thus implied by all objects without exception. Even when something is supposed to be non-existent, this very non-existence cannot be proved in the absence of knowledge.[7]
>
> The second feature of the Advaita analysis of consciousness lies in its insistence that consciousness is always distinct from the object of consciousness. The things, therefore, should not be identified with the consciousness which makes them its objects. From this follows two corollaries; namely – that consciousness cannot be its own object and that every object of consciousness is unconscious or material.[8]

Consciousness has, however, been regarded as the ultimate

---

[6] Chakrabarti, K.K., 2001, *Classical Indian Philosophy of Mind*, p. 271.

[7] Mukerji, A.C., 1938, *The Nature of Self*, p. 110.

[8] Ibid., pp. 110-11.

principle of revelation for which alone the objects of the empirical world have become meaningful. In this context, it is observed that consciousness is "the centre of the whole world comprising the objects, the senses and the mind, and it has neither inside nor outside, it is altogether a mass of knowledge".[9]

This "occupies the central place of the universe, inasmuch as all objects owe their meaning and significance to the relations in which they stand to the self that essentially is consciousness".[10] It is known as "the Centre Theory of Self".

Consciousness as Foundational Knowledge

Pure consciousness is treated as the foundation on which existence gets unified with it. In that, the primacy of consciousness is admitted over the dynamics of existence.[11] It may be stated that "the notion of consciousness is so elementary that it cannot possibly be resolved into others more simple. It cannot, therefore, be brought under any genus – any more general conception; and consequently it cannot be defined. ... It may, however, be philosophically analysed."[12] When the empirical contents are abstracted from the consciousness, one is likely to experience pure consciousness, being the Absolute Reality (i.e. *Brahman*). This is treated as the foundation through which the entire universe is known.

Unity of Ātman or Brahman (Pure Consciousness)

Brahman, *Ātman* and matter, explained through consciousness in such a logical and consistent manner are rarely found in other places. This is evident from the following observation:

> When the concentricity of consciousness remains in its innate

---

[9] Mukerji, A.C., 1938, op. cit., p. 112.

[10] Ibid.

[11] Singh, S.P., 2004, op. cit., p. 58.

[12] Bart, W.H., 1995, *Philosophy of Knowledge*, vol. I, pp. 191-92.

> status as holding to itself in the midst of the convulsions of the space–time continuum, it is called *Ātman*. The position in which it happens to break the barrier of space–time continuum by means of the power of its concentricity, it comes to be called *Brahman*. Lastly, when the concentricity of consciousness gets lost in the convulsion of the space–time continuum itself, it assumes the form of matter. Getting reduced to matter also, however, it tends to assert its concentricity in the formation of the particles out of the waves of energy followed by organization of the particles into atoms and eventually into living beings with their all out attempt to retain their individuality of conscious existence in all its concentricity. This is where *Ātman* reappears as *jīvātman* with all possible distractions on the concentricity of consciousness in it on the one hand and the inverse attempt on its part to get revived it to the original one, on the other. This common tendency of the *jīva* to come to itself in the intensest possible concentricity of consciousness, goes veritably to suggest that concentricity is the innate tendency of consciousness.[13]

It is further explained:

> *Ātman* is a specific formulation of consciousness characterized by concentricity; when concentricity breaks down, *Ātman* becomes a coincident either to *Brahman* upward or to matter below. But concentricity being innate to consciousness, its breakdown can never be absolute.[14]

All individual *jīvātmans* are parts or reflection of supreme self known as *Brahman*, which in essence happens to be pure consciousness. However, *Ātman* is also referred to as *Sat–Cit–Ānanda*, but in essence is pure consciousness. It may be stated that *Ātman* has been compared with the *Brahman* in Advaita Vedānta. Therefore, *Ātman*, as *Sat–Cit–Ānanda* has been described below.

---

[13] Singh, S.P., 2004, op. cit., pp. 255-56.

[14] Ibid., p. 255.

ĀTMAN AS SAT

The existence of *Ātman* is well known from the fact that everybody feels, "I exist" and this concept persists at all levels of consciousness and that is why it is said that *Ātman* is eternal and it knows no change,[15] whereas the body, senses, mind, etc. undergo transformations moment by moment, for they are subject to change.

This has been, further, clarified that

> I, who have had dreams and then fell asleep happily, am now wide awake – such is the experience of everyone. It is in this way that the continuity of *Ātman* is experienced. There can therefore be no doubt as to the existence of *Ātman*.[16]

ĀTMAN AS CIT

Since *Ātman* is constituted of pure consciousness, it illumines the intellect and that which the intellect surveys.[17] Further, *Ātman* has been compared with the sun. It is stated that "*Ātman* is compact of consciousness just as the sun is compact of light".[18] This has been explained as follows:

> It is not the light of sun, nor of the moon, nor the flash of lighting, nor the dull blaze of fire that illumines this world entire. It is by the reflex of light of consciousness that the world is made manifest. The light which illumines the world entire is the light of *Ātman*.[19]

According to Vedānta, *Ātman* (pure consciousness) neither is doer nor enjoyer. The adjuncts like mind, *buddhi* and ego become

---

15 Swami Tattwananda, 2002, *The Quintessence of Vedānta of Śrī Śaṅkarācārya*, p. 230.

16 Ibid.

17 Ibid., p. 232.

18 Ibid.

19 Ibid., p. 234.

doer and enjoyer.[20] In other words, the empirical self (*jīvātman*) is doer and enjoyer.

ĀTMAN AS BLISS (ĀNANDA)

Pure consciousness itself is bliss, which is being experienced during dreamless sleep when the mind is merged with consciousness. After waking one immediately says: "I was sleeping happily, I know nothing then."[21] This recollection presupposes experience. So in sleep there was experience of bliss and it is revealed by the consciousness itself.

THE NON-DUAL NATURE OF ĀTMAN

The supreme *Ātman* is referred to as *Sat–Cit–Ānanda* (existence, conscious, bliss). These terms do not possess either the attributes or the qualities of *Ātman*[22] which transcends all qualities. However, these terms indicate "The thing in itself, just as heat and light indicate the real nature of fire".[23] Further, *Sat-Cit-Ānanda* have their combined connotation as mentioned earlier.

PROOF OF ĀTMAN

Ātman being pure consciousness is a *svayamsiddha* reality. In this context, it is stated:

> *Svayamsiddha* reality which is presupposed by all proof and disproof and which falls beyond the region equally of logical justification and refutation. ... This *svayamsiddha* character of consciousness follows from its self-illuminosity or *svatah prakāśatva*. Proof is quite unfit to establish it; for, proofs and other means of evidence and validity have themselves to be proved by self-luminous consciousness.[24]

---

[20] Sinha, J.N., 2006, *Indian Philosophy*, vol. II, p. 487.

[21] Swami Swahananda, 2001, *Pañcadaśī*, p. 452.

[22] Swami Tattwananda, 2002, op. cit., p. 254.

[23] Ibid.

[24] Saksena, S.K., 1971, *Nature of Consciousness in Indian Philosophy*, pp. 143-44.

Mind and Consciousness

The experience is related to mind; for in deep sleep one does not have any experience, but after awakening from sleep one remembers immediately that I have slept well. This is mainly because in the waking state the mind starts working. The sleep state indicates two things: (i) pure consciousness witnesses the sleep; and (ii) the mind recollects immediately that "I slept" well after waking up from sleep. If there was no persistence of pure consciousness witnessing sleep, it would not have been possible for the mind to remember immediately the experience of sleep. It is rather a well-known fact that the mind remembers only those events which have been experienced earlier. This in a way gives supportive evidence to the fact that the mind works in the shadow of past experience. However, without the functioning of the mind, it would be difficult to acquire knowledge.

Pure consciousness alone will not give rise to empirical knowledge.[25] But it also to be recognized that without a reflection of pure consciousness in the mind (which is known as *cidābhāsa* in Vedānta) the mind will not be in a position to gain experience because it is treated as unconscious. But this relationship between pure consciousness and mind may be explained by using the method of co-presence and co-absence (*anvaya-vyatireka*).

This in turn suggests that if pure consciousness exists, the entire world exists, if pure consciousness does not exist, all else including mind will be non-existent. In other words, the mind has no existence apart from pure consciousness.

That apart, the fact remains that the manifestation of consciousness in the human being has been perceived by the Vedānta as functioning in two phases: the outer and the inner. The former operates through five sense organs, whereas the latter discerns as *antaḥkaraṇa* (mind). This has four kinds of mental states, viz. doubt, certitude, egoism and recollection.

[25] Grimes, J., 1992, op. cit., p. 18.

Owing to this diversity of states, it plays different roles, although the mind is one.[26] When the mind starts doubting, this indecisive state is known as the *manas*. In the decisive state (certitude), the mind is referred to as intellect (*buddhi*). When the mind works having some reference to self in the judgement such as "I am happy", it is known as ego (*ahaṁkāra*). Further, in the state of recollection of the past events or experience, the mind works as *citta* constituting the instrument.

The concept of *antaḥkaraṇa* (mind) in the Vedānta is based on the view that the mind is created by consciousness, so as to act as an organ of interconnection between the outer and the inner. In this context, it is stated:

> While *citta* represents consciousness as narrowed down in its range and *ahaṁkāra* is rooted in the concentricity of consciousness as such, *buddhi* reflects the decisiveness of consciousness operating on the stuff provided by the shifting *manas*. Considered inversely, the sensory datum gathered from outside by *manas* through senses is being processed by *buddhi*; owned by *ahaṁkāra*, and finally merging into consciousness through the agency of *citta*. This is how, explains the Vedāntin, consciousness projects itself individually and universally outside as also gets back the projection to itself both ontologically and epistemologically and thus opens out the entire phenomenon of the world along with life in it.[27]

According to the Vedānta anything other than *Ātman* must be non-conscious.[28] *Ātman* being pure consciousness, it may be said that anything other than pure consciousness (in the sense of *cit*) is unconsciousness (*acit*).[29] Since the mind happens to be the object of consciousness, it is treated as *jaḍa* (insentient).[30] This

---

[26] Swami Madhavananda, 2000, *Vedānta Paribhāsā*, p. 32.

[27] Singh, S.P., 2004, op. cit., pp. 74-75.

[28] Swami Jagadananda, 2000, *Upadeśa Sāhasrī of Śrī Śaṅkarācārya*, p. 65.

[29] Woodroffe, J., 2001, *The World as Power*, p. 103.

[30] Ibid., p. 114.

shows that treating the mind as unconscious (*jaḍa*) in the Vedānta is basically a definitional problem. The mind in its functional form is both consciousness and unconsciousness. The same thing may be elaborated. The *cit* is pure consciousness, whereas mind is both conscious and unconscious. In that, mind and matter both are *cit*, as is evident from the following observation:

> The substance again of both mind and matter is *cit*, the Supreme Consciousness and Pure Experience itself. Mental process is a veiling or (relative) unveiling of *cit* which is itself unchanged. Consciousness appears, however, to undergo change because of the modifications of mind of which it is the changeless substratum.[31]

It seems that when the mind reaches at its base, which is known as sublimal or subconscious mind. This state of mind, opens the gate of pure consciousness, the Absolute Reality. In this state, one is really moving in *cit* (pure consciousness) existing in *cit* and functioning in *cit*, where there is no dualism of mind and matter.[32] Therefore, it may be said that in the Absolute Reality (i.e. pure consciousness), there is no duality of any kind. This is the stage, where consciousness reverts to its innate tendency of concentricity.

The reverse side of concentricity or the integrated state is the differential aspect, in which manifestation of pure consciousness takes place through the medium of mind. It means that the integrated consciousness becomes differentiated consciousness due to the modifications of the mind which creates not only duality: the knower and the known but also triplicity, the knower, knowing and the known, with a view to gain individual experience as mentioned in the introduction. But this is a relative state where pure consciousness being the Absolute Reality becomes the many due to modifications of the mind. In such a situation, pure consciousness (*cit*) is itself veiled.

---

[31] Woodroffe, J., 2001, op. cit., p. 112.

[32] Ibid., p. 422.

While manifesting through modifications of the mind, pure consciousness (*cit*) does not loose its capacity as the knower.[33] That is why according to the Vedānta in the ultimate analysis, it is pure consciousness that is the knower, because without its reflection in the mind, the mind itself cannot gain experience of any kind.

Consciousness and Manifestation

When pure consciousness reflects in the *antaḥkaraṇa* (the mind or internal organ), it is known as the *cidābhāsa*; which gives rise to the ego (*ahaṁ*). This consciousness associated with the eternal organ is capable of reflection which takes place during our waking and dream experience. "In our waking experience there is 'I' which functions as knower (*jñāta*), as doer (*kartā*), as experiencer (*bhoktā*): it functions, that is to say, as the subject of knowledge, as the agent of action and as the experiencer of the consequences of action."[34] This shows that the consciousness becomes intentional when it is associated with the mind.

However, the intentional consciousness is mostly associated with "I" which limits the functioning of consciousness because it is tied up with objects: internal or external involved in the physical world. This is explained below:

> By cutting the knot of the ego, consciousness ceases to be personal, it is spread out infinitely, and becomes identical with the world which is a content of the transcendental consciousness – arising from it and again withdrawing into it. So long as consciousness is ego-centric, all thoughts, feelings and actions are directed towards furthering the interests of ego. But when consciousness is universe-centric, thoughts and actions no longer serve the interests of a single individual, they become disinterested. As there is no sense of want there is no

[33] Woodroffe, J., 2001, op. cit., p. 115.

[34] Balasubramanian, R., 2004, "Advaita Vedānta on the Problem of Enworlded Subjectivity", p. 84.

> longer any feeling of pleasure or pain: there is only a sense of fullness, unvarying and undying.[35]

All manifestations are based on duality: the knower and the known, the observer and the observed. This is created by the mind with a view to gain the experience from the empirical world. The mind is mainly capable of discursive knowledge which understands everything through differentiations and distinctions. Therefore, without creating duality in the sphere of knowledge, the mind cannot gain experience. The manifestations of consciousness take place mainly in the empirical world, which has only relative existence.

Since the Vedānta has recognized only pure consciousness as the Absolute Reality or the foundation of all things, people generally think that the phenomenal world as treated by Śaṅkara is an illusion. This seems to be a misunderstanding: for, Śaṅkara has accepted the existence of phenomenal world as true as long as the knowledge of *Brahman* being the self of all has not risen. It is stated that "as long as true knowledge does not present itself, there is no reason why the ordinary course of secular and religious activity should not hold on undisturbed".[36] Further, in the commentaries on the *Gauḍapāda-Kārikās*: 24th and 25th of the *Māṇḍūkya Upaniṣad*, Śaṅkara has clearly stated that the reality may be viewed from two standpoints: (i) viewed from the point of view of relational experience (*yukti-darśana*); and (ii) from the point of view of experience of ultimate-being (*bhūta-darśana*). "Śaṅkara is emphatic and uncompromising on the point that at the former level of experience there is no escape from the admission of the reality of external objects which alone can account for the diversity of our ideas and subjective experiences, but at the level of the latter experience, the very distinction between the subjective and the objective vanishes."[37] This

---

35 Bhattacharyya, S., 2004, "Phenomenology and Indian Philosophy", p. 72.

36 Shrivastava, S.N.L., 1968, *Śaṅkara and Bradley*, p. 116.

37 Ibid., op. cit., p. 117.

clearly shows that the external world in which manifestations of consciousness take place is treated by Śaṅkara as real only in relational sense, whereas in the Absolute Reality, the duality of the phenomenal world does not exist at all.

In the reflective consciousness, the mind is involved as an instrument. Therefore, consciousness in reflection becomes *pramātṛ-caitanya* (knower).[38] It may be stated that the Vedānta has also recognized the concept of *sākṣī-caitanya* (witness consciousness), which in itself does not decide about the right or wrong, its main function is to reflect its own light. In this context, the deciding factor happens to be the *pramātṛ-caitanya* (knower).[39] However, in the reflection the *pramātṛ-caitanya* (knower), is not separate from the *sākṣī-caitanya* (witness) consciousness: the former depends upon the latter. Whatever is known to *sākṣī-caitanya*, it also becomes known to *pramātṛ-caitanya* (knower). The witness consciousness reflects the modifications of mind, which are unknown to *pramātṛ-caitanya*, but are known to witness consciousness.[40] Therefore, an inference may be drawn that the reflective consciousness knows the objects mainly through the light which it receives from the witnessing consciousness (*sākṣī-caitanya*).

The above relationship may be explained in a more forceful manner through the concepts of pre-reflective consciousness and reflective consciousness as propounded by Sartre on the basis of phenomenological considerations. Sartre has tried to explain the concept of pre-reflective consciousness through his memory of reading. In this context, it is stated:

> I have just read a story, and I recall my reading in seeking to account for experience. There was pre-reflective consciousness

[38] Swami Madhavananda, 2000, op. cit., p. 14.

[39] Manju, 1986, *Advaitavāda and Śūnyavāda*, p. 53.

[40] Ibid.

> of the book, of the heroes of the novel; furthermore, there was an inner awareness of consciousness of all this. This inner awareness of consciousness is called "non-positional consciousness of itself", i.e. self-consciousness. Neither consciousness of objects nor self-consciousness was anyway experienced as related to the ego.[41]

This shows that the ego does not appear in the pre-reflective consciousness. So is the case with Vedānta; there is no ego in pure consciousness.

In the Sartrean framework, the ego appears only in the reflective consciousness.[42] Therefore, it may be said that the pre-reflective consciousness is egoless, and it is the non-positional self-consciousness. Whereas the reflective consciousness has the ego and in that it becomes the positional consciousness. This is explained in the following observation:

> All consciousness is positional in that it transcends itself in order to reach an object, and it exhausts itself in this same positing. All that there is of intention in my actual consciousness is directed toward the outside, toward the table; all my judgements or practical activities, all my present inclinations transcend themselves; they aim at the table and are absorbed in it. ... However, the necessary and sufficient condition for a knowing consciousness to be knowledge of its objects, is that it be consciousness of itself as being that knowledge.[43]

The reflective consciousness cannot be separated from the pre-reflective consciousness. This is evident from the fact that "every positional consciousness of an object is at the same time a non-positional consciousness itself".[44] In this context, it has been

[41] Medhidhammaporn, P., 1995, op. cit., p. 25.

[42] Ibid., p. 31.

[43] Sartre, J.-P., 1984, *Being and Nothingness*, p. 11.

[44] Ibid., p. 13.

further clarified that "reflection has no kind of primacy over the consciousness reflected-on. It is not reflection which reveals the consciousness reflected-on to itself. Quite the contrary, it is the non-reflective consciousness which renders the reflection possible; there is pre-reflective cogito which is the condition of the *Cartesian Cogito*."[45]

However, there seems to be some problems regarding the treatment of transcendental consciousness by Sartre. In this context, it has been observed:

> The difficulty arises only when Sartre denies the role of the transcendental consciousness as the unifying principle of the intentional acts. Sartre argues that transcendent object intended by consciousness gives unity to the different intentional acts. His argument is not convincing. It appears that Sartre who banishes the transcendental "I", the permanent factor underlying all our acts of consciousness, by the front door brings it back inside through the back door. At every stage in his explanation he tacitly assumes the existence of such a permanent consciousness in all our acts of consciousness.[46]

The reflective consciousness or empirical consciousness is basically intentional because it is tied up with the objects. It always works with the mind as a medium in the waking condition. Such consciousness is identified with cognition or thought in the framework of "I" consciousness. It also ought to be recognized that the empirical consciousness is limited by the mind which mostly works with the past experiences.

Further, the distinction is made between pure consciousness (*Brahman*) in itself and pure consciousness (*Brahman*) in the universe in the Vedānta. The *Brahman* itself is the transcendent beyond manifest-ation, whereas *Brahman* in the universe is

---

[45] Sartre, J.-P., 1984, op. cit., p. 13.

[46] Balasubrahmaniam, R., 2004, op. cit., p. 87.

the transcendent in manifestation.[47] The distinction between *Brahman* in universe and *Brahman* beyond manifestation are like two sides of one reality. In other words, pure consciousness being the one Absolute Reality becomes many in the manifestation which operates in the relative world. In fact, in the world, things are always changing in the process of becoming. What is constant in this process of becoming is pure consciousness being the Absolute Reality (*Brahman*). This has been summarized in the most elegant way: "what is incomplete in the relative world of becoming is completed in the absolute world of being".[48]

Distinction between Brahman in Itself and Brahman in the Universe

Brahman (Pure Consciousness) in Itself	*Brahman (Pure Consciousness in Universe) for Itself*
Ātman	*Jīvātman*
Indeterminate (*nirākāra* (formless)) consciousness	Determinate (*sākāra*) form of consciousness
Integrated consciousness	Differentiated consciousness
Pre-reflective consciousness	Reflective consciousness
Witnessing consciousness	Witnessed consciousness
Mindless consciousness	Mindful consciousness
Sleeping state	Waking state

Pure consciousness is treated as the Absolute Reality. This is mainly because it becomes the theory of everything in perceiving the entire universe. It is also the unity of opposites. The proof of pure consciousness is based on the deep-sleep experience. On waking from deep sleep, one recognizes that he has slept blissfully. On this evidence, the whole *brahma-vidyā* (i.e. the knowledge of the Absolute Reality) is based. Here the

---

[47] Radhakrishnan, S., 2009, *The Principal Upaniṣads*, p. 70.

[48] Ibid., p. 86.

main purpose is briefly to show that the deep-sleep experience has been given due importance in knowing pure consciousness by the Advaita Vedānta. This is evident from a comparison of sleep experience with Kant's concept of "transcendental unity of apperception". It is stated that "the self disassociated not only from the body but also from the mind rests in itself. It is then immediately conscious of itself, not conscious of itself as returning to itself in reflection. It is then identical with what Kant calls "transcendental unity of apperception".[49] According to Kant, it is mere thought and fringe of empirical consciousness. Whereas Bhattacaryya regards it *as concrete reality not merely thought*[50] (emphasis added by italics).

Theory of Five Kośas: Realms of Knowledge

ANNAMAYA-KOŚA (MATTER AND LIFE)

The creatures that dwell on the earth are produced from food. When they are born, they grow by food and at the end, they merge in food. Therefore, it is called the medicine for all.[51] *Annamaya-kośa* is made of the five elements – earth, water, fire, air and ether – that constitute the physical world. These elements sustain and nourish particular cells. "The atoms of earth go to form bones, of water blood, of fire gastric processes, of air respiration, and of ether support for all these subsheaths."[52] This shows that subtle elements pervade and sustain the gross ones. These elements should not be confused with the scientific concept of atom.

The gross body of human being is known as *annamaya-kośa*, the sheath of food. It is composed of essence of food and is meant

---

[49] Bhattacharyya, K.C., 1983, *Studies in Philosophy*, p. 18.

[50] Ibid.

[51] Swami Gambhirananda, 2004, *Taittirīya Upaniṣad with Commentary of Śaṅkarācārya*, p. 88.

[52] Swami Yogeshwaranand Saraswati, 1987, *Science of Soul*, p. 48.

of the enjoyment for the individual soul. It is also observed that happiness is always go together with food. However, "the eternal value of food is considered a medicine for all and also as an all-healing medicine. Food can sustain our health and can cause disease as well. It becomes an all-healing medicine for everyone when one's self-existence and the value of food are brought together unitively."[53]

PRĀṆAMAYA-KOŚA (VITAL SHEATH)

The life of all creatures depends on the vital force. Therefore, it is called the life of all.[54] *Prāṇamaya-kośa* keeps the physical sheath engaged in different activities and infuses the life into it. In the absence of vital force, physical body cannot live for a single minute.

For preceding the physical body (*annamaya-kośa*), the *prāṇamaya-kośa*, becomes indeed the embodied self. Further, as compared with the vital body (*prāṇamaya-kośa*) there is another internal self-constituted by the mind.[55]

Prāṇa-vidyā (knowledge of vital forces) has two aspects: universal and individual. On the universal scale, the air is the point of merger of water, fire, sun and moon. Whereas in the case of the individual, *prāṇa* is the merging point of speech, sight, hearing and making and unmaking of determinations. This is evident from the state of sleep in which speech, sight, etc. are merged into *prāṇa*.[56]

The other characteristic of consciousness is the instinct of self-protection. It is formed by the permeation of consciousness in life under the domination of the vital. "This is evident from the instinct of self-preservation being confined to the protection

---

53 Swami Muni Narayana Prasad, 2009a, *The Taittirīya Upaniṣad*, p. 106.

54 Swami Gambhirananda, 2004, op. cit., pp. 92-93.

55 Ibid., p. 93.

56 Singh, S.P., 2004, op. cit., p. 210.

of the vital, that of procreation to the promotion of the vital and that of possession of the feeling of the vital."[57] In this process, the consciousness becomes the source of rebirth. In the Buddhist philosophy the self has not been admitted directly, but the consciousness is treated as the medium of rebirth. In the case of Vedānta, it is clearly stated that when pure consciousness descends in human beings it becomes *jīvātman*, through which rebirth takes place.

MANOMAYA-KOŚA (MIND SHEATH)

The *jīvātman* always reflects through the mind, which is known as *citta* in Yoga and *antaḥkaraṇa* (inner instrument) in the Vedānta. It is stated:

> One part of this inner instrument is somewhat gross, this is the *sūkṣma śarīra* (the subtle or astral body). It has two parts, the first being action-predominating known as *manomaya-kośa* (mind sheath), the second, which is knowledge predominating, is known as *vijñānamaya-kośa* (intellect sheath). But these powers of knowledge and action do not belong to the sheaths themselves in which they manifest.[58]

The centre from which the power or energy arises is *jīvātman*. This is explained below.

> *Jīvātman* is related to *citta* from infinity (rebirth after liberation – *mokṣa*), from the very commencement of each creation in the form *bimba–bimbī bhāva* (relationship of reflector and reflection), the relationships of owner and owned and *bhogya–bhoktṛ bhāva* (relationship of enjoyer and the enjoyed). *Citta* is also in contact with *ahaṁkāra* and *jīvātman* takes the work from *ahaṁkāra* at every moment.[59]

It may, however, be stated that "the human mind is a creation of consciousness so as to act as an organ of interconnection

---

[57] Singh, S.P., 2004, op. cit., p. 223.

[58] Swami Yogeshwaranand Saraswati, 1987, op. cit., p. 92.

[59] Ibid., p. 112.

between the inner and the outer, the physical and the spiritual, the individual and the world".[60] In fact, "*citta* can serve as the gateway to pure consciousness",[61] which is referred to as *Ātman*.

It is, thus, evident that it is *citta* which works for *jīvātman* and becomes the substratum of all the *saṁskāras*, *vāsanās* (dispositions) and *smṛti* (memory) in the seed form. In fact, *citta* being in close association with *jīvātman*, has special luminosity and is very active. "It appears to be ever conscious. It is ever generating life force in the form of subtle *prāṇa*. It is the revealer of the nature of *jīvātman*. It is described as *madhyama pariṇāmī* because it is subject to contraction and expansion."[62]

Generally, it is stated that "knowledge is inherent in the mind".[63] This is partially correct in the sense that without reflection of pure consciousness in the mind, it may not be possible to obtain the knowledge of external object. Yet, without the functioning of the mind, neither knowledge nor experience is possible. However, "the mind is regarded primarily as cognitive, and impulses, emotions, desire, etc. are regarded as forces invading the cognitive faculty".[64]

According to the *Taittirīya Upaniṣad*, of that preceding *prāṇamaya-kośa*, this *manomaya-kośa*, is embodied self; "as compared with this mental body, there is another internal self-constituted by valid knowledge".[65] This internal self is known as *vijñānamaya-kośa*.

Before discussing *vijñānamaya-kośa*, it may be mentioned that according to the Vedānta, consciousness (i.e. *cit*, *caitanya*)

---

[60] Singh, S.P., 2004, op. cit., p. 74.

[61] Ibid., p. 78.

[62] Swami Yogeshwaranand Saraswati, 1987, op. cit., p. 111.

[63] Swami Bhajananda, 2009, Knowledge and Consciousness: An Integral Approach", p. 91.

[64] Ibid., p. 90.

[65] Swami Gambhirananda, 2004, op. cit., p. 98.

has two aspects: the immanent and the transcendent. In the above discussion of three *kośa*s all the types of the knowledge are manifestations of consciousness immanent in matter, in life and in the mind.[66] It may, therefore, be said that immanent consciousness is limited by the body, *prāṇa* (vital) and mind in above three *kośa*s (sheaths). When the limitations – body, senses and mind – are transcended, one may realize an unlimited, unconditional aspect of consciousness.[67]

VIJÑĀNAMAYA-KOŚA (INTELLECT SHEATH)

Of that preceding *manomaya-kośa* (mental) one, this *vijñānamaya* (cognitive) sheath is an embodied self. As compared to this cognitive body, there is another internal self-constituted by the bliss.[68]

Consciousness at the transcendent level becomes an ontological or metaphysical principle as the Ultimate Reality.[69] According to the Advaita Vedānta, reality is pure consciousness, which is non-dual without any differentiation. This consciousness is known as *astitva-jñāna* (ontological knowledge). It can be explained as "I am" therefore "I think", which happens to be just reverse to Descartes approach known as "I think therefore I am".

The existence of pure consciousness (*Brahman*) has been supported by the fact that the pure consciousness is the self of all: "for everyone feels that his Self exists, and he never felt that I do not exist".[70] The same thing has been said in different words in the commentary on verse III.2.7 of the *Muṇḍaka Upaniṣad*. It is stated that "each is conscious of one's own identity as "I" the

66 Swami Bhajananda, 2009, op. cit., p. 92.

67 Ibid.

68 Swami Gambhirananda, 2004, op. cit., p. 101.

69 Swami Bhajananda, 2009, op. cit., p. 92.

70 Swami Gambhirananda, 2000, *Brahmasūtra Bhāṣya of Śrī Śaṅkarācārya*, p. 12.

specific consciousness is called here *vijñānātmā* – which also becomes one with the Imperishable Reality, the Self".[71]

How to attain the transcendental knowledge? Or how to know the knower? In verse 1.1 of the *Kena Upaniṣad* the question is revised as to who is the real agent in the individual? This has been answered in the commentary of verse 1.2 of the same Upaniṣad. In that it is stated:

> There is the Eternal Reality behind the mind, life and senses, the mind of the mind, the life of the life. *Brahman* is not an object, subject to mind, speech and the senses. He who knows it will gain life eternal and not the partial satisfactions of the earthly life. Here in the world of space and time we are always seeking the Beyond, which is above space and time. There, we possess the consciousness that is beyond space and time.[72]

ĀNANDAMAYA-KOŚA (BLISS SHEATH)

It is stated that when *citta* (mind) is illumined by the light, it suggests:

> The individual soul undergoes contraction and expansion every moment through infusion of consciousness. Because of contraction and expansion on one hand, there is constant emergence of knowledge and action, and, on the other hand, the individual soul experiences its existence every moment in the form of *asmi* (I am) caused by the process of contraction and expansion. By the ceaseless vision of the reaction of the light of self-reflecting in the mirror of *citta*, there arises an experience of supremely *sāttvika* nature in *citta*, which is termed *ānanda* (bliss).[73]

This bliss being endowed with changing attributes should not be confused with the supreme bliss of pure consciousness

[71] Swami Muni Narayana Prasad, 1998, op. cit., p. 122.

[72] Radhakrishnan, S., 2009, op. cit., p. 581.

[73] Swami Yogeshwaranand Saraswati, 1987, op. cit., p. 230.

(*Brahman*).[74] It is further stated that "the sheath of bliss, though close to *Ātman* cannot be *Ātman* itself".[75]

The above five sheaths (*kośas*) have solved the body and soul problem. It will be discussed below. However, all these sheaths are basically modifications of the premordial matter (*prakṛti*). They do not possess Absolute Reality.[76] That is why consciousness has to transcendent all these sheaths, so as to reach its concentricity being its true nature. In fact, it becomes pure consciousness (*Ātman*), the unchanging Absolute Reality, witnessing all the three states of consciousness: waking, dreaming and sleeping. Further, it is the pure consciousness (*Ātman*) that enables one to break the bondage of relative world and attains supreme Blessedness.[77]

Five Kośas as Solution of Body–Mind Problem and Gaining Different Kinds of Knowledge

In the *Taittirīya Upaniṣad*, the most important problem of Body (matter) and Soul (consciousness) has been solved in a unique manner. This may be seen from the following observation:

> If *annamaya* is the body, *prāṇamaya* becomes its soul. If *prāṇamaya* is the body, *manomaya* becomes its soul. If *manomaya* is the body, *vijñānamaya* becomes its soul. If *vijñānamaya* is the body, *ānandamaya* becomes its soul. All these are conditional. We find it impossible to say absolutely which is the body and which is the soul. What we see, instead of a division, there is a hierarchy of entities, one end of which appears to be the body, and the other end appears to be the soul. The entire range as a whole is neither matter nor mind, but something that transcends both.[78]

---

[74] Swami Nikhilananda, 2008, *Self Knowledge of Śrī Śaṅkarācārya*, p. 88.

[75] Ibid., p. 89.

[76] Ibid., p. 88.

[77] Ibid., p. 90.

[78] Swami Muni Narayana Prasad, 2009a, op. cit., p. 132.

Although the above statement seems to be confusing, if one goes deeper into the problem, one may get an interesting insight. In this context, it is observed:

> The word used here for body is *śarīra*, which means "the perishable form". The word for soul is *Ātman* which means the imperishable reality that pervades the entire form, just as gold pervades the form of an ornament. Here what we see is not the duality of the body and soul, but the unity of imperishable Reality and the perishable form which the former assumes.[79]

It may, however, be stated that these observations are in conformity with the commentary of Śaṅkarācārya on the *Taittirīya Upaniṣad*.[80]

The above *kośa*s of the *Taittirīya Upaniṣad* have recently been interpreted in a slightly different, but in a more interesting way. It has been observed that each layer of body (*kośa*) corresponds to a particular level of knowledge or knowing. This is given in Table 6.2.

Koṣas and Their Relevant Knowledge

Kośa	*Described as*	*Knowledge*
Annamaya	Physical body - matter	Physics
Prāṇamaya	Vital body - life and *prāṇa*	Biology
Manomaya	Mental body - mind	Psychology
Vijñānamaya	Intellectual body - soul	Theology
Ānandamaya	Blissful or spiritual - spirit	Mysticism

Source: Quoted by Swami Jitātmānanda, 1993, *Holistic Science and Vedānta*, p. 31.

The above description has, however, been summed up as follows:

> The higher transcends but includes the lower and not vice versa. Thus, life transcends but includes matter; mind

[79] Swami Muni Narayana Prasad, 2009a, op. cit., p. 132.

[80] Swami Gambhirananda, 2004, op. cit., pp. 99-104.

> transcends but includes life; soul transcends but includes mind, and spirit transcends but includes soul. At that point, however, asymptotic at infinity, we have reached a paradoxical limit; spirit is that which transcends everything and includes everything. Or, in traditional terms, spirit is both completely transcendent to the world and completely immanent in the world – and this is the most notorious (and unavoidable) paradox of spirit.[81]

The implication of above observation regarding the mind–body problem is that when the mind transcends to higher, i.e. *vijñānamaya* which is known as self-consciousness, but it includes the mind along with *prāṇamaya* as the body. In self-consciousness, both the mind and body get united. It may, therefore, be said that the mind–body problem gets resolved in self-consciousness which is embodied in human being.[82]

---

81 Swami Jitātmānanda, 1993, *Holistic Science and Vedānta*, p. 32.

82 Misra, V.N., 2019, *Phenomenal Consciousness and Mind–Body Problem in East–West Perspective*, p. 156.

7

Perceptual Knowledge in Advaita Vedānta

Introduction

PERCEPTION is twofold: external and internal. The external perception is known by any of the five sensory organs such as hearing, sight, touch, taste and smell. Whereas the mental perception of pain and pleasure, of knowledge, ignorance, love, hate, etc. are internal. However, "internal perception is again twofold: (i) relative to the perceiving self, and (ii) relative to the states of the mind."[1] It may, therefore, be said that the perception is not only the principle means of physical knowledge,[2] but it is also the primary source of human knowledge.[3] Perceptual knowledge has three distinct phases: (i) regarding the physical objects, (ii) regarding the mental states, and (iii) regarding the knowing self.[4] All these aspects are discussed in this chapter.

Internal Perception

It is observed that "a brain surgeon can watch with his eyes a patients' cerebral movements, but not his mental operations".[5] The former is external, whereas the latter are internal. It is pointed out that none of the sense organs can perceive one's

---

[1] Swami Satprakashananda, 2001a, *Methods of Knowledge According to Advaita Vedānta*, p. 41.

[2] Ibid., p. 36.

[3] Ibid., p. 37.

[4] Ibid., p. 42.

[5] Ibid., p. 40.

mind. "What is psychical and not perceptible to the senses can, thus, be distinguished from the physical objects and their properties as internal."[6]

Any individual can observe his mental condition directly from inside, whereas others can know it indirectly through its physical expression. It is observed: that "the proof of such mental traits as joy, love, guiltiness, and so forth, is inner experience and not outer behaviour which may even belie the internal state."[7] This is explained below:

> In experiencing happiness which is a state of the mind, a person is aware of himself as its experiencer, as is evident from such expressions as I feel happy, I am happy. But he ascribes to himself the mental state, although he is distinct from it as its experiencer. Every individual is more or less aware of himself as a doer and as an experiencer. But in his self-recognition no subject–object relation is involved. The self shines of itself and is not objectified. ... This means that he is aware of the empirical self, the ego, but not of the changeless luminous self ever distinct from the psychophysical adjunct as its witness.[8]

In the Advaita Vedānta's view the mental states of pain like pleasure, fear, hope, love and hate are illuminated directly by the witness self without any intermediary. These are manifested by the witness self, i.e. unaided by an agency.[9] Now the question is how is this knowledge known in such a situation?

According to the Advaitins, the nature of knowledge happens to be self-manifest.

> Every knowledge, whether perceptual or inferential, has a subjective side of pure awareness (*cit* or *saṁvit*) which is the life and core of the self itself, so that nothing stands

---

[6] Swami Satprakashananda, 2001a, op. cit., p. 40.

[7] Ibid., p. 41.

[8] Ibid.

[9] Ibid., p. 42.

> between knowledge and the self (that is to say, no mediation is necessary) and consequently knowledge must necessarily be immediate or self-manifest. But there is another side to knowledge in which reference to the object is all important. It is from this side that we divide knowledge into two classes, immediate and mediate, though from the former point of view knowledge can be said only to be immediate. Now from this latter point of view, knowledge being about an object, is immediate or mediate according as the object is known immediately or mediately. Knowledge of the pot, from this objective standpoint, can be said to be immediate, when the condition referred to above is satisfied, and the object is related to the subject thereby. Thus this condition does not conflict with the fundamental Vedāntic position that knowledge in its subjective aspect (*cit*) is immediate or self-manifest, so long as we remember the two aspects of knowledge, the subjective consciousness which is self-manifest, and the objective mode (*vṛtti*) which is illumined by the former.[10]

Still one may ask, "How do you know that knowledge is self-manifest"? The reply is that "we can infer the self awareness of knowledge from the testimony of our memory. At a subsequent moment I can judge not only that "I remembered the table" but also that "I remember to have perceived the table". Both these memory judgements are undoubtedly based on past perceptional knowledge alone".[11]

In reality, however, knowledge neither needs to be, nor can be an object either of itself or any of other knowledge. "Self-manifestation of knowledge means that knowledge can behave as being immediate without being an object of knowledge. This would be an exact rendering of the explanation of the term *svaprakāśatva* (self-manifestation)."[12]

---

[10] Datta, D.M., 1998, *The Six Ways of Knowing*, pp. 115-16.

[11] Ibid., p. 117.

[12] Ibid., p. 118.

External Perception

According to the Vedānta, sense organs are *prāpyakārī*[13] in the sense that they apprehend the objects through their contacts. The visual organ and the auditory organ go out to apprehend their objects. Whereas the olfactory organ, the gustatory organ and the tactual organ appropriate their objects remaining in their seats. However, "each organ has a particular location except the organ of touch which extends all over the body".[14] Further, each sense organ is produced by a subtle element, whose distinctive property has the power to reveal. This is stated in Table 7.1. The actual organs are imperceptible. "We perceive or act through them, but we never perceive them. Their existence, however, is inferable."[15]

The Subtle Element and Distinctive Property of the Sense Organs

Sense Organ	Composed of Sattva Aspect of Subtle Element	Specific Property of Manifestation
Sight	*Tejas* (light or fire)	Colour
Hearing	*Ākāśa* (ether)	Sound
Taste	*Ap* (water)	Taste
Smell	*Kṣiti* (earth)	Smell
Touch	*Vāyu* (air)	Touch

Source: Swami Satprakashananda, 2001a, *Methods of Knowledge*, p. 50.

Contact of Sense Organs with Their Respective Objects

On the basis of above statement, the sense perception may be explained as follows:

1. In the case of sight and hearing, the object does not come

---

[13] Sinha, J.N., 2008, *Indian Psychology*, vol. I, p. 25.

[14] Swami Satprakashananda, 2001a, op. cit., p. 48.

[15] Ibid., p. 49.

in direct touch with corresponding sense organs but they operate through vibrations.[16] In fact, presence of light vibrations acting on retina of the eye produces the impressions of form and colour.[17] However, the organ of hearing and the organ of vision being the nature of ether (*ākāśa*) and light (*tejas*), respectively, both move instantly and freely. The organ of vision locates its object in space.[18] In the case of hearing, the sound vibrations act upon the drum of the ear, producing thereby sensation of sound through which the nature of sound is known, even without seeing the sound-producing objects.[19] It is, however, observed:

> Physicists tried to discover "ether" by physical means and naturally could not find it because it is not material in the ordinary sense. It is mental in nature and therefore called *cidākāśa* (mental space). Being above the material state, it cannot be affected or discovered by physical means. So physicists had to conclude that there was no ether as previously supposed and light existed and travelled in empty space. According to occultism, there is a basic medium called *ākāśa*, but it is mental in nature, the stuff in which the mind works.[20]

It is, thus, evident that it is the mind which cognizes the sensation created by the objects in the sense organs resulting thereby in the sense perception.

2. In the case of smell, taste and touch, there is direct contact of objects with the corresponding sense organs, creating thereby sensations. For instance, "to feel the smell the particles of the odorous substance should be in contact

[16] Taimni, I.K., 1987a, *Glimpses into the Psychology of Yoga*, p. 383.

[17] Taimni, I.K., 1999, *The Science of Yoga*, p. 174.

[18] Swami Satprakashananda, 2001a, op. cit., p. 53.

[19] Ibid.

[20] Taimni, I.K., 1987a, op. cit., pp. 392-93.

with the mucous membrane of the nose. In order to feel the taste, the substance in solution should come in contact with the taste buds."[21]

3. The organ of touch gets its object in actual contact. The sensation of heat depends upon moving atoms and molecules on the skin.[22]
4. The sense perception does not depend only on the senses, but it also requires the mind to attend the object.[23] Now "modern research also shows that seeing is not a mere passive act like light falling on the lens of a camera; the retina plays an active role in selecting, filtering and transmitting to brain the sensory input in the eye. At any rate it is now well established that seeing is a dynamic and an intentional act."[24] These facts show that eye sees but the mind cognizes.

Mental Mode of Advaita Vedānta

There are three different views in the Advaita Vedānta as how the mental mode (*antaḥkaraṇa vr̥tti*) gets united with the external object, leading thereby to its perception.[25] These views are stated below:

i. *Āvaraṇa-bhaṅga* (removal of ignorance hiding the object from the subject);
ii. *Ciduparāga* (tinging the subject consciousness with the object); and
iii. *Abhedābhivyakti* (unity of consciousness among *pramātr̥-caitanya, pramāṇa-caitanya* and *prameya-caitanya*. They become

---

[21] Taimni, I.K., 1987a, op. cit., p. 383.

[22] Taimni, I.K., 1999, op. cit., p. 175.

[23] Safaya, R., 1976, *Indian Psychology*, p. 115.

[24] Swami Bhajananda, 2009, "Knowledge and Consciousness", p. 70.

[25] Swami Satprakashananda, 2001a, op. cit., p. 97.

one in consciousness in the sense that the same consciousness gets transformed into three).

It may, however, be stated that in the case of *abhedābhivyakti*, the three functions are just the differentiated aspects of pure consciousness reflecting in three different ways.

It is observed that "this method of *abhedābhivyakti* is open to serious objection. One may say, since the object, a jar for instance, is perceived as non-different from the subject-consciousness, why does not the perceiver have such experience as 'I am a jar' or 'In me is a jar' instead of there is jar."[26] This question can be answered in two ways: (i) fusing state; and (ii) wholeness. Both are discussed below:

While commenting on *Yogasūtras* III.3, it is stated:

> Everything in manifestation has two forms. An external form expressing its superficial and non-essential nature which is called *rūpa* and an internal form which constitutes the very essence or substance of its true nature which is called its *svarūpa*. ... With the disappearances of the mental *svarūpa* a faculty higher than the intellect comes into play, and the perception of the reality hidden beyond the object takes place through the instrumentality of this faculty which perceives by becoming one with the object of perception. The perceiver, the object of perception and perception become fused in one state.[27]

This shows that perceiver, perceiving and perceived all three become one in consciousness. In other words, the same consciousness gets differentiated into three spheres.

The approach of wholeness is adopted in the Buddhist philosophy. It is stated below:

> Consciousness has three parts: perceiver, perceived and wholeness. The subject (*darśana-bhāga*) is the first aspect of perception. The second is the object of perception

---

[26] Swami Satprakashananda, 2001a, op. cit., p. 105.

[27] Taimni, I.K., 1999, op. cit., pp. 282-83.

> (*nimitta-bhāga*). The third aspect, the base of both subject and object, is wholeness (*svabhāva-bhāga*). Subject and object are born at the same time. When the snail sends up its antennae, he sends up both at the same time. Consciousness can manifest or fail to manifest, depending on whether both the perceiver and the perceived aspects manifest. When consciousness manifests, we say it exists. When it doesn't manifest; we say it does not exist. But this idea of existing and not existing causes us to suffer. The subject of perception manifests at the very moment that the object of perception manifests, and neither is possible without the base. Wholeness is everything.[28]

It is thus evident that in the wholeness of consciousness, perceiver and perceived have no separate existence. One cannot exist without other.

Now the question arises that if the perceiver, perceiving and perceived are one, why are they treated separately? This may be answered by the fact that the experience happens to be the result of the coming together of the subjective and the objective side. In the case of perception, it is only when the integrated state of consciousness is broken into triplicity of perceiver, perceiving and perceived, the individual experience takes place. In this context, the following observation is worth noting:

> In order to understand the nature of experience it is also necessary to remember that the continued existence or maintenance of any mental phenomenon is not possible unless consciousness or the mind is attached to or involved in what is created through the faculty of *buddhi*, the power of perception. It is this essential involvement of consciousness which connects the subject and the object and produces experience in all cases.[29]

---

[28] Hanh, 2008, *Understanding Our Mind*, p. 167.

[29] Taimni, 1998a, *The Secret of Self Realization*, p. 38.

Cognitive Process of External Perception

It is stated:

> Consciousness is immanent in every phase of existence. While it is hidden in all physical objects, it is manifest more or less in every sentient being. In a human individual it finds expression as distinct self-awareness, which is the only immediate and direct cognition in the strict sense. An object becomes directly known through its association with the immediacy of subject consciousness. The mental mode brings about the association.[30]

The above statement is further explained by the fact that pure consciousness alone is responsible for the manifestation of all objects (including light).[31] But it is only possible when the veil of ignorance (*ajñāna*), that is the darkness of non-consciousness that hides object before perception is removed.[32]

The mind experiences the external world, but this is possible mainly due to the light of pure consciousness. Therefore, an inference has been drawn that pure consciousness is all that exists. In reflection, it becomes many. All differentiations are mainly appearances. In this context, it has been observed that "anything we perceive is but a form appearing as an entity because of the underlying reality".[33] This reality is pure consciousness. It has, however, been asserted that "what we perceive as a chair is pure consciousness apparently limited by the chair form".[34] This has been illustrated by several examples.

---

30 Swami Satprakashananda, 2001a, op. cit., p. 98.

31 Ibid., p. 99.

32 Ibid.

33 Ibid., p. 84.

34 Ibid.

Pure Consciousness and Its ApparentlyLimited Forms

Perceiving Items as Pure Consciousness	*Apparently Limited by**
Chair	Chair form
Fire	Fire form
Heat	Heat form
Sound	Sound form
Ear	Ear form
Mental Modifications	*Particular Mental Mode*
Happiness	Mental mode to happiness
Mind	Mind form
Cognition	Cognitive mode of mind

* The limiting forms are mere superimpositions and have no existence apart from pure consciousness.

Source: Swami Satprakashananda, 2001a, op. cit., p. 84.

In the above statement, it is, however, difficult to understand perceiving the chair as pure consciousness at the first instance.

But if one goes deeper into the problem in the Vedāntic terms, it could be easily explained as follows:

> While consciousness, as identical with knowledge, is always conceived to be about some object, *caitanya*, as the undifferentiated reality, does not necessarily imply the existence of some object. In its isolated character, it may be described only as self-shining. This characteristic of *caitanya*, in its pure aspect, is not altogether absent in the stage of differentiation. It is in virtue of this fundamental quality that an object appears and the subject knows. Appearance and knowledge are but the two differentiated sides of the same neutral fact of immediacy. In other words, the appearance of *caitanya* as object to *caitanya* as subject, or the knowledge on the part *caitanya* as subject of *caitanya* as object, has to be credited to the fundamental self-manifesting characteristics of *caitanya*.[35]

[35] Datta, D.N., 1998, op. cit., p. 74.

However, the above observation of perceiving the chair as pure consciousness limited by the form of chair may be supported by two facts: one is based on the Vedic vision, and the other is from the Kashmir Śaivism. Both the arguments are state as follows:

i. When we receive the stimulus from the external world, it forms the image reaching to the sense organ. This in turn gets transformed into the object. In this context, it is stated:

> Transcription of the stimulus into the perceived object is the crucial point of coming together of the subject and the object. Here the source of the stimulus assumes the form of object perceived through the intermingling of the subjective with the objective. What happens in the event of intermingling is that by way of transcribing the stimulus into the object of perception, it is actually the consciousness which comes to assume the form of the object which otherwise in itself remains imperceptible to us even after we have the notion of having perceived it. A simple generalization of this process is sure to lead us to the conclusion that whatever we perceive in the external world, apart from what actually it is, is simply a projection of our own consciousness, on that imperceptible and inexplicable something. Though a sheer projection of consciousness, our percept, however, is felt as very much existing there outside to us in all its material correctness and tangibility.[36]

ii. It is pointed out that:

> The events which constitute the universe are always internal events happening within consciousness because their essential nature is consciousness itself. We can only account for the fact that things appear if there is an essential identity between consciousness and the object perceived. If physical objects were really totally material, that is, part of a really independent of, and external to,

[36] Singh, S.P., 2004, *Vedic Vision of Consciousness and Reality*, p. 15.

consciousness, it could never be experienced.[37]

Perceptual Illusion

An object like silver perceived can neither be real, for, it is sublated by the knowledge of the nacre, nor it can be unreal because it is perceived.[38] Therefore, an object like silver is indefinable (*anirvacanīya*), as existent or non-existent. The theory of *anirvacanīya khyāti* is advocated by Advaita Vedānta. It has recently been observed that the theory of *anirvacanīya khyāti* (i.e. the inexplicability of appearance) in a way is derivable from the Buddhist's view of *ātma-khyāti*,[39] which is nothing but the revelation of awareness itself.[40]

However, the illusory object according to Advaita Vedānta arises from ignorance (*ajñāna*), which happens to be just the opposite of knowledge. It is associated with the substratum being pure consciousness as mentioned earlier. In fact, pure consciousness underlies each and every phase of existence. "While it is concealed in all physical objects, it shines as conscious self in sentient beings. ... An object is perceived when the light of consciousness that shines in a living individual, being manifest in his mental mode conforming to the object, withdraws its veil of *ajñāna* and makes it cognizable."[41]

The object has apparent existence (*prātibhāsika-sattva*), which is distinct from the empirical existence (*vyāvahārika-sattva*). However, "an empirical object exists prior to its being perceived and afterwards, but the illusory object lasts as long as its perception lasts. It is coterminous with its cognition."[42]

---

37 Dyczkwoski, M.S.G., 2006, *The Doctrine of Vibration*, p. 47.

38 Swami Satprakashananda, 2001a, op. cit., p. 133.

39 Matilal, B.K., 1986, *Perception*, p. 190.

40 Ibid., p. 184.

41 Swami Satprakashananda, 2001a, op. cit., p. 134.

42 Ibid., p. 133.

It seems that illusion is also created by the mind, which functions within the experience of the past. This fact has not been directly acknowledged by Advaita Vedānta, although it is mentioned that the true nature of object is not perceived because it is veiled by the images created by the mind, which works through the past as mentioned in the Abhidharma of Buddhist philosophy.[43]

[43] Halder, 2001, *Some Psychological Aspects of Early Buddhist Philosophy*, p. 52.

8

Self-knowledge of Advaita Vedānta

Introduction

HUMAN beings experience daily three states: dreamless sleep, dreaming and waking. It has been asserted that the true nature of the Absolute Reality may be known by discriminating these three states.[1] However, these three states are of consciousness and not of mind, which has been derived from the consciousness. Therefore, the states are basically concerned with the nature of awareness rather than its contents. It may be stated that awareness is treated as an expression of consciousness.[2] In fact, awareness itself is nothing but consciousness. This framework of treating these three states – dreamless sleep, dreaming and waking – of consciousness is expected to provide a better understanding of their roles in locating the nature of the Absolute Reality.

It has, however, been observed that "dream and waking represent the dynamic modes of pure consciousness and what is regarded as sleep is but pure consciousness free from the imposition of subject and object, pure and unalloyed".[3] Since pure consciousness requires the absence of a duality of subject and object at the same time, this may be possible mainly in the experience of sleep in which there is no duality.

---

[1] Alston, A.J., 1997, *The Method of the Vedānta*, p. 95.

[2] Taimni, I.K., 1987a, *Glimpses into the Psychology of Yoga*, p. 164.

[3] Iyer, K., 1991, *Vedānta or Science of Reality*, p. 70.

However, *turīya* state transcends all three states of consciousness: sleep, dream and waking. In that it becomes transcendental consciousness under which transcendental unity of self-consciousness may be realized. This is likely to lead to liberation (*mokṣa*). It may be mentioned here that *turīya* state also transcends *kāraṇa-śarīra* (causal body) of Vedānta.

Liberation as Self-Realization

There is immediate liberation in the case of enlightenment in which one experiences pure consciousness. This is referred to as *Brahman/Ātman* according to Vedānta. The immediate liberation takes place mainly because the metaphysical knowledge comes simultaneously along with enlightenment. This is, however, known as, "liberation while yet alive (*jīvanmukti*)", evident from the following observation:

> It is also called "liberation while yet alive" (*jīvanmukti*) because from the empirical standpoint, it appears to be acquired by someone still living, and to last as long as his life does. His remaining in the Absolute as the Absolute on the death of the body is referred to by various figurative expressions such as final release (*vimukti*), dissolution in the Absolute (*brahmaṇy-apyaya, brahma-nirvāṇa*), realization of the Absolute (*brahma-bhūya*), attainment of the Absolute (*brahma-sampatti*), final peace (*kṣema*) and the state of non-return (*apunarāvṛtti*). These terms draw attention to the absence of any remnant of merit or demerit which might occasion another body. But liberation in the strict sense is, "immediate liberation only".[4]

Liberation is the realization of *Ātman* (pure consciousness). When it descends in human beings it becomes self-consciousness (*jīvātman*). This *jīvātman* when experiences pure consciousness (*Ātman*), it becomes liberated in the sense that there will be no rebirth again in *saṁsāra* (empirical world). However, *Ātman* is

---

[4] Alston, A.J., 1997, op. cit., p. 161.

disembodied and eternal. "It is eternally liberated. Liberation is its ontological nature. It is unchangeable, eternal, omnipresent, unmodifiable, eternally fulfilled, undivided, self-luminous, supermoral, non-temporal and disembodied. It transcends virtue and vice. It transcends the past, the present and the future."[5] This is further assured in the following observation:

> Unembodiedness is inherent in the Self in accordance with such Vedic text as, "Having mediated on the self as bodiless in the midst of bodies, as permanent in the midst of the impermanent, and as great and pervasive, the wise man ceases to grieve" (Ka. 1.ii.22), "For that *Puruṣa* (infinite Being) is without vital force (i.e. organs of action) and mind (i.e. organs of perception)" (Mu. II.i.2), "For this infinite Being is unattached" (Br. IV.iii.5). Hence it is proved that the unembodiedness, called liberation, is eternal and different from the results of works that have to be performed. Among things permanent, some are changefully permanent, with regard to which the idea, "That very thing is this one", does not get sublated even though the thing goes on changing, as for instance the earth according to those who say that the world is permanent, or the three constitutes of matter (*sattva, rajas* and *tamas*), according to the Sāṁkhyas. But this one is unchangingly permanent in an absolute sense. It is all-pervasive like space, devoid of all modifications, ever content, partless, and self-effulgent by nature. This is that unembodiedness, called liberation, where the idea of the three periods of time does not exist and virtuous and vicious deeds cease along with their effects (happiness and sorrow).[6]

That apart, the fact remains that *jīvātman* is hidden by *avidyā* (ignorance). Therefore, when *avidyā* (ignorance) is removed by *vidyā* (knowledge), *mokṣa* is realized.[7] This has been further

---

5 Sinha, J.N., 2006, *Indian Philosophy*, vol. II, pp. 577-78.

6 Swami Gambhirananda, 2000, *Brahmasūtra Bhāṣya of Śrī Śaṅkarācārya*, verse 1.1.4, pp. 27-28.

7 Sinha, J.N., 2006, op. cit., p. 578.

assured by another statement that *avidyā* is destroyed by its natural opposite, perfect knowledge (*vidyā*).[8] It may, however, be noted that "liberation is different from the result of work, it is being unrelated to virtue and vice".[9] This has been explained herein:

> Liberation is the same as *Brahman* about which this deliberation is started. Had liberation been spoken of (in the scriptures) as being supplementary to action and had it been asserted as a thing to be achieved, it would become impermanent. In that case liberation would become some sort of an excellent product amidst a horde of above-mentioned products of work standing in graded order. But all who believe in liberation admit it to be eternal. Thus (since liberation is the same as *Brahman*), it is not proper to talk of *Brahman* as though it formed a factor in some action.[10]

It is observed that "in liberation the soul exists in a state of inseparableness from the supreme self".[11] In other words, the supreme self is non-separate from the individual soul. However, "the soul manifests in its own real nature of pure consciousness, still (its possession of) the earlier form, the divine majesty of (the qualified) *Brahman* that is known from such reasons as Upaniṣadic reference is not denied from the empirical point of view; and hence there is no contradiction".[12]

The Locus of Ignorance

The locus of ignorance is a bit controversial issue. According to Sureśvara, the locus of ignorance is *Brahman/Ātman*. Whereas according to Vācaspati, the seat of ignorance happens to be the individual soul.

---

8 Potter, K.H., 1998, *Encyclopedia of Indian Philosophies*, vol. III, p. 33.

9 Swami Gambhirananda, 2000, op. cit., p. 28.

10 Ibid.

11 Ibid., p. 898.

12 Ibid., p. 901.

However, if the locus of ignorance is *Brahman*, the non-duality of *Brahman* becomes doubtful because the Reality becomes two: *Brahman* and ignorance.[13] This objection has been replied by the Advaitins as follows:

> *Avidyā* is not anything real – it is false. What is real can never be negated. But *avidyā* gets negated with the knowledge of *Brahman*. Therefore, *Brahman* and *avidyā* do not belong to the same category of reality. *Avidyā* only appears to be real so long as we do not have the knowledge of *Brahman*.[14]

It is, however, observed:

> The *jīva* has no possibility of obtaining knowledge. Ignorance must be in place where it is doing its work of concealing knowledge. That is its legitimate work. And knowledge must be able to arise from *avidyā*'s destruction. But if *avidyā* is located in the *jīva*, then knowledge can never arise and liberation will be rendered impossible (as well as Śruti rendered useless).[15]

It means that if *jīva* has ignorance, knowledge can never arise. This argument may be equally applied to *Brahman* in its *saguṇa* aspect. If the location of ignorance is in *Brahman*, is it possible to gain enlightenment (liberation) by realizing *Brahman*? It seems that Madhusūdana Sarasvatī has probably realized the problem in the location of ignorance in *Brahman*. This seems to be the reason that he has explained the concept of ignorance as having its locus in *jīva* without involving mutual dependence in his *Advaita Siddhiḥ*. In this context, it is stated:

> *Avidyā* is made known by consciousness (*caitanya*), while the *jīva-caitanya* is self-luminous and self-revealed. Thus, it does not require the knowledge of *avidyā* to be known and there is no mutual dependence involved. Lastly, though *avidyā* is dependent on the *jīva-caitanya*, the *jīva-caitanya* does not rest on

---

[13] Bhattacharyya, K., 1992, *Advaita-Siddhiḥ of Madhusūdana Sarasvatī*, p. 57.

[14] Ibid.

[15] Grimes, J., 1992, *The Naiṣkarmayasiddhi of Sureśvara*, p. 157.

> *avidyā*. Thus, there is no mutual dependence. Nor can we say that one cannot be conceived of without the other: for though the existence of *avidyā* cannot be thought of apart from the existence of *caitanya*, the *jīva-caitanya* can be thought of apart from the existence of *avidyā*.[16]

It is thus evident that ignorance works at the individual level (subjective). Its counterpart *māyā* functions at the cosmic level (objective). It is, therefore, observed that "even as *Brahman* and *Ātman* are one, so are *māyā* and *avidyā* one".[17]

Three States of Consciousness (Sleep, Dream and Waking)

Before examining *turīya* being the fourth state, which is treated as means of liberation, the examination of three states – sleep, dream and waking – is important because these states explain three quarters of *Ātman*.[18] Therefore, these states are explained below.

METAPHYSICS OF SLEEP CONSCIOUSNESS

Dreamless sleep happens to be just the opposite of the waking state, which is characterized by the duality of subject and object, and the mental modifications/differentiations associated with perception of gross objects. Whereas in the dream state there is no perception of gross objects. The activities and experiences of both the states – waking and dreaming – are unified in dreamless sleep. These conscious experiences being the forms of thought become a thick mass of consciousness in dreamless sleep. This state of deep sleep is referred to as *prajñāna-ghana*, i.e. a thick mass of unified consciousness.[19] In the state of

16 Grimes, J., 1992, op. cit., p. 155.

17 Radhakrishnan, S., 2002, *Indian Philosophy*, vol. II, p. 587.

18 Swami Nikhilananda, 2000, *The Māṇḍūkya Upaniṣad* I.6.9, p. 45 (Note 1: Fourth quarter).

19 Ibid., p. 22.

deep sleep, not only the duality of subject and object but also manifoldness (discrimination) of variety are absent.[20] The most significant aspect of deep sleep is desirelessness, although it is only relative, because desires remain in deep sleep but they are dormant and "hence unnoticed by the self on account of itself lying in dormancy".[21]

It may, however, be stated that beyond three *guṇas* – *rajas, tamas* and *sattva* – "there is the undifferentiated, the *avyaktam*, where three *guṇa*s remain in a germ state before creation. That is the cause of these two bodies.[22] *Suṣupti* (dreamless sleep) is the state of that causal body. In this state, intellect remains in sleep."[23] Although the mind recedes to the base of subtle body, it continues to exist in its subtle form, like a seed. "The proof of this can be found in everybody's experience – that the mind when we wake up, still remembers: 'I knew nothing'."[24]

One sleeps mainly because the mind reaches to the base of the subtle body. This base of subtle body happens to be the causal body of Vedānta. In fact, the causal body subsists after the gross physical body and the subtle body.[25] However, the causal body happens to be the vehicle of pure consciousness (*Ātman*) in dreamless sleep. Although the causal body is an unmanifested state, it is conceived of "as root of the manifested (*vyakta*) which is only its effect (*kārya*)".[26] The cause pre-exists in the effect. This is the causation theory of Sāṁkhya. It is, however, accepted by Vedānta.

---

[20] Swami Nikhilananda, 2000, op. cit., p. 22.

[21] Singh, S.P., 2004, *Vedic Vision of Consciousness and Reality*, p. 24.

[22] Two bodies are: subtle body and causal body.

[23] Swami Turiyananda, 2007, *Vivekacūḍāmaṇi of Śrī Śaṅkarācārya*, verse 120, p. 53.

[24] Ibid., verse 121, p. 53.

[25] Safaya, R., 1976, *Indian Psychology*, p. 219.

[26] Rene, G., 1981, *Man and His Becoming According to Vedānta*, p. 104.

Dreamless sleep has, however, been referred to as *cetomukha*, because it happens to be the doorway to the cognition of the two other states of consciousness known as dream and waking. The *ceta* is the perceiving entity characterized by empirical consciousness leading to the experience of dreams, etc. Therefore, it is called *cetomukha*. It is also called *prajñā* because it is conscious of all previous states of consciousness experienced in waking and dream.[27]

While commenting on *Māṇḍūkya* VII, Śaṅkara had shown that although the three states – waking, dream and sleep – are changing and negatable, "The consciousness which is present therein is constant and invariable. Change of one state to another cannot affect the unchanging nature of consciousness itself. Therefore, pure consciousness is real."[28]

The reality of pure consciousness is based on the sleep experience of consciousness, which happens to be undifferentiated, distinctless and non-dual absolute consciousness. Pure consciousness being the Absolute Reality, it is referred to as *pāramārathika-satya* in Vedānta.

Further, based on the Gauḍapāda's *kārikā* IV.45, Śaṅkara had concluded that the Ultimate Reality is consciousness which is unborn, immovable and not of the character of material objects. "It is the consciousness which, being free from birth, change, etc.; is all peace therefore non-dual."[29] One can have a dim experience of pure consciousness in dreamless sleep as bliss.

The following observation regarding the sleep experience is worth noting:

> In psychological investigations of a conscious subject, or during introspection, the act of investigation disturbs the mental state under investigation. *Suppose one wants to find out how he actually*

[27] Swami Nikhilananda, 2000, op. cit., pp. 23-25.

[28] Ibid., p. 55.

[29] Ibid., p. 262.

> *goes to sleep. So long as he is alert (awake, so that he finds out how sleep comes to him), the very fact of alertness prevents him from going to sleep. We can never know how we actually go to sleep. That is impossible in the very nature of things.*[30] (emphasized by *italics*)

The above observation on sleep shows that the sleep is the most complex state. In this state, one may experience pure consciousness, on which the entire universe depends in the sense that it is known mainly due to consciousness. One may accept or may not accept the sleep state as experience of pure consciousness. Śaṅkarācārya has, however, taken deep sleep as the unity of subject and object. On waking from sleep one realizes that "I slept well". This was not acceptable to Rāmānuja, founder of the Viśiṣṭādvaita school of Vedānta. According to him, a person on waking from sleep says only that "I slept well" and has no consciousness of anything. Therefore, Rāmānuja denied the persistence of pure consciousness in the deep sleep. This has already been discussed in Chapter 1.

DREAM CONSCIOUSNESS

The perceiving objects in the dream state are transitory, but in the waking state they appear to be permanent, indicating thereby some difference between the two. In the latter, the senses cooperate in contacting the external objects, but not in the former. In the dream state, "there are no such objects as chariots there, in dream. Nor are animals to be yoked to them, such as horses; nor roads for the chariots".[31] But in the waking state these are there. As a result, their functioning leaves some impressions in the mind in the waking state. These accumulated impressions work in the dream state without the presence of objects. That is why it is stated:

> When he dreams, he takes away a little of (the impressions of)

[30] Kothari, D.S., 2002, "Atom and Self", p. 314.

[31] Swami Madhavananda, 1997, *The Bṛhadāraṇyaka Upaniṣad*, verse IV.iii.10, p. 444.

> this all-embracing world (the waking state), himself puts the body aside and himself creates (a dream body in its place), revealing his own lustre by his light and dreams. In this state, the man himself becomes the light.[32]

It seems that in the dream state the self in itself, having withdrawn from the external world, starts operating in the light of innate consciousness. In this state, consciousness gets concentrated well within itself and becomes highly creative.[33] It is further observed:

> Consciousness tends to objectify itself in various ways. This is evident not only from the act of perception but also from the experience of the state of dream. In the state of dream, the person concerned remains stuck to his bed all the time and yet undergoes experiences involving almost as much tangible an objective environment around him as in the waking state with all its sensibility, variety and physical substantiality.[34]

It may, however, be stated that, "dream vision is a kind of memory, whereas the visions of the waking state are forms of perceptions (through the valid means of knowledge)".[35]

A representative analysis of dreams is advocated in the *Vedānta-Paribhāṣā*. This is evident from the statement that, "I saw a chariot in a dream". Although the chariot, etc. experienced in a dream are also illusory and persist as long as the illusion lasts.[36] There is no denying the fact that the author of *Vedānta-Paribhāṣā* does not follow Śaṅkarācārya and holds the presentative theory of dream.[37] Yet, the fact remains that Śaṅkarācārya has advocated

---

32 Swami Madhavananda, 1997, op. cit., verse IV.iii.9, p. 440.

33 Singh, S.P., 2004, op. cit., p. 23.

34 Ibid., p. 15.

35 Swami Gambhirananda, 2000, op. cit., verse II.ii.29, p. 423.

36 Swami Madhavananda, 2000, *Vedānta-Paribhāṣā of Dharmarāja Adhvarīndra*, p. 57.

37 Safaya, R., 1976, op. cit., p. 231.

mainly the representative theory of dreams. This is evident from commentary on Gauḍapāda's *kārikā* 1.4. This states that "the *Taijasa* is called the *antaḥprajñā* or conscious of the internal because his consciousness in dream becomes aware of the mental states, which are impressions left by the previous waking state".[38]

In the *Praśna Upaniṣad* also the representative theory of dreams has been advocated in very precise manner. It is stated:

> In dreams we experience seeing many things, hearing many things, tasting many things and so on, the concerned sense organs remaining non-functioning, while the dreaming mind plays their role. All the objects experienced have mind alone for their source; those objects are also enjoyed by the same mind. Dream could, therefore, be defined as the state in which both subject and object arise from mind, wherein the subject also enjoys the object. Śaṅkara puts the same in another fashion by saying that dream is the state in which senses merge with mind, while the mind remains itself not merged with anything.[39]

Despite the fact that on waking, the dream objects turn to be false, yet the treatment of dream as perception provides the directness and immediacy to objects in the dream experience itself. This immediacy and certainty of objects in the dream experience provides an empirically real fact.[40] This has been supported by Śaṅkarācārya's commentary on the *Chāndogya Upaniṣad*. It is stated:

> Objects perceived in the waking state also are accomplished by mental ideas only. ... Therefore, it is surely admitted that things mental and external are related to each other as cause and effect, like a seed and its sprout. Although the mental (images) originate from external things, and the external things originate from the mind, still, in one's own Self, they

---

[38] Swami Nikhilananda, 2000, op. cit., p. 19.

[39] Swami Muni Narayana Prasad, 1999, *Praśna Upaniṣad*, verse IV.5, pp. 128-29.

[40] Indich, W.M., 2000, *Consciousness in Advaita Vedānta*, p. 84.

are never false.[41]

From this, an inference has been drawn that "Śaṅkara extends the discussion of philosophically relevant experience beyond the waking state and its conditions".[42]

Having examined the various concepts used in Upaniṣads to explain the dream experience now it appears that when the Vedāntic vision is pursued seriously, both the waking state and dreaming state are the states of mental activity. "If any difference in detail can be discovered, it is no more than the difference between one mode of thought and another."[43]

When each state is viewed from its own standpoint, it emerges that "thinking, feeling and the perception of tangible objects are activities common both to waking and dreaming experience".[44] However, the tangible objects are absent in dream state; but when their position in waking state is examined seriously, they turn out to be the mental ideas only. Thus, the tangible objects perceived in the waking states have no independent existence. "They exist as notions in the perceiver's mind; and thus between mind and matter the destination is unreal, as it is also between the thought and the perception of a tangible object. If this is granted, then to be awake has no meaning and there is no waking state: it is all a dream. But a dream, so called only from the standpoint of an inexistent waking state, is also a misnomer."[45]

WAKING CONSCIOUSNESS

The mind and senses are active in the waking state, so as to bring the knowledge or awareness of the external world to human beings. In the *Māṇḍūkya Upaniṣad*, the waking state has

---

41 Swami Gambhirananda, 2003, *Chāndogya Upaniṣad*, verse III.5.4, p. 607.

42 Indich, W.M., 2000, op. cit., p. 85.

43 Levy, J., 2004, *The Nature of Man According to the Vedānta*, p. 19.

44 Ibid.

45 Ibid., p. 20.

been compared with *Vaiśvānara*,[46] which has two words: *vaiśvā* and *nara*. The former is related to *viśva*; referred to as cosmic system, whereas the latter (*nara*) is known as individual human. In other words *viśva* pertains to universal (*samaṣṭi*) and *nara* as particular individual (*vyaṣṭi*). "If these two form the two extreme poles of a situation, then *Vaiśvānara* is the unitive or non-dual consciousness functioning in the waking state. This life-situation forms the *jāgrat* sphere of activity of consciousness."[47]

In the waking state, we remain conscious of the external world (*bahiḥ-prajñaḥ*) and the gross objects are being experienced through nineteen facets, which include the five sense organs, the five motor organs, the five forces and the mind, known as *antaḥkaraṇa* in Vedānta. It has four aspects: *manas, buddhi, ahaṁkāra* and *citta*. So nineteen facets are involved in the waking state for obtaining the knowledge of the external world.

The peculiarity of the waking state is that it is mostly outwardly oriented (*bahiḥ-prajñaḥ*). In this context, it is stated that "it remains conscious of everything outside, yet unaware of itself. A subject can know objects while being ignorant of what the subject is. Such is the nature of waking state. All such objects put together form the world or *viśva*; and the individual subject who knows this *viśva* is a human being or *nara*."[48] However, the waking state represents the dynamic modes of pure consciousness, in which the external world and human beings are interacting with each other, so that experience is gained by human beings. In this state, the duality – subject and object – is involved in the act of knowledge. Therefore, waking consciousness provides only relative knowledge of things. The experience or knowledge from the external world is possible mainly because human beings have the capacity to perceive the external world.

---

[46] Swami Nikhilananda, 2000, op. cit., verse 3, p. 13.

[47] Swami Muni Narayana Prasad, 2009b, *Īśāvāsya and Māṇḍūkya Upaniṣads*, p. 91.

[48] Ibid., p. 92.

Causal Body of Human Being and Causal Consciousness

CAUSAL BODY

It is observed that "the causal body owes its name to the fact that in it reside the causes which manifest themselves as effects in the lower planes".[49] This is mainly because the experiences of past lives are stored in the causal body, which has two main functions:

i. "To act as a vehicle for the Ego: the causal body is the body of *manas*, the form aspect of the individual, the true man, the Thinker."[50]

ii. "To act as a receptacle or storehouse for the essence of the man's experiences in his various incarnations. The causal body is that into which is woven everything which can endure, and in which are stored the germs of qualities, to be carried over the next incarnation."[51]

Every individual has a causal body, which constitutes individuality. This body will last through the whole of the human evolution. It is observed that "the causal body is a true register – *the only true register* – of the growth of the man of the stage of evolution to which he has attained".[52] However, the causal body is the organ for abstract thinking. "In the thinker, thus, is the store of experiences, reaped in all our past lives, harvested through many rebirths."[53]

The following observations regarding the causal body may be worth stating:

i. The causal body is the form aspect of the individual. In this context, it may be noted that when by the power of the Self

[49] Powell, A.E., 2000a, *The Causal Body and the Ego*, p. 89.

[50] Ibid.

[51] Ibid.

[52] Ibid., p. 90.

[53] Ibid., p. 91.

preparing its own habitation, the matter of the mind plane begins slowly to evolve, then there is a downpouring from the great ocean of *ātman–buddhi*, which is ever brooding over the evolution of man, and this, as it were, meets the upward-growing, unfolding mind stuff, comes into union with it, fertilizes it, and at that point of union the causal body, the individual, is formed.[54]

ii. Life after life, century after century, millennium after millennium, this evolution of individual proceeds, and in aiding its growth by conscious effort we are working in harmony with the divine will, and carrying out the purpose for which we are here. Nothing good that is once woven into the texture of this causal body is ever lost; nothing is dissipated; for this is the man who lives forever.[55]

The causal body is treated as repository of kārmic impressions which are accumulated in the course of many lives. In this context, the following observations are worth noting:

> Out of this dense store there arise not only the characteristics that determine each individual being but also the forms that appear in his or her consciousness in the shape of the empirical world-forms, moreover, that are shared with other members of our species and even to some extent with other species whose world-experience is in part similar to our own. Thus behind the conscious mind there lies a vast hinterland of unconscious memory, which is the real source of each individual being. Rebirth comes about when a group of accumulated impressions or "Kārmic seeds" (*karmabījas*) come together and stir into activity, while a further group (forming *sañcita-karma*) remains dormant. The awakening impressions form *prārabdha-karma*, the portion of *karma* that finds expression in course of a single lifetime; emerging from the causal body in the shape of formative forces (*saṁskāras*) – predisposed capacities and

[54] Besant, A., 2000, *Man and His Bodies*, pp. 106-07.

[55] Ibid., p. 114.

patterns of thought and behaviour – they constitute the subtle body of the new individual being. *Prārabdha-karma*, once launched into manifestation, must play itself out: even the liberated person (*jīvanmukta*), until physical death, remains subject to *prārabdha-karma*, which, like an arrow once has left the bow, must complete its course.[56]

CAUSAL CONSCIOUSNESS

It is explained as:

> Causal consciousness thus deals with the essence of a thing, whilst the lower mind studies its details. With the mind, we talk round a subject, or endeavour to explain it; with the causal consciousness, we take up the essence of the idea of the subject, and move it as a whole, as one moves a piece when playing chess. The causal plane is a world of realities: we no longer deal with emotions, ideas or conceptions, but with thing in itself.[57]

The thinker, with his causal consciousness dwells within himself, engrossed with deeper aspects of life and thought, "seeking to understand causes rather than troubling himself with effects, and approaching nearer and nearer to the recognition of the One that underlies all the diversities of external nature".[58] It is, further, explained as follows:

> It is only when consciousness has withdrawn from the lower bodies, and is once more centred in the ego, that the final result of the incarnation just concluded is known. Then it is seen what new qualities he has acquired in that particular little cycle of his evolution. At that time also, a glimpse of the life as a whole is obtained: the ego has for a moment a flash of clearer consciousness, in which he sees the result of the life just completed, and something of what will follow from it in his next birth.[59]

---

[56] Cross, S., 2014, *Schopenhauer's Encounter with Indian Thought*, p. 140.

[57] Powell, A.E., 2000a, op. cit., p. 105.

[58] Ibid., p. 106.

[59] Ibid., p. 129.

Means of Liberation

TURĪYA

Turīya is the fourth state, as distinct from the other three states: waking, dreaming and sleep. This is explained as follows:

> The fourth state is eternal and the other three states come and go in it. In *turīya* there is an awareness that the mind has merged in its source, the Heart and is quiescent there, although some thoughts still impinge on it and the senses are still somewhat active. In *nirvikalpa* the senses are inactive and thoughts are totally absent. Hence the experience of pure consciousness in this state is intense and blissful. *Turīya* is obtainable in *savikalpa samādhi*. . . . The bliss which is enjoyed unconsciously in sleep is enjoyed consciously in *turīya*, that is the only difference. The bliss enjoyed in the waking state is second-hand, it is an adjunct of the real bliss (*upādhi-ānanda*).[60]

However, *turīya* is treated as transcendental undifferentiated knowledge. It is distinguished from different levels. This is explained below on the basis of verse I.vii of the *Māṇḍūkya Upaniṣad*:

> *Turīya* is not that which is conscious of the internal (subjective) world, nor that which is conscious of the external (objective) world, nor that which is conscious of both, nor that which is a mass all sentiency, nor that which is simple consciousness, nor that which is insentient (it is), unseen (by any sense organ), not related to anything, incomprehensible (by the mind), uninferable, unthinkable, indescribable, essentially of the nature of consciousness, constituting the Self alone, negation of all phenomena, the Peaceful, all Bliss and the Non-dual. This is what is known as the fourth (*turīya*). This is the *Ātman* and it has so be realized.[61]

---

60 Godman, D., 1992, *Be As You Are*, p. 150.

61 Swami Nikhilananda, 2000, op. cit., pp. 47-48. It may be noted that "by the statement that *turīya* is not a mass of all sentiency, it is denied that it is the condition of deep sleep which is held to be a causal condition on account of one's inability to distinguish the truth from error (in deep sleep)." – p. 50

While commenting on the above *sūtra*, it is observed that "the consciousness which is present therein is constant and invariable. Change of one state to another cannot affect the unchanging nature of consciousness itself. Therefore, pure consciousness is real."[62] This shows that *turīya* is realization of pure consciousness, which happens to be *Brahman/Ātman* according to Vedānta. In other words, *turīya* is nothing but the realization of *Brahman/Ātman*. This experience is enlightenment.

In *turīya*, there is the cessation of illusion. In that, the attributes which characterize the three states – waking, dreaming and dreamless sleep – are negated, Hence it is ever peaceful without any manifestation of change and all bliss. In this context it is observed that "as it is non-dual, i.e. devoid of illusory ideas of distinction, therefore, it is called *turīya*. ... This, indeed, is the *Ātman* and it should be known."[63] *Ātman* is related to *turīya*.

In the *Bṛhadāraṇyaka Upaniṣad*, liberation is defined as:

> Liberation is not an effect – it is but the destructions of bondage, not a created thing. ... Production, attainment, modification and purification are the functions of work. In other words, work can produce or bring within reach or modify or purify something; it has no other functions besides these. ... And liberation is not one of these; we have already said that it is hidden by ignorance.[64]

It is, thus, from the above observation we come to know that liberation (*mokṣa*) can neither be produced nor be attained. In this context, it is stated that "liberation is the natural condition of consciousness, while the activity which appears to bring this realization about actually fails to effect consciousness at all."[65] This may be, reassured by Śaṅkara's views on self-knowledge.

---

[62] Swami Nikhilananda, 2000, op. cit., p. 55.

[63] Ibid., pp. 51-52.

[64] Swami Madhavananda, 1997, op. cit., verse III.iii.1, p. 312.

[65] Indich, W.M., 2000, op. cit., p. 107.

It is stated that "though *Ātman* is an ever-present reality, yet because of ignorance it is unrealized. On the destruction of ignorance *Ātman* is realized. It is like the case of the ornament on one's neck."[66]

The realization of *Ātman* which is pure consciousness means the liberation (*mokṣa*) according to Vedānta. It is further explained as follows:

> The *yogī* endowed with complete enlightenment sees, through the eye of knowledge, the entire universe in his own Self and regards everything as the Self and nothing else. ... The tangible universe is verily *Ātman*: nothing whatever exists that is other than *Ātman*. As pots and jars are verily clay and cannot be anything but clay, so to the enlightenment, all that is perceived is the Self.[67]

However, the following two observations regarding *turīya* are worth noting:

i. "*Turīya* transcends the conditions of space, time and causality."[68] In such a situation, it becomes an impersonal immortality, an undifferentiated eternal awareness.[69]
ii. *Mokṣa* is a state of eternal rest, equilibrium and continuity as opposed to the struggle, imbalance and contradictory nature of *saṁsāra*.[70]

Turīya state is also treated as transcendental consciousness, because it transcends three states of consciousness: sleep, dream and waking. This transcendental consciousness is the transcendental unity of self-consciousness as mentioned in

---

66 Swami Nikhilananda, 2008, *Self Knowledge of Srī Śaṅkarācārya*, verse 44, p. 168.

67 Ibid., verses 47 and 48, p. 171.

68 Indich, W.M., 2000, op. cit., p. 105.

69 Ibid., p. 106.

70 Ibid.

the introduction. In that, it becomes like *Ātman* of Vedānta. Therefore, the realization of transcendental unity of self-consciousness is also likely lead to liberation (*mokṣa*). In this context, the following observation deserves attention:

> This is the highest state called *turīya* (the fourth), the state of direct perception of the Absolute (*sākṣātkāra*), perfect intuition (*samyag-jñāna*), intuitional consciousness or experience absolute (*anubhava*). This is the goal of all experience (*anubhavāvasānaṁ*). It is of the nature of perception, as the Self witnesses itself directly. It is the state of self-realization. It corresponds to the *samādhi* of Yoga. Herein the individual Mind mingles with the universal Mind, the individual consciousness in the Cosmic Consciousness. *Jīva* in *Īśvara*, *Ātman* in *Brahman* and *vyaṣṭi* in *samaṣṭi*.[71]

The *turīya* state is also treated beyond *ānandamaya-kośa* of the *Taittirīya Upaniṣad*. *Ānandamaya-kośa* is equated with the *kāraṇa-śarīra* (causal body) of Vedānta. This, along with the other *kośas*, is stated below:

Pañca Kośas and Their Relationship with Śarīra-traya, Avasthā-traya and the Mode of Self

Pañca Kośas	*Śarīra-traya (Three Śarīras)*	*Avasthā-traya (Three States)*	*Mode of Self*	
			Vyaṣṭi (Microcosm)	*Samaṣṭi (Macrocosm)*
Ānandamaya	Causal body	Deep sleep (*suṣupti*)	*Prajñā*	*Īśvara*
Vijñānamaya *Manomaya* *Prāṇamaya*	Subtle body (*sūkṣma-śarīra*)	Dream (*svapna*)	*Taijasa*	*Hiraṇya-garbha*
Annamaya	Gross body (*sthūla-śarīra*)	Waking (*jāgrat*)	*Vaiśvānara* or *Viśva*	*Virāṭ*

Source: Swami Atmapriyananda, 2006, *Bhavamukha*, p. 287

[71] Safaya, 1976, op. cit., pp. 232-33.

On the basis of the above statement, it is observed:

> Beyond the casual (*kāraṇa)* is the Great Cause (*mahākāraṇa*) which is the *turīya caitanya*. *Turīya* is the Absolute, Transcendental, Infinite, *Hiraṇyagarbha* is the first born or *prathamaja*. It is at the stage of *Hiraṇyagarbha* that the relative world of names and forms appears. Beyond *Īśvara* or *Saguṇa-Brahman* is the Absolute or *Nirguṇa-Brahman*.[72]

It is, thus, evident that the realization of *turīya* state is liberation (*mokṣa*), according to Advaita Vedānta. However, the self-realization in the simple language, based on the discourses of Bhagavan Ramana Maharshi, is stated below:

> The state we call realization is simply being oneself, not knowing anything or becoming anything. If one has realized, one is that alone which "is" and which alone has always been. One cannot describe that state. One can only be that. Of course, we loosely talk of Self-realization, for want of better term. How to realize or make real that which alone is real? Realization is nothing to be gained afresh; it is already there. All that is necessary is to get rid of the thought "I have not realized". Realization is already there. The state free from thoughts is the only real state. There is no such action as realization.[73]

---

[72] Swami Atmapriyananda, 2006, "Bhavamukha", p. 287.

[73] Ramana Maharshi, 1999, *Absolute Consciousness*, pp. 136-37.

9

Perception and Self-consciousness in Yogācāra Vijñānavāda of Buddhist Philosophy

Introduction

THERE are two faculties by which one acquires knowledge: (i) the faculty of external perception; and (ii) self-consciousness, which is the faculty of internal experience.[1] Since the external world is not accepted by the Yogācāra Vijñānavāda, the representative theory of perception is advocated. This theory has several limitations. However, without external world what one perceives are mere images of the objects depending upon its impressions which get imprinted on the consciousness. As a result, perception becomes quite complicated in the case of Yogācāra Vijñānavāda Buddhist philosophy. The main reason for such a complicated theory of perception has recently been attributed to the fact that the Buddhists did not acknowledge the existence of separate spirit entity.[2]

There is no denying the fact that the Buddha had evolved the philosophy of Anātmavāda (no soul or self). Yet, several concepts like *bhavaṅga citta* and *ālaya-vijñāna*, which are introduced later with a view to deliver the religious discourses consistent and logical in the sense that without enduring any entity like self which causes rebirth in *saṁsāra* (physical world), *nirvāṇa* has no meaning. In the present context, self-consciousness

---

[1] Bart, W.H., 1995, *Philosopy of Knowledge*, vol. II, p. 190.

[2] Mookerjee, S., 1993, *The Buddhist Philosophy of Universal Flux*, p. 338.

is representing the Self in perception. This is mainly because self-consciousness is treated as *jīvātman* (i.e. self) according to Advaita Vedānta school of Indian philosophy.

However, according to Bart,

> Perception is the power by which we are made aware of the phenomenon of the external world. Self-consciousness is the power by which we apprehend the phenomenon of the internal. The objects of the former are all presented to us in Space and Time: space and time are thus two conditions: the two fundamental forms of external perception. The objects of the latter are all apprehended by us in Time and in Self: time and self are thus the two conditions – the fundamental forms, of internal perception or self-consciousness. Time is thus a form or condition common to both faculties; while space is a form peculiar to the one, self a form peculiar to other.[3]

It is, thus, evident that self-consciousness is in a way representing self in the internal perception. Further, "in regard to self-consciousness – the faculty of internal perception – philosophers have been more harmonious than in regard to external perception".[4]

Self in Tattvasaṁghraha

The self-cognition of cognition has not been accepted by Śāntarakṣita in the *Tattvasaṁgraha*, which is the basic treatise of the Sautrāntika Vijñānavāda school of Buddhist philosophy. The main reason for not accepting the self-cognition of cognition is stated below:

> One and the same entity, which is impartite in form, cannot have three characters. Hence, the only right view is that the self-cognition of the cognition is due to its being the very nature of consciousness.[5]

---

[3] Bart, W.H., 1995, op. cit., vol. II, pp. 190-91.

[4] Ibid., p. 190.

[5] Jha, G., 1986, *Tattvasaṁghraha of Śāntarakṣita* vol. II, Texts 2001-02, p. 950.

According to Śāntarakṣita, the self-cognition means that it does not require any other cognition to cognize it. Yet, it is not uncognized.[6] It is further explained in another study that "the nature of self-awareness is self-evident. It is known to all".[7] Let us see how Śāntarakṣita himself has defined the self in the same study at another place:

> That alone is the knowledge of self, which consists in the perception of pure self. As there in the only cognition is that of pure consciousness freed from all adventitious impurities.[8]

The pure self in the above passage is referred to as *viśuddhātman*.[9] It may further be noted that *prabhāsvaramitam cittam*, in verse 210 of Dharmakīrti's *Pramāṇavārttikam* is also referred to as the real self. It is stated that "the real self is self-luminous consciousness; all impurities are adventitious".[10]

The above observations suggest that self is represented by self-consciousness, which is involved in internal perception. Therefore, the conclusion that there is no self or soul entity involved in the Buddhist theory of perception does not seem to be appropriate.

External World and Object of Perception

EXTERNAL WORLD

There is some controversy regarding the external world among different schools of Buddhism. According to the Yogācāra Vijñānavāda, the external world does not seem to have independent existence. Even, "if it exists, we have no way of

---

6 Jha, G., 1986, op. cit., vol. II, Text 2012, p. 954.

7 Sinha, J.N., 1999, *Indian Realism*, p. 13.

8 Jha, G., 1986, op. cit., Text: 3535, p. 1543.

9 Sharma, C.D., 2003, *A Critical Survey of Indian Philosophy*, p. 325.

10 Shah, N.J., 1967, *Akalanka's Criticism of Dharmakirti's Philosophy*, p. 174.

knowing that it exists",[11] whereas "the Sautrāntika seemed to have allowed the possibility of the external world".[12] In this context, the Buddhist theory of atomism (Pramāṇavāda) is discussed below.

Atomism

Atoms are treated like the data of sensory perceptual consciousness, where the material object is a "functional construction out of these atomistic data".[13] The atoms are phenomenal elements rather than physical elements. These are treated as substantially real (*dravya sat*), whereas the material objects like the pot or the table are imagined to be real (*saṁvṛtti sat*).[14]

According to the Yogācāra Vijñānavāda, atom stimulants cannot be perceived, because they do not appear in consciousness.[15] Whereas the Sautrāntika is of the view that the gross pot is visible because it is "made up of the cluster of the subtler atomic constituents. They are what we call the atom-visibles, that is, the visible atomic data."[16]

In view of the above observations, let us see how Vasubandhu and Diṅnāga view the atomic theory as it emerged in the Vaiśeṣika school of Indian philosophy. The view of Vasubandhu as stated in the auto-commentary on the verse 11 of *Viṁśatikā-Kārikā* is stated below:

> The Vaiśeṣika believed that spheres like material form (*rūpa*), which holds one to one correspondence with the concepts of material form, represent a unity (*eka*) in terms of a molecule,

---

[11] Matilal, B.K., 1997, *Logic, Language and Reality*, p. 221.

[12] Ibid.

[13] Ibid.

[14] Ibid.

[15] Ibid., p. 226.

[16] Ibid.

> i.e. an entity that consists of parts (*avayavīrūpa*). However, in terms of atoms it is a plurality (*aneka*).[17]
>
> Vasubandhu argues that a whole is not perceived apart from its parts. Even so, a molecule is nowhere perceived independent of its constituents. Similarly, the object is not a unity of atoms or parts. Neither is it a plurality, for the atoms that go to constitute a molecule are also not perceived either as individual units (*pratyeka*) or an aggregate (*saṁhata*).[18]

However, Vasubandhu has denied the validity of the atomic theory of the Vaiśeṣika. This is stated in the auto-commentary on the verse 12 of Vaiśeṣika. It is observed that:

> When an atom has to combine with six others from six directions, it has to possess six facets. For one atom cannot occupy the space of another. However, if each atom were to occupy an identical space and by definition an atom has no magnitude, then aggregate itself would be a mere atom. In fact, an aggregate would not be perceived if parts are separate from one another (*paraspara-vyatirekād*).[19]

Diṅnāga has, however, argued that "the atoms being formless, themselves cannot contribute the form or image to the corresponding cognitive state. Thus, the atoms do not satisfy the second condition for being the objective support of consciousness."[20] However, Diṅnāga has also reached to the conclusion that "the so-called *ālambana* or objective support does not lie outside consciousness. But in the *Pramāṇasamuccaya*, Diṅnāga developed his doctrine of *sva-saṁvitti*, self-consciousness or self-awareness."[21] This doctrine is explained below:

> The doctrine of self-consciousness states that in each act

---

17 Kalupahana, D.J., 1992a, *The Principles of Buddhist Psychology*, p. 182.

18 Ibid., pp. 182-83.

19 Ibid., p. 183.

20 Matilal, B.K., 1997, op. cit., p. 236.

21 Ibid.

> or moment of consciousness there are not only two forms or appearance, the forms of compression (*grāhaka*) and the comprehensible (*grāhya*), but also a self-comprehension or self-cognition where both these forms are registered. For Diṅnāga, self-cognition is a kind of mental perception which constitutes an integral part of each episode of awareness. Each episode of awareness in the consciousness series is ultimately real and self revealing in character while it reveals both the object form and its compression.[22]

It is, thus, evident that in each event of self-consciousness, there are three aspects; the object aspect, its cognition and self-awareness (*grāhya, grāhaka* and *sva-saṁvitti*). All the three are integral parts of one momentary state of consciousness. This is explained as follows:

> Since there is the invariable fact that the object-form is never apprehended without its cognition-form being apprehended, it is argued that one should not be distinguished from other. What then, accounts for the particularity and variety of our different cognitive states? The answer is amazingly simple. It is not the external world but the internal *vāsanā*, individual backlog of our personal history, our mental dispositions, the residual forces of our past actions, coupled with the ingrained, beginning-less, *avidya* "wrong notions".[23]

However, according to Dharmakīrti, all things are momentary. "As a result a thing is already destroyed when the perception of it takes place. How could then it be held that the perception grasps a thing for the thing is not there be grasped by it."[24] In order to avoid this difficulty, Dharmakīrti has suggested that:

> An external thing causes its own perception, that is, is the object of perception inasmuch as it has the power to leave behind, through the sense-channel, its own impression

---

[22] Matilal, B.K., 1997, op. cit., p. 237.

[23] Ibid., p. 238.

[24] Shah, N.J., 1967, op. cit., p. 207.

> in consciousness. Thus what we directly perceive is this impression; the object is at best inferred from this impression or copy. The perception of an external thing is therefore only the perception of an impression or copy in the mind, which copy of impression is supposed to represent faithfully the external thing. This raises the question as to what the immediate cause of perception exactly is. The copy is to be considered as the immediate cause of perceptual cognition and the perceptual cognition as such is the result. But the copy in the cognition and the cognition as such are really identical. So, how could they be related as cause and effect. In reply it is said that as a matter of fact the copy in the cognition is the determinant and the cognition as such is what is to be determined on the basis of this copy. But who determines it on the basis of the copy? It itself cannot determine itself because it is indeterminate. So, for this purpose it requires the determinate cognition arising in its wake. Unless and until the cognition is determined it is as good as non-existent because it cannot lead to successful purposive action and attainment of the desired object. It becomes efficient when it is, for example, ascertained as "cognition-of-the-blue-object" by the determinate cognition. Hence only those indeterminate cognitions that generate determinate cognitions in their train are valid and efficient. If the indeterminate cognition does not generate determinate cognition in its wake, then the consciousness-of-the-object remains unascertained and consequently the indeterminate cognition remains inefficient with regard to its object. It might be urged that if it be so, then the indeterminate cognition is valid only when it is coupled with the determinate cognition and not in its pristine form of pure sensation.[25]

According to Diṅnāga, the external reality exists as a unique particular (*svalakṣaṇa*). "This unique particular is so atomic as to have no extension in space or persistence in time."[26]

---

25 Shah, N.J., 1967, op. cit., p. 207.

26 Pandit, M.L., 2008, *The Buddhist View of Knowledge and Reality*, p. 235.

OBJECT OF PERCEPTION: UNIQUE PARTICULAR

The object of perception happens to be the unique particular, meaning thereby an entity be unique that is not shared by anything else. This is interpreted as the thing in itself.[27] It is stated that:

> The peculiarity of Diṅnāga's doctrine about the particular and the general consists in its conception of the particular as the unique. The existence in every direct cognition of something unique by being present to me in perception, is also pointed by Bosanquet, *Logic* 1.76. Here it assumes the role of the thing in itself, it is the absolute particular, the limit of all synthetic construction. It represents a single moment (*kṣaṇa*). It has no extension in space (*deśa-ananugata*), no duration in time (*kāla-ananugata*), it is similar to nothing (*sarvato-vyāvṛtta*), it is unique (*trailokya-vyāvṛtta*).[28]

The unique particular is perceived directly (direct perception), without any distortion or delusions. The object of cognition is, however, double in the sense that it is perceived in two moments: (i) the first moment, happens to be pure sensation; and (ii) the moment of reflection by which one realizes that one has perception of something (this is blue) on the basis of sensation; which is known as the unique particular, i.e. the thing in itself.

It may be noted that the unique particular in the form of pure sensation is cognized as indeterminate perception (*nirvikalpaka pratyakṣa*), which is treated as the Ultimate Reality. The indeterminate perception is always preceded to determine perception. It is explained as follows:

> Since the determinate perception is of a generalized nature, it means that the objects being the construction of the mind, do not represent the external reality as it is in itself. Thus, whatever is cognized in and through the determinate perception has no ontological value, because determinate perceptions do

---

[27] Stcherbatsky, T., 1996, *Buddhist Logic*, vol. II, p. 33.

[28] Ibid., n. 3, p. 33.

> not give the exact picture of the perceived. It is an unreal constituent, namely the generalized nature of perception, which is involved in determinate perception. However, it is through the indeterminate perception that reality as it is in itself is cognized. It is so because in this cognition it is the unique particular (*svalakṣaṇā*) that is involved. Although we may not be conscious of indeterminate in thought, it always precedes determinate perception.[29]

The most intriguing is that the unique particular as given in indeterminate perception, it is not possible to cognize it since it ceases to be before it is reached.[30] However, it has also been observed:

> The sense consciousnesses can reach the realm of things in themselves in combination with mind consciousness, as long as they are functioning directly with their objects of perception. A baby looks at toy in a way that does not use her mind very much – there is no comparison, remembering or judging. She has not yet learned to think. This toy is not as colourful as that toy. I like that toy better: She simply enjoys the form of the toy (the sense-object) that her eyes (sense-base) make contact with. That way of looking is the direct mode of perception, and through it the realm of things in themselves can be reached.[31]

This observation may be further supported by the Tibetan Buddhist philosophy. It is stated:

> When we bring a baby into a temple, the baby directly sees all the objects, and images, but, it does not think, "Oh, that is a throne, that is the Buddha" instead it has a direct experience of the temple. During meditation, we should have this direct experience without thoughts and concepts, and experience self-knowledge.[32]

---

[29] Pandit, M.L., 2008, op. cit., pp. 219-20.

[30] Ibid., pp. 220-21.

[31] Hanh, T., 2008, *Understanding Our Mind*, p. 150.

[32] Rinpoche, T., 2001, *Transcending Ego*, p. 35.

The above concepts of indeterminate perception (*nirvikalpaka pratyakṣa*) and determinate perception (*savikalpaka pratyakṣa*) are more or less similar to the Vedāntic version. In this context, it is observed that "there is in *nirvikalpaka pratyakṣa*, the awareness of existence (*sattā*) alone. This existence becomes afterwards differentiated in *savikalpaka pratyakṣa* through the activity of the mind."[33]

SENSE PERCEPTION AND SENSATION

Sense perception is categorized as the entire class of perception to consciousness through the medium of sense organs. Once the object is presented, its function is exhausted. "So the first presentation is alone authoritative with regard to objective reality."[34] In another way, it is stated "cognition which is free from conceptual content and is not erroneous is sense perception".[35]

The thing which comes with the sense organ at one moment does not last in the second moment but somehow its image gets imprinted on the consciousness. However, "this mental image is regarded as a faithful representation and exact copy of the extra mental reality existing in its own right".[36] As against this background, let us see how the six sense organs are generating perceptual consciousness, which are treated as sensations on basis of *Abhidharmakośa* of Vasubandhu. This is presented in the following table.

---

[33] Datta, D.M., 1998, *The Six Ways of Knowing*, p. 83.

[34] Moorkerjee, S., 1993, op. cit., p. 296.

[35] Jha, G., 1986, op. cit., p. 615.

[36] Mookerjee, S., 1993, op. cit., p. 338.

Perceptual Consciousness Generated by Six Sense Organs

The Occurrent (1)	*The Locus of Organ* (2)	*The "Object" Complement or Support* (3)
Visual awareness	Faculty of vision	The visible (colour shape)
Auditory awareness	Faculty of hearing	Sound
Olfactory awareness	Faculty of olfaction	Smell
Gustatory awareness	Faculty of tasting	Taste
Tactile awareness	Faculty of touching	Touch
"Mental" awareness	Faculty of cognizing = mind	Mindables = *dharma*

Source: Matilal, B.K., 1986, *Perception*, p. 241.

The above table indicates that on the basis of faculty of vision in column (2), and colour and shape in column (3), visual awareness, arises in column (1). It may be stated that the five phenomenal properties; the visibles known as *rūpa* (matter), sound, smell, taste and touch are our immediate sensory awareness. These are our sensible phenomena in the sense that:

> The colour expanse, for example, is a case of veridical perception, for it owes its origin to the phenomenon as its "objective" complement.
>
> This dependence of the perceptual awareness upon its objective complement constitutes the minimal "causal" connection required by the Buddhist *pratyaya* theory. Even the colour expanse is only a phenomenon, for that it is not the ultimately real entity. The ultimately reals (also called the substantially reals) are the atomic constituents of these phenomena or sensibilia. Our familiar chair has, therefore, first to be resolved into (or dissolved into) a set of familiar

> sensibilia, and then the gross sensibilia are in turn resolved into cluster of atomic sensibilia.[37]

In other words, first five sense awarenesses mentioned in the above statement are merely sensations. These sensations of different sense organs are mainly concerned with present objects mainly because sense organs have the tendency to grasp present objects; they do not grasp the objects of past and future.[38] However, the objects; known by sense organs are cognized by mind, which relates these objects with its past experience. The mind works mainly with past.[39] In fact, sensations of sense organs when come in contact with mind consciousness, may be defined as cognition.[40] As mentioned above, when the objects of the (column 3) of Table 9.1 come into contact with the sense organs (column 2), the resultant different awarenesses of sense organs arise (column 1).

These are referred to as sensations. In the next stage, when these sensations become the objects of mind (*mana*), resulting process turns out to be the *manosaṁjñā* (mind's perception), which is immediately followed by *mano-vijñāna* (mind awareness).[41]

The two processes – formation of sensations and their resultant *mano-vijñāna* – are described in *kārikā* 17 of *Abhidharmakośabhāṣyam*. It is stated that "all consciousness which has just perished receives the name of *manodhātu*; in the same way, a man is both son and father; the same vegetable element is both fruit and seed".[42] It is further explained by the fact that

---

37 Matilal, B.K., 1986, op. cit., p. 242.

38 Swami Yogindrananda, 2005, *Pramāṇavārttikama of Dharmakīrti*, vol. II, p. 597.

39 Haldar, A., 2001, *Some Psychological Aspects of Early Buddhist Philosophy*, p. 52.

40 Ibid., p. 51.

41 Ibid., p. 44.

42 Pruden, L.M., 1991, *Abhidharmakośabhāṣyam*, vol. I, p. 75.

five sense consciousnesses have their support from five material organs such as organ of sight, but the sixth mental consciousness does not have such support. "Consequentially with a view to attributing a point of support to this consciousness, one calls *manas* or *manodhātu*."[43] However, there is no *manas* distinct from consciousness.[44]

It is further stated that "the mind is termed *citta* because it accumulates (*cinoti*): it is termed as *manas* because it knows (*manute*) and it is termed *vijñāna* because it distinguishes its object (*ālambanam vijñānāti*)".[45] However, the mind and mental states have support as they rely on the organs (organ of sight, mental organ, etc.).[46] According to Vijñānavādins, the eye does not see, it is the visual consciousness that sees. Whereas the Vaibhāsikas attribute seeing to the eye organ.[47]

Vijñānavādins do not believe in the external world. Therefore, the question arises that what is the source of sensations according to Yogācāra Vijñānavāda.

Source of Sensation in Yogācāra Vijñānavāda

According to Yogācāra, the origin of sensations lies "within the psychic continuum in subconscious impressions (*vāsanās*). The variety of sensations is due to the variety of subconsciousness impressions."[48]

Here we are mainly concerned with the sole impression in perception. According to Dharmakīrti, a sense object has the power to leave its impression in the form of image in

---

[43] Pruden, L.M., 1991, op. cit., vol. I, p. 75.

[44] Ibid., p. 74.

[45] Ibid., p. 205.

[46] Ibid.

[47] Ibid., p. 115.

[48] Sinha, J.N., 1999, op. cit., p. 10.

the consciousness through the sense channel. This peculiar efficiency of a sense object of perception has been explained as follows:

> What really is immediately perceived is not the external object but a copy or image of it imprinted on the consciousness. And this mental image is regarded as a faithful representation – an exact copy of the extramental reality existing in its own right. It is evident therefore that external reality can never be an immediate object of perception but can at best be mediately known – in other words, it can only be inferred by its supposed likeness presented in the idea. Perception of an external object is, therefore, only the perception of the idea believed to be a copy or picture of the same.[49]

This representative perception is fairly comparable to Descartes representative theory of perception. However, it may further be supported by Kant's observation. In that, "the sensation is tied up with the cognitive receptivity or the capacity of human mind to receive the senses in the form of representation. This innate capacity of human is intertwined, according to Kant, with sensibility."[50]

It is further explained that "it is due to the sensibility that the world is perceived in the form of representations, which, for Kant, are the ontological 'stuff' generated by the perceiving subject. How this stuff springs up is one of the greatest riddles in epistemology."[51]

The representative theory of perception indicates that everything happens as inner episode within the mind. Now the question arises whether is it possible for everything to happen without any influence from outside? The inner happening in the mind is quite often being justified by the dream experience in which action also takes place. But the fact, however, remains that

---

[49] Mookerjee, S., 1993, op. cit., p. 338.

[50] Sinari, R.K., 2007, *The Paradox of Being Human*, p. 123.

[51] Ibid., p. 125.

the consciousness of waking state gives rise to dream-infusing consciousness.[52]

MOMENTARY PERCEPTION

Time and space are treated in Buddhist philosophy as one.[53] It is captured in the point instant. In this context, it is stated that "every point instant may be viewed as particle of time, as particle of space and as a sensible quality, but this difference is only a difference of our mental attitude towards that point-instant. The point-instant itself, the ultimate reality cut loose from all imagination is qualityless, timeless and indivisible."[54]

However, there are differences regarding the point instant, required for completing the process of perception. Vasubandhu has distinguished two moments: (1) the moment of contact between the sense organs and the object; and (ii) the moment of reflection by which one realizes that one has the perception of something. This reflective awareness is known as perception. Whereas according to Diṅnāga the moment instant consists of not only two forms, compression (*grāhaka*) and comprehensible (*grāhya*), but also it includes self-consciousness in which both forms are revealed.

This has been reassured by Dharmakīrti's explanation based on the concept of self-cognition. These observations indicate that three aspects – the object aspect, its cognition and self-awareness – are involved in forming one momentary state of perception, rather than only two sub-moments in the process of perception as mentioned by Vasubandhu.

However, in another study, it is observed that the first moment is pure sensation, whereas in the second moment happens to be the mental sensation both together constitute

---

52 Swami Yogindrananda, 2005, op. cit., p. 860.

53 Hanh, T., 2008, op. cit., p. 201.

54 Stcherbatsky, T., 1996, op. cit., vol. I, p. 85.

indeterminate (*nirvikalpa*) perception. In third point moment, when perception takes place constructed images, it becomes determinate (*savikalpa*) perception.[55] This shows that three submoments form one point instant.

The momentariness has, however, been criticized by the Buddhist assumption that things are destroyed without a cause. In this context, the following observation may be worth noting:

> Uddyotakara asserts that nothing is destroyed without a cause. When it is stated that there is no cause of destruction what it means is either that there is no cause of destruction at all (*vināśo nāsti*) or that destruction is eternal (*nityaḥ*) because there is no cause (*akāraṇatvāt*). Now, if there is no destruction at all everything would become eternal and the cognition of the destruction will be without any basis and hence impossible. If destruction is eternal, no effect will be produced because destruction is equivalent to non-existence (*abhāva*). Again whatever effect is produced becomes simultaneously existent with destruction and all opposition between existence and non-existence being cancelled, the things become eternal.[56]

---

[55] Stcherbatsky, T., 1996, op. cit., vol. II, p. 312.

[56] Kher, C.V., 1992, *Buddhism as Presented by the Brahmanical System*, p. 50.

10

Quantum Physics and the Buddha Nature

Introduction

THE quantum physics has already been discussed in the earlier chapter. Here, we are mainly concerned with the Buddha Nature having bearing on the quantum physics.

The Buddha Nature is described as *tathatā* (suchness), which is treated as emptiness and it is dependently co-arise. This has been compared with the quantum physics, whose field being vacuum is also treated as emptiness. In view of these observations, it is stated that, "the void (*śūnya*) of the Buddhists and the vacuum of the quantum physicists are identical".[1] It may also be mentioned here that the field has been treated by Einstein as the only reality.[2]

In the quantum physics, the world is treated in terms of universal flux of events and process.[3] This may also be compared with the Buddhist's doctrine of universal flux, which is explained on the basis of the proposition that "whatever is existent is momentary".[4]

David Bohm has, however, treated the reality as process in the quantum physics. In this context, it is observed:

I regard the essence of the notion of process as given by the

---

1 Panda, N.C., 2008, *Māyā in Physics*, p. 123.

2 Levy, P., 2019, *A Physics of Possibilites*, p. 83.

3 Bohm, D., 2012, *Wholeness and the Implicate Order*, p. 12.

4 Mookerjee, S., 1993, *The Buddhist Philosophy of Universal Flux*, p. 24.

> statement: Not only is everything changing, but all is flux. That to say, *what is*, is the process of becoming itself, while all objects, events, entities, conditions, structure, etc. are forms that can be abstracted from this process.[5]

It is, further, observed that, the reality being independent of thought is ultimately unknown and unknowable.[6] Yet, Bohm wants to know "for an understanding of how reality and consciousness are related".[7] Here it may be pointed out that consciousness itself is reality, according to Advaita Vedānta of Indian philosophy.

Consciousness (*cit*) meets the most important criterion of reality, namely, non-contradiction. The real is that which does not contradict itself nor is it contradicted by anything else.[8] In this context, it may be pointed out that there is only consciousness which cannot be contradicted with absolute certainly. This is mainly because even the absence of consciousness has to be testified by consciousness itself. It is stated that "consciousness alone does not appear to be; it is. For, in the case of consciousness, appearance and reality coincide."[9] Here, it may be mentioned that pure consciousness itself is reality,[10] its appearance or manifestation is changing and negatable. Further, pure consciousness is reality, which is ever unborn, immovable and free from the character of materiality: it is all peace and

---

5 Bohm, D., 2012, op. cit., p. 61.

6 Ibid., p. 78.

7 Ibid., p. xii.

8 Swami Satprakashananda, 2004, *The Universe, God and God Realization*, p. 167.

9 Mohanty, J.N., 1995, "Some Aspects of Indian Thinking on Being" in edited book by Sprung, M., p. 150.

10 Swami Nikhilananda, 2000, *The Māṇḍūkya Upaniṣad with Gauḍapāda's Kārikā and Śaṅkara's Commentary*, verse 7, p. 55.

non-dual.[11] In fact, pure consciousness happens to be both: *Brahman* and *Ātman* as mentioned earlier. According to Śaṅkara, "consciousness as eternal, transcendent existence is unchanging, uncaused and homogeneous".[12]

However, according to Vijñānavāda school of Buddhist philosophy, when the *ālaya-vijñāna*, "returns to itself, it becomes the *dharmakāya* of the Buddha, the non-dual (*advaya*) principle, the Absolute".[13] The *ālaya-vijñāna* being the storehouse in which all seeds (*bījas*) of one's mental and physical activities are accumulated since the beginningless past. This is treated as soul in disguise in the Buddhist philosophy.[14]

The concept of "I am" (self-awareness) is quite important in Vijñānavāda of Buddhist philosophy. This is mainly because it represents thought which has been explained very well in the Vedānta school of Indian philosophy. In this context, the following observations are worth stating:

> Consciousness becomes itself only when it begins to stir and the thought *I am* arises. Why does consciousness arise at all? For no apparent reason other than it is its nature like the wave on an expanse of water; "the causeless cause" says Maharaj. Simultaneously, along with the primal thought *I am*, springs into existence the entire manifested universe in a split-second. When consciousness, which is impersonal in rest, manifests itself by objectifying itself as phenomena.[15] It is further stated that there is no power on earth that is greater than this consciousness, this sense of presence *I am*.[16]

The manifestation of consciousness is, however, treated as an

---

[11] Swami Nikhilananda, 2000, op. cit., p. 262.

[12] Indich, W.M., 2000, *Consciousness in Advaita Vedānta*, p. 26.

[13] Matilal, B.K., 1997, *Logic, Language and Reality*, op. cit., p. 346.

[14] Stcherbatsky, T., 1996, *Buddhist Logic*, vol. I, op. cit., p. 114.

[15] Balsekar, R.S., 1998, *Pointers from Nisargadatta Maharaj*, p. 221.

[16] Ibid., p. 222.

objective aspect of subjective awareness.[17] In this context, it is observed:

> Noumenon, being pure subjective, cannot see itself as noumenon. The phenomenal manifestation, therefore, is not something from outside, projected by noumenon, but is an objectivization as manifestation on and within itself.[18]

This shows that the essential identity between noumenon and phenomena is innate in human being.

The Absolute Reality: Buddha's Nature as Tathatā (Suchness)

Tathatā has two aspects: conditioned and unconditioned. The former is manifested in the empirical sphere. It is relative existence and operates in dualism of subjects and objects. "It should always be remembered that suchness, whether conditioned or unconditioned, remains unchanged. It is absolute sameness in all phenomenon. It is uncreated and eternal."[19] Whereas the unconditioned suchness represents the highest truth (*paramārtha satya*). However, it is stated that "in the original texts like the *Prajñāpāramitā*, from which passages are now cited in support of *tathatā* refer only to the unconditioned".[20]

Tathatā is treated as the absolute suchness in the *Ratnagotra-vibhāga*. It is again explained in two ways as stated below:

> *Samalā tathatā* designates that aspect of Reality "mingled with defilement" and is the *Ratnagotra's* consistent term for the *tathāgatagarbha*, while *nirmala tathatā* is its expression for Reality "apart from defilement", and is thus synonymous with the *dharmakāya*.[21]

---

[17] Balsekar, R.S., 1998, op. cit., p. 225.

[18] Ibid., p. 226.

[19] Dutt, N., 1978, *Mahāyāna Buddhism*, p. 278.

[20] Ibid., p. 280.

[21] Brown, B.E., 1994, *The Buddha Nature*, p. 251.

Tathatā itself affirmed as perfectly pure essence, unconditioned nature of all reality. In this context, it is observed that:

> Such an emphasis upon the primary subjectivity of *tathatā* as embryonic absolute knowledge or the germinal essence of Buddhahood (i.e. as *garbha* or *gotra*) tended inevitably to minimize the uniqueness of the phenomenal subject. According to the *Ratnagotra* then, the Buddhist transformation process is primarily the emergence of *tathatā*'s perfect self-consciousness, its movement to perfect self-understanding, from hiddenness to manifestation.[22]

Tathatā is treated as the pure essence, the fundamental nature, the basic substratum, the unborn, undying, permanent, steadfast, eternal and ultimate ground of *saṁsāra* and *nirvāṇa*.[23] It is further observed:

i. The necessary movement of *tathatā*'s inner convergence upon itself, the stages towards its final and perfect self-comprehension, includes all the teachings and instructions, the prescriptions and praxis embodying the entire *dharma*. *Tathatā* is the truth which animates and finds self-expression in all formulations and specifications of the Buddhist path.[24]

ii. *Tathatā*'s self-objectifying knowledge of itself is the truth of all things. Under the primary axiom of "impermanence, ill, not-self", *tathatā* manifests an important insight into the conditioned relativity of phenomenal existence; it is a wisdom revealing the non-substantiality (*śūnyatā*) of things, and thus dispelling a form of ignorance that seizes upon the determinate as indeterminate, the relative as absolute.[25]

---

22 Brown, B.E., 1994, *The Buddha Nature*, p. 252.

23 Ibid., p. 257.

24 Ibid.

25 Ibid., pp. 257-58.

iii. *Tathatā*'s advance towards total and perfect self-awareness progresses through the innumerable varieties and forms, degrees and levels of self-reflective wisdom constituting the path of the *dharma*. At each stage, by its efficacy as innate absolute knowledge, it attains a proportionate self-liberation from the obscurative force of ignorance through the instrumentality of its self-formations. But these latter, while the vehicles of its self-representation, are never (independently) the adequate media for the perfect self-manifestation of *tathatā*. Instead, they are the necessary moments of self-transcending absolute wisdom as it approaches the goal where the form in which *tathatā* appears for its own perfect self-consciousness corresponds completely to its essence. Only as omniscient wisdom, unrestricted by the contours and moulds of material existence, does *tathatā* universally perceive itself as the fundamental and original purity of all things, intrinsically free from the concealing defilements.[26]

Critical Comments

In the context of above observations, some critical comments are the most important. These are stated below.

i. Since the perfect self-awareness of *tathatā* takes place in and through human consciousness. The *Ratnagotra* failed to adequately explain how finite, particular consciousness functions with, and is transformed into the infinite universal and absolute consciousness. It neglected to elaborate a generic structure of consciousness that would account for the coherence of such a relationship. While the *Ratnagotra* clearly indicates that the Innate Mind (*citta prakṛti*) is the fundamental noetic substratum common to ordinary beings and Buddhists alike, it sustains no detailed analysis of its active interplay with and upon the

---

[26] Brown, B.E., 1994, op. cit., p. 258.

phenomenal mind. The whole question of how the latter becomes individuated out of, but not separate from, that primordial stratum of pure awareness, is not addressed by the Śāstra, its answer and the subsequent question as to precisely the Innate Mind becomes compromised and defiled as the individual consciousness strays from its identity with it, demands a knowledge of the structural dynamics animating the processes of sensory awareness, intelligible apperception, ideal conceptualization and objective creativity. Together, these represent the essential phases as a coherent morphology of phenomenal consciousness; they are critical mental determinations and as such, must be considered in any discussion of *tathatā*'s self-realization in and through human consciousness.[27]

ii. The above observations may be explained through the purification of consciousness. In the Buddhist's philosophy consciousness gets purified by going through four spheres (*bhūmi*s) of consciousness, viz. *kāmāvacāra-citta-bhūmi, rūpācāra-citta-bhūmi, arūpāvacārī-citta-bhūmi* and *lokuttara-citta-bhūmi*. These spheres of consciousness will be discussed later.

iii. In the contest of purification of consciousness, the following observation is worth stating:

> The beings are polluted because of pollution of consciousness and they are purified because of purification of consciousness. Consciousness alone is responsible for pollution and purification of beings. Therefore, understanding sincerely the important role of consciousness one should make right efforts to remove the pollution of consciousness by utilizing every moment of life with complete awareness.[28]

[27] Brown, B.E., 1994, op. cit., pp. 259-60.

[28] Tiwary, M., 1968, *Nāmarūpa-Paricchedo*, p. 70.

iv. The above observation in way indicates that nothing is uncreated so long as human consciousness is involved.

It is stated that *tathatā* (suchness) is nothing but pure consciousness realized in spiritual experience.[29] According to Vasubandhu, consciousness manifests itself as subject and object. It is, further, explained as:

> All forms (*rūpa*) and fields of experience are nothing but the manifestation of the dormant seeds in consciousness (*vijñapti*). Things are unreal only in relation to the real which is consciousness. Pure consciousness is not grasped by intellect. But its existence cannot be denied as it is the basis of all existence. Reality is pure consciousness. The *dharma*s that appear as subject and object are imagination (*parimalpita*) or at best conditioned and relative (*paratantrā*). In the absolute reality (*parinispatti*) there is neither subject nor object, the state being only indicated as suchness (*tathatā*) of *dharmas*.[30]

The relationship between the *ālaya-vijñāna* and the *tathatā* being the nature of consciousness is very well explained in the Hsuan-tsang's treatise on the doctrine of mere consciousness (*Vijñapti-mātratā*). The Yogācāra school of Buddhist philosophy had categorically denied the dualism of matter and consciousness, object and subject, but established one reality; mere-consciousness (*vijñapti-mātratā*). This is evident from the following observation:

> Consciousness is the essential nature of phenomena and *tathatā* is the essential nature of consciousness. Thus, the self-transparency of *tathatā* in the totality of phenomena is the self-recognition of consciousness in the multiplicity of its forms. For, to say that consciousness is the sole reality is not to consign material existence to the realm of illusion, but to interpret its sensible shapes and contours as the immanent developments and structural modalities of consciousness itself. Illusion is to imagine the independent self-subsistence of those sensible

---

[29] Ganguly, S., 1992, *Treatise in Thirty Verses on Mere Consciousness*, p. 10.

[30] Ibid.

> forms apart from consciousness, when they are instead, the integral patterns of that one reality. Phenomena are forms of consciousness and as such are real. Their objectivity is only the mode of its appearance (i.e. consciousness). They seem to be "out there" possessing independent self-subsistence; in fact, that is only the way in which the *ālaya-vijñāna* projects its contents, its own ideal self-determination of "universal *bījas*". Since the *ālaya* is the noetic aspect of *tathatā*, the latter can know itself as the indeterminate, unconditional nature of all things because they are the radically ideal manifestations or transformations from within itself.[31]

Dharmakāya

Dharmakāya is triple, three *kāyas*. These are: (i) *Svabhāvikakāya*, (ii) *Saṁbhogakāya*, and (iii) *Nirmānakāya*.

Dharmakāya is used in opposition with *tathāgata* as something that transcends the nature of the five *dharmas*, being furnished with things issuing from the highest knowledge (*prajñā*), and itself abiding in the realm of magical appearances (*māyāviṣaya*). Here we may consider all these terms, synonyms, *dharmakāya*, *tathāgatakāya* and *tathāgata*. *Tathāgatakāya* is reforced to also when the *bodhisattva* attains a certain form of meditation whereby he finds himself in accord with the suchness of things and its transformations. The *tathāgatakāya* is realized when all his mental activities conditionally working are extinguished and there takes place a radical revolution in his consciousness. The *kāya* is no less than the *dharmakāya*.[32]

As Suzuki has mentioned *Dharamakāya* has following seven characters:

> Briefly stated, they will think of the *dharmakāya* by picturing to themselves its seven characteristics, which constitute the faultless virtues and essential functions of the *kāya*. (1) Think

---

[31] Brown, B.E., 1994, op. cit., p. 264.

[32] Suzuki, 1999, *Studies in the Laṅkāvatāra Sutra*, op. cit., pp. 316-17.

> of the free, unrivaled, unimpeded activity of the *dharmakāya*, which is manifested in all beings; (2) Think of the eternality of all perfect virtues in the *dharmakāya*; (3) Think of its absolute freedom from all prejudice, intellectual and affective; (4) Think of those spontaneous activities that uninterruptedly emanate from the will of the *dharmakāya*; (5) Think of the inexhaustible wealth, spiritual and physical, stored in the Body of the Dharma; (6) Think of its intellectual purity which has no stain of one-sidedness; (7) Think of the earthly works achieved for the solution of all beings by the *tathāgata*s who are reflexes of the *dharmakāya*.[33]

In the context of the will of the *dharmakāya*, the following observations are worth stating:

> The *dharmakāya* assumes three essential aspects as reflected in our religious consciousness: first, it is intelligence (*prajñā*); second, it is love (*karuṇā*); and third, it is the will (*praṇidhānabda*). We know that it is intelligence from the declaration that the *dharmakāya* directs the course of the universe, not blindly but rationally; we know again that it is love because it embraces all beings with fatherly tenderness; and finally we must assume that it is a will, because the *dharmakāya* has firmly set down its aim of activity in that good shall be the final goal of all evil in the universe. Without the will, love and intelligence will not be realized; without love, the will and intelligence will lose their impulse; without intelligence, love and the will will be irrational. In fact, the three are coordinates and constitute the oneness of the *dharmakāya*.[34]

The *dharmakāya* has also been interpreted as "a soul, a willing and knowing being, one that is will and intelligence, thought and action. It is, as understood by the Mahāyānists, not an abstract metaphysical principle like Suchness, but it is a living spirit, that

---

33 Suzuki, D.T., 2000, *Outlines of Mahāyana Buddhism*, pp. 234-35.

34 Ibid., pp. 238-39.

manifests itself in nature as well as in thought."[35]

The formation of *dharmakāya* is that stage in which consciousness is merged in the universal consciousness or soul devoid of any attribute.[36] However, the *dharmakāya* has been compared with the *Brahman* of Hinduism.[37]

Svābhavikakāya

In the *svabhāvikakāya*'s state of transformation, consciousness is totally awakened in the original state of suchness (*tathatā*). In this state, the witnessing consciousness and that which is witnessed are one and the same. "The entire World Process then arises, moment to moment, as one's own Being, outside of which, and prior to which nothing exists."[38]

Saṁbhogakāya

Saṁbhogakāya is of two kinds:

i. *Svasaṁbhogakāya* is consisting of the infinite real qualities created by the accumulation of immeasurable merits and wisdom cultivated by the *tathāgatas* during the *asaṁkheyakalpas*.[39]

ii. *Parasaṁbhogakāya* – the *tathāgata* by means of *samatā-jñāna* manifests a body possessed of subtle and pure qualities. This body displays supernatural power by the *bodhisattvas*.[40]

However, the *saṁbhogakāya* has been compared with the subtle body of Sāṁkhya–Yoga philosophy. It has been further

---

[35] Suzuki, D.T., 2000, op. cit., pp. 222-23.

[36] Barborka, G.A., 1998, *The Divine Plan*, p. 448.

[37] Capra, F., 1989, *The Tao of Physics*, p. 110.

[38] Wilber, K., 2004, *The Ātman Project*, p. 86.

[39] Ganguly, S., 1992, op. cit., p. 135.

[40] Ibid.

compared with the *vijñānamaya-kośa* of the *Taittirīya Upaniṣad*. *Saṁbhogakāya* is also compared with the concept of overmind of Aurobindo.[41] However, in order to know the overmind, the underlying linkages among supermind, overmind and mind are important. Therefore, these linkages are described briefly here:

The fundamental nature of supermind is that all its knowledge is originally a knowledge of identity and oneness.[42] Whereas the mental awareness (i.e. mind) has its own subjective existence, which is only a partial derivative and superficial action of the self.[43] Further, the knowledge of the supermind is real because it is a total knowledge and has a transcendental vision.[44]

The knowledge obtained by mind on the contrary is limited. Mind cannot grasp the universal.[45] The other important difference between the two is that the supermind is the knower and creator of its own truth, whereas the mind of man is only knower and creator in the half-light and half-darkness of mingled truth and error.[46] However, the supermind directly knows the truth consciousness, a divine power of immediate inherent and spontaneous knowledge, an idea holding luminously all realities.[47]

When consciousness moves inward below the surface mind, one discovers an inner being, a soul, an inner mind, an inner life, an inner subtle physical entity which is much larger in its potentialities, more powerful, more capable of manifold

---

41 Williamson, R.K., 2004, op. cit., p. 79.

42 Aurobindo, Sri, 2002, *The Synthesis of Yoga*, p. 786.

43 Ibid., p. 787.

44 Ibid.

45 Ibid., p. 788.

46 Ibid., p. 790.

47 Ibid., p. 788.

knowledge and dynamism than the surface mind.[48]

Nirmāṇakāya

This is a body of transformation of the Buddha, who manifests himself as a *nirmāṇakāya* in response to the earnest desire of his followers with a view to end their sufferings. However, the *nirmāṇakāya* is based on the conception of *manomayakāya* (mind-made body or the will body).[49] Therefore, it may be said that in *nirmāṇakāya*, the five senses and *mano-vijñāna* are involved.

Nirmāṇakāya has recently been compared with the gross body (*sthūla-śarīra*) of Sāṁkhya–Yoga philosophy. This is explained as follows:

> The gross realm, the *nirmāṇakāya* – the realm of ordinary walking consciousness is simply composed of all those levels which are based on, or centred around, or take as their final referent the gross physical body and its constructs of ordinary space and time. The physical or axial body itself is called the "gross level" and all aspects of the psyche that reflect this level are called the gross reflecting mind.[50]

According to Aurobindo at the physical level, the consciousness of human beings is limited by the mind.[51] This mind has been evolved out of ego, creating thereby the superficial mentality.[52] Because it mainly works to satisfy desire which is related to seek for power and knowledge in the worldly affairs, it ultimately results in human suffering. Those who want to get rid of suffering, the Buddha teaches them how to end suffering by transforming himself into *nirmāṇakāya*. His teaching is basically related to *nirvāṇa*, which happens to be the Absolute Reality.

---

48 Aurobindo Sri, 2001, *The Life Divine*, p. 291.

49 Suzuki, D.T., 1999, op. cit., p. 145.

50 Williamson, R.K., 2004, op. cit., p. 73.

51 Aurobindo, Sri, 2001, op. cit., p. 288.

52 Ibid., p. 234.

Purification of Consciousness

Purification of consciousness is required mainly for those who want to experience the Absolute Reality, which would result in: (i) the end of suffering; and (ii) attainment of *nirvāṇa*. Consciousness has to be purified mainly because it (*citta*) contains all seeds (*bījas*), that are capable of perpetuating existence from beginningless time. This consciousness is referred to as *ālaya-vijñāna* (storehouse of consciousness) by the Yogācāra Vijñāna school of Buddhist philosophy.

However, forces of habit (*vāsanā*) operating in human beings from beginningless time create the limitations in the functioning of consciousness. Things are not perceived as such, but they are influenced by the mental images created by circumstances and some mental conditioning. In such a condition, the perception becomes quite illusory. The consciousness defiled by mental blemishes will not provide a proper understanding of reality. Therefore, one has to purify his consciousness for attaining *nirvāṇa* (freedom from the world). Consciousness gets purified by going through the four phases and "each level speaks of a stage, where it has reached in achieving purity".[53]

KĀMĀVACĀRA-CITTA-BHŪMI (SPHERE)

Kāma means desire. *Avacāra* is known as that which moves. Thus, *kāmāvacāra citta* is consciousness which is influenced by desire.[54] In this category, consciousness happens to be restless: one moves from one object to another. This creates attachment with various objects. In fact, the desire creates various defilements, resulting thereby into sufferings.

The *kāma bhūmi* is the sensuous place of existence for ordinary persons who are influenced more by sensuous desires, which, in turn generate craving sense pleasure. However, these limitations may be overcome by the practising of concentration

---

[53] Tiwary, M., 1988, op. cit., p. 29.

[54] Ibid.

meditation. One can purify consciousness of these hindrances, so as to reach to the second level.

RŪPĀVACĀRA-CITTA-BHŪMI

In this sphere, consciousness arises from the object associated with form and colour. There are five psychic factors constituting the trance (*jhānaṅga*). These are: (i) *Vitakka* (initial application) on some thought, the doubt is inhibited; (ii) *Pitti* (rupture) by which aversion is suppressed; (iii) by feeling of happiness (*sukha*) distraction and worry are removed; (iv) *Ekaggatā* (one-pointedness) by which sensuous desire is suppressed. When one reaches the fifth stage (v) of *rupāvacāra-jhāna* consciousness, purification of consciousness starts by removing major defilements and wavering. One may proceed through one-pointedness for the realization of right understanding (*pana*) and then move to *arūpāvacāra-citta-bhūmi*.[55]

ARŪPĀVACĀRA-CITTA-BHŪMI

Arūpāvacāra-citta is the subtle consciousness of formless objects as compared to *rūpāvacāra-citta*, in which consciousness happens to be gross objects as mentioned above. However, four types of consciousness arise in *arūpāvacāra-citta-bhūmi*, viz. (i) infinite space, (ii) infinite consciousness; (iii) nothingness; and (iv) neither perception nor not perception. These are stated below.

While concentrating on objective forms, one develops the internal power to transcend them. Once objects get removed, it becomes all-pervading. The object is like a curtain, when it is removed, one can see the infinite space in his own consciousness. This consciousness dwelling upon the infinite space is known as *ākāśanañcāyatana-citta*.

The infinite space in a way is a mere concept, because it is the consciousness which manifests like infinite space. Therefore, the infinite consciousness becomes the objects of the second stage

---

[55] Tiwary, M., 1988, op. cit., p. 56.

of *arūpāvacāra bhūmi*. It is known as *vijñānañcāyatana citta*. From this, one can go to the third stage of nothingness.

In the stage of nothingness, effort is made to realize that even consciousness is not an independent unit; for, consciousness arises as an object forming a moment as a complex of a number of psychic factors.[56] It is, therefore, inferred that the consciousness also has no substance like the banana tree that has no substance in it. Consciousness is like *Dhamma-puñja*. "Pondering like this, the nothingness of consciousness is understood and realized. This type of nothingness of the consciousness becomes the object of third type a *arūpāvacāra* moral consciousness."[57] It is known as *akiñcannāyatanā citta*. Having achieved this stage, one goes still higher.

The fourth stage of *arūpāvacārā citta* is known as *nevasanna-nasannāyatanā citta*, dwelling upon there is neither perception nor not perception. In this state, the mind becomes too subtle. It loses its discriminating capacity to see itself as subject and that other as the object. "It rather remains one-pointed within itself. It does not remain as a consciousness because it does not function as grasping the object. It does not remain as not consciousness; because it is not extinct but remains as immensely pure consciousness being one-pointed on itself."[58]

Further, "this state of the consciousness is very subtle as well as penetrative through the nature of reality. It is with this, one may very easily proceed for realization of right understanding."[59]

LOKUTTARA-CITTA-BHŪMI

The above three *bhūmis* of consciousness are termed as *lokīya citta*; mundane consciousnesses. As compared to them, *lokottara-citta*

---

[56] Tiwary, M., 1988, op. cit., p. 58.

[57] Ibid., p. 59.

[58] Ibid., pp. 59-60.

[59] Ibid., p. 61.

is supramundane consciousness. The mundane consciousnesses of above spheres are accumulating states, whereas *lokuttara-citta* is the eliminating one.[60]

The word *lokuttara* is derived from *loka* = world, and *uttara* = beyond, transcendent to. This is defined as follows:

> The concept of "world" is threefold: the world of living beings (*sattaloka*), the physical universe (*okasaloka*), and the world of formations (*saṅkhāraloka*), that is, the totality of conditioned phenomena, physical and mental. The notion of world relevant here is the world of formations, that is, all mundane phenomena included within the five aggregates of clinging. That which transcends the world of conditioned things is the unconditioned element, *nibbāna*, and the types of consciousness that directly accomplish the realization of *nibbāna* are called *lokuttara-citta*, supramundane consciousness.[61]

The above supramundane consciousness in a way is pure consciousness. It may be stated that *nirvāṇa* is the realization of pure consciousness.

However, in the supramundane plane, some polluted forces in the form of seeds remain in the consciousness, although in much reduced forms. Yet, there is a possibility to emerge again in the favourable situations. Therefore, in order to get rid of the polluted forces, and to avoid repeated births in this world, it is essential for the Yogācāra to finally eradicate the defilement so that consciousness can attain *nirvāṇa*, a state of eternal bliss.[62] In the supramundane, ten fetters are uprooted. These are given below:

1. *Sakkāya-diṭṭhi* (belief in the existence of permanent soul)
2. *Vicikicchā* (doubt)

---

[60] Medhidhammaporn, P., 1995, *Sartre's Existentialism and Early Buddhism*, p. 152.

[61] Bhikkhu, Bodhi, 1999, *A Comprehensive Manual of Abhidhamma*, p. 31.

[62] Tiwary, M., 1988, op. cit., p. 63.

3. *Sīlabbataparāmāsa* (clinging to rituals and rites)
4. *Kāmarāga* (sensuous pleasure)
5. *Paṭigha* (ill-will)
6. *Rūpāraga* (desire for becoming a divine being in the *rūpaloka*)
7. *Arūparāga* (desire for having existence in *arūpa-brahmaloka*)
8. *Māna* (conceit)
9. *Uddhacca* (restlessness)
10. *Avijjā* (ignorance).

These defilements are not destroyed at one attempt. Their destructions vary in four stages of sainthood such as stream-winner (*sotappana*), once returner (*sakadagāmī*), never returner (*anāgāmī*) and liberated being (*arahant*).

Universal Flux

QUANTUM PHYSICS

The universal flux as the quantum physics is explained below:

> There is a universal flux that cannot be defined explicitly but which can be known only implicitly, as indicated by the explicitly definable forms and shapes, some stable and some unstable, that can be abstracted from the universal flux. In this flow, mind and matter are not separate substances. Rather, they are different aspects of one whole and unbroken movement. In this way, we are able to look on all aspects of existence as not divided from each other, and thus we can bring to an end the fragmentation implicit is the current attitude toward the atomic point of view, which leads us to divide everything from everything in a thorough-going way. Nevertheless, we can comprehend that aspect of atomism which still provides a correct and valid form of insight; i.e. that in spite of the undivided wholeness is the flowing movement, the various patterns that can be abstracted from it have a certain relative autonomy and stability, which is indeed provided for by the

universal law of the flowing movement.[63]

Buddhist Philosophy

The doctrine of universal flux holds that "all existents are momentary, existing only for the moment and disappearing in the next moment".[64] This has been described in two ways: (i) In Abhidharma, every effect is originating merely depending upon what is called *pratyaya* (or *hetu*). It means that, "the Buddhists reduced causal dependence to nothing more than a mere sequence, a very loose relation usually expressed in the formula: if *x* is, *y* arises."[65] (ii) Momentariness of *ālaya-vijñāna*. Both are described below.

Six Hetus in Abhidharma

These *hetu*s are *kāraṇa-hetu, sahabhū, saṁprayutaka, sabhāga, sarvatraga* and *vipāka*.

Kāraṇa-hetu is reason for existence; *sahabhū-hetu* is coexistence cause; *sabhāga-hetu* is parallel cause; *saṁprayukta-hetu* is associated cause; *sarvatraga-hetu* is universal cause and *vipāka-hetu* is retributive cause.[66]

KĀRAṆA-HETU

Kāraṇa-hetu happens to be the cause of all *hetu*s as mentioned above. This is merely because it is the generating cause. In this context, it is stated that "eye and colour are the *kāraṇa-hetu* of the consciousness of sight; as food is with regard to body. The seeds, etc. with regard to the sprout, etc."[67] However, all *dharma*s are *kāraṇa-hetu* with regard to all, with the exception that "A

---

63 Bohm, D., 2012, op. cit., p. 14.

64 Mookerjee, S., 1993, op. cit., p. 39.

65 Matilal, B.K., 1997, *Logic, Language and Reality*, p. 288.

66 Pruden, L.M., 1991, *Abhidharmakośabhāṣyam*, vol. I, p. 255.

67 Ibid., p. 256.

dharma is not a *kāraṇa-hetu* of itself."[68]

SAHABHŪ-HETU

In the category of *sahabhū-hetu*, all conditioned *dhramas* are included, which are is mutual relationship of causality.[69] It is observed that "in any given molecule the inter-causal influence of the atoms of the four great elements is called *sahabhū-hetu*".[70] According to the Sarvāstivādins, "the lamp arises with its light; the sprout, growing in the light, arises with its shadow. Now a lamp is the cause of its light and sprout is the cause of its shadow. Thus, cause and effect can be simultaneous."[71] However the Sautrāntikas criticize the doctrine of coexistent causes. In that it is stated that "one does not prove a similar relationship between simultaneous things. You should then demonstrate that all *dharmas* arisen together can be of a cause and effect relationship."[72]

SAṀPRAYUKTAKA-HETU

This is caused by the mind and its mental states through association. In that, mind and mental states are *saṁprayuktaka-hetu*.[73] It is further clarified that "the mind and mental states which have the same support are, among themselves, *saṁprayuktaka-hetu*". Same signifies single or undivided.[74] *Saṁprayuktaka-hetu* is also *sahabhū-hetu*. What is the difference between these two causes are explained below:

> Some *dharmas* are called *sahabhū-hetu* because they are mutually the results of one another. As companions in a

---

[68] Pruden, L.M., 1991, op. cit., p. 255.

[69] Ibid., p. 257.

[70] Chaudhary, S., 1983, *Analytical Studies of the Abhidharmakośa*, p. 110.

[71] Pruden, L.M., 1991, op. cit., p. 260.

[72] Ibid.

[73] Ibid., p. 272.

[74] Ibid.

> caravan travel thank to the support that they give one another, in the same way, the mind is the result of mental states, and the mental states are the result of the mind.[75]

However, the essential condition for *saṁprayuktaka-hetu* is the sameness of *āśraya, ālambana, ākāra, kāla* and *dravya*.[76]

SABHĀGA-HETU

It is defined as homogeneity. The cause is always antecedent to the effect. This is applicable to all *dharmas* of the same category.[77] *Sabhāgatā* indicates a feature or likeness or homogeneity among human beings. It is found in every human being. However, "according to the Sautrāntikas, *sabhāgatā* is not *dravyasat* or real".[78] The following observation is worth noting:

> *Sabhāgatā* indicates the abstract basis of personality phenomenon or uniqueness of *astitva* in general. This view seems to be supported by *koṣa* which holds that *sabhāgatā* in a sense forms the abstract and subtle potentiality of an individual. *Saṁskāra* of *sabhāgatā*, thus, accounts for an individual's uniqueness. *Sabhāgatā* links up the moments after moments of existence (*bhāva*), extending over the different cycles of birth and death. *Sabhāgatā* may be interpreted then both as the potentiality and manifestation of entire *bhāva* or existence which is only disrupted at the time of *nirvāṇa*. ... *Sabhāgatā* as a *citta viprayukta dharma* may be similarly understood as a substratum of individual's life (*jīvita*) functioning alongwith mind (*citta*).[79]

SARVATRAGA-HETU

This is known as universal causes. "Universals are only the

[75] Pruden, L.M., 1991, op. cit., pp. 272-73.

[76] Chaudhary, S., 1983, op. cit., p. 111.

[77] Ibid.

[78] Halder, A., 2001, *Some Psychological Aspects of Early Buddhist Philosophy*, p. 125.

[79] Ibid., pp. 126-27.

cause of defiled *dharma*s; they are the cause of defiled *dharma*s in their own categories and other categories (*nikāya* II.52.B)".[80]

VIPĀKA-HETU

It is heterogeneous cause, this has been explained in two ways:

i. "*Vipāka* is the name assinged to the states of consciousness and their concomitant, which are the results of volitions; or to the matured volitions themselves."[81]

ii. *Vipāka-hetu* signifies either cause of *vipāka* or cause which is *vipāka*. In the first case, the *vipāka* is the result of the operation indicated by the root *vi-pac*. In the second place, "the *vipāka* is that which becomes ripe (*vipacyate*), that is to say, the action arrive at the moment when it gives forth a result".[82]

Ālaya-Vijñāna and Momentariness

Ālaya-vijñāna "is the ever-changing dynamic 'link' like the subterranean current of water in the ocean: the *Triṁśikā* calls it *dhruva* 'an ever-changing constant' (verse 30). It is ever-changing everlastingness."[83] However, the changes are momentary. Each moment on the basis of the Buddha statement has three sub-moments: arising (*uppāda*), presence (*thiti*) and dissolution (*bhaṅga*).[84] These three sub-moments are misinterpreted by the Sautrāntikas by saying that "it is the series that Blessed One means to designate as conditioned; for quite clearly he does not attribute the three marks to each moment of the series".[85]

According to the Sautrāntikas there are only two sub-moments:

---

[80] Prudent, L.M., 1999, op. cit., p. 273.

[81] Sayadaw, L., 1997, *The Manuals of Buddhism*, p. 53.

[82] Pruden, L.M., 1991, op. cit., p. 275.

[83] Matilal, B.K., 1997, op. cit., p. 346.

[84] Bhikkhu Bodhi, 1999, op. cit., p. 156.

[85] Pruden, L.M., 1991, op. cit., p. 241.

arising and passing away, which form the momentary series. The first sub-moment (i.e. arising) gets destroyed completely; nothing is left in this preceding moment. Once destroyed, the new entity has come in its place. The latter may be similar to the former, but not the same. This happens to be "the doctrine of universal-momentariness, the point, where there remains no being but only becoming".[86]

In such a momentary homogeneous series two things are happening: (i) in the complete destruction of the preceding sub-moment before the succeeding sub-moment, there is no time for any activity to leave its impressions. As a result, it may not be possible to accumulate impressions in the storehouse of consciousness, which is known as the *ālaya-vijñāna*; and (ii) being a homogeneous series, it may not be possible to arise the *karma* because the *karma* is a specific and a particularized job.[87] The problem of circularity is also involved in this series.

In relation to cause and effect, the following observation may be noted:

> If effect is supposed to be produced from a cause that has become defunct, the effect will be destitute of a cause as defunct entity is a pure non-entity. And if it be conceived to be originated by a living cause, the cause must be conceded to exist for more than one moment. So the Buddhist is placed between horns of a dilemma. If he admits the former alternative, he cannot explain causation; if the latter alternative is accepted, he gives up his doctrine of universal flux.[88]

The observation on the unity of consciousness generated by the homogeneous series is equally intriguing. It is stated that "in reality, however, our consciousness does not possess unity at all; it is nothing but an ever-flowing unimpeded procession

---

[86] Kher, C.V., 1992, *Buddhism as Presented by the Brahmanical Systems*, p. 16.

[87] Balsys, B., 2006, *Karma and the Rebirth of Consciousness*, p. 4.

[88] Mookerjee, S., 1993, op. cit., p. 62.

of unique conscious moments, each sharply divided from the other. The unity of consciousness is only an illusion, generated by the homogeneity of the conscious units coupled with their uninterrupted career, their ceaseless continuum, which experiences no check and never comes to an abrupt end."[89] However, the fact is that consciousnesses itself comes to us with a unified structure. Kant called this unity as the transcendental unity of self-consciousness. This has already been mentioned in Chapter 1 (n. 12).

How to reconcile the above critical observation within the existing momentary framework? Some light may be thrown by examining the cause–effect relationship in each moment-instant as explained by the Buddhist scholars like Diṅnāga, Dharmakīrti and Hsuan-tsang. We hope that their observations will help us to reconcile the above criticisms of the momentary homogeneous series.

RECONCILIATION

The relationship between the preceding moments as cause to the succeeding moment is known as *samānāntara-pratyaya*. This requires the atomic data (a gross body, such as a table, may be thought of as an atom cluster) to emerge at a point instant simultaneously and without gaps to disappear at the next moment.[90] Since atoms being substantially or ultimately reality can cause the corresponding consciousness.[91] But it has been argued by Diṅnāga as follows:

> The atoms being formless themselves cannot contribute the form or image to the corresponding cognitive state.[92] For this purpose Diṅnāga developed the doctrine of self-consciousness (*sva-saṁvitti*). The moment instant consists of not only two

[89] Mookerjee, S., 1993, op. cit., pp. 82-83.

[90] Matilal, B.K., 1997, op. cit., p. 225.

[91] Ibid., p. 236.

[92] Ibid.

> forms: comprehension (*grāhaka*) and comprehensible (*grāhya*), but it also includes self-consciousness in which both forms are revealed. "Self-cognition is a kind of mental perception which constitutes an integral part of each episode of awareness. Each episode of awareness in the consciousness series is ultimately real and self-revealing character, while it reveals both the object form and its comprehension."[93]

The above observation may be further supported by Dharmakīrti's explanation based on the principle of self-cognition. "Every cognition of an external object is at the same time a cognition of that cognition. Every feeling and every volition are, on the one side, connected with some object, but they also are, on the other side, self-conscious. We are thus possessed of an "awareness of our awareness".[94]

On the basis of above observation, an inference has been drawn that "in each event of awareness, according to the doctrine of self-cognition, there are three aspects: the object aspect, its cognition and self-awareness (cf. *grāhya*, *grāhaka* and *sva-saṁvitti*). All the three are internal parts of one momentary state of consciousness."[95] Now the question arises, how our different cognitive states would be accounted for? This may be explained not by the external world but by our internal impression (*vāsanā*), our mental dispositions, the residual forces of our past actions coupled with an ingrained beginningless, *avidyā*, wrong notions.[96] It may be noted that self-cognition and self-consciousness are one and the same thing.

It is thus evident from the above observations that without admitting the doctrine of self-cognition and its appearance into the object aspect and self-awareness aspect in a moment-instant,

---

93 Matilal, B.K., 1997, op. cit., p. 237.

94 Stcherbatsky, T., 1996, *Buddhist Logic*, vol. I, p. 163.

95 Matilal, B.K., 1997, op. cit., p. 238.

96 Ibid.

it is difficult to account for recollection caused by memory impression of a past experience. According to Diṅnāga, unless a cognition is self-cognized, it can never be recollected.[97] Once self-cognition is admitted, each moment-instant itself becomes unity because it contains both: object appearance and cognition appearance. This may be supported by another observation which states that in cognition three elements – pure consciousness, an object and a sense organ – are involved.[98] Pure consciousness is here referred to as self-cognition. These observations indicate that each cognition is self-cognized.

The doctrine of self-cognition is, however, criticized by Kumārila on the ground that the cognition cannot be both: the cognizer and the cognized. It is stated that "if the momentary cognition reveals itself to itself, it must take such form as 'I am blue', instead of 'this is blue'. But we find that a cognition always appears as pointing to 'this' which is other than itself. The functioning of cognition is directed outwards (*parāvr̥tti*) and not inwards (*pratyāvr̥tti*) as the idealist theory implies. Therefore, the identity of the cognizer and the cognized is impossible."[99] In reply to this, Diṅnāga has said that "this theory leads to an infinite regress because to make recollection possible the second piece of cognition must be recognized by the third piece of cognition and so ad infinitum".[100] Jayanta also criticizes the doctrine of self-cognition because it is not self-luminous. Therefore, it is not an acceptable theory.[101] Whatever may be the criticism of self-cognition, the fact remains that this is the most important contribution of Buddhist logicians.

---

97 Matilal, B.K., 1997, op. cit., p. 243.

98 Stcherbatsky, T., 1996, op. cit., vol. I, p. 173.

99 Bhatt, G., 1989, *The Basic Ways of Knowing*, pp. 35-36.

100 Matilal, B.K., 1997, op. cit., p. 243.

101 Ibid., p. 244.

The concept of self-consciousness has, however, been justified by Sartre, an existentialist philosopher of the twentieth century. He states:

> The necessary and sufficient condition, for a knowing consciousness to be knowledge of its object, is that it to be consciousness of itself as being that knowledge. This is a necessary condition, for if my consciousness were not consciousness of being consciousness of the table, it would then be consciousness of that table without consciousness of being so. In other words, it would be a consciousness ignorant of itself, an unconscious, which is absurd. This is a sufficient condition.[102]

Now coming back to the cause and effect relationship in the moment-instant, it may be explained in a better way by taking into consideration the Chinese version of the *Treatise on Thirty Verses* (*Triṁśikā*) of Vasubandhu. According to Hsuan-tsang, when consciousness is born, its manifestation has two aspects: (i) the perceiving (*darśana*), and (ii) the perceived (*nimitta*) portions. The former discriminates the seeming subject (what can cause), and the latter discriminates the seeming object (what is caused). However, there is another functional aspect of consciousness that supports the perceiving and perceived divisions. "This is called self-corroboratory aspect (*sva-saṁvitti-bhāga*). It is the realization by the consciousness of itself. If this was lacking, there would be no way of remembering the various manifestations of mind and its activities."[103] This implies that all three portions of consciousness operate simultaneously in the moment-instant. As a result, the moment-instant becomes complete in itself and forms unity because both, subject and object as cause and effect respectively, are included in it.

---

[102] Sartre, J.-P., 1984, *Being and Nothingness*, p. 11.

[103] Ganguly, S., 1992, op. cit., p. 139.

Dividing consciousness into different portions is an absurdity, because consciousness in any way cannot be divided. But looking into at the problem seriously from the empirical point of view, this division into different manifestations provides a better understanding of the self-consciousness. It could be fairly compared with the concept of pre-reflective and reflective consciousness as developed by Sartre. The pre-reflective consciousness is comparable to perceiving (*darśana*) portion. Whereas the perceived (*nimitta*) portion may be compared with the reflective consciousness. The pre-reflective consciousness is the cause of the reflective consciousness which in a way is the effect of the former.

It emerges quite clearly from the above discussion that each moment-instant contains not only subject and object, which are treated as cause and effect, respectively, but also another functional aspect of consciousness that supports the perceiving and the perceived aspects. This is known as the self-corroborating aspect (*sva-saṁvitti-bhāga*) under which both subject and object are revealed. Each point-instant in the consciousness series turns out to be ultimately real. Since each point-instant includes subject and object, i.e. cause and effect, it becomes unity in itself. When the consciousness series is formed on the basis of such point-instants, each point-instant becomes a bead in the chain. Further, such series may turn out to be heterogeneous rather than homogeneous. However, the criticism of the homogeneous series under which *karma* does not arise, because it is a particularized job and will not be applicable to the suggested approach in which each point-instant will be an independent unit and it will differ from another point-instant. In this case, the series in all probability may turn out to be heterogeneous.

The above suggestion may be supported by Sartre's observation that the momentary instants of consciousness are unity in itself. It is stated that "each instant of consciousness is new existence, which does not arise out of prior instant. The rapid succession of instants constitutes one stream of experience. The instants are unified."[104] This unity is, however, treated as real and it is called the "unity within duration".[105]

---

[104] Medhidhammaporn, 1995, op. cit., p. 21.

[105] Ibid., pp. 21-22.

Epilogue

It has been recently observed that thought has created thinker. Each thought carries out with it the potential for self-awareness. Thought thinks itself. As against these observations, this study is reassuring that thought without thinker is merely an unreal abstraction and thought developing itself into a thinker is a sheer fiction.

We have examined thinker as thinking being and self-conscious being. Both are one and the same thing in the sense that thinking is not possible without conscious human being. But it also ought to be recognized that conscious human being cannot live without thinking of something. Thought becomes the object of my self-consciousness. In other words thought gets objectified of my self-consciousness. Yet, thinker and thought both may be distinguished in self-consciousness.

However, thinking is the most important because it includes both the subject (thinker) and the object of thought. So is the case with knowing and perceiving. It has also been observed that thinking certainly leads to knowing. Yet, according to Kant, we can think about things in themselves, but we cannot know them. The other observation in equally intriguing. It is stated that I cannot be the thinker, for the thinker as such is the object of consciousness and not the self, otherwise I could not remember having thought. This shows that consciousness and the self are two different notions. Whereas according to the Vedānta, self-consciousness and the self are one and the same thing. Self-luminous consciousness being eternal, there is nothing irrational in the theory that identifies with the self. A distinction between the two may, however, be allowed itself as we use the term *anubhava* (consciousness, knowledge) to denote the self in relation to object; while we speak of the self simply, when the relationship is not emphasized between self-consciousness and object.

Thought has, however, been distinguished from the sense. It is observed that physical objects live and move and have their being mainly in a world of rational conceptions which can be entered only for thought. Whereas we see a special order or mental activity which works over sense data into rational forms. From this point of view, thought might be defined as a process whereby the mind works over the raw material of the sensibility into the forms of intelligence. These observations show that thought as an object or a product is objectively valid. Whereas thought as a mental activity working through sense data is known as a thought process which happens to be the subjective aspect of thought.

The mental state itself causes the higher order thought (HOT) to occur. According to Rosenthal the higher order thoughts are themselves conscious. This is, indeed, difficult to understand how HOT can be conscious. This is mainly because thought happens to be the object of self-consciousness. Even abstract thoughts and generalizations are the objects of self-consciousness. As such they are distinct from introversion. It may be, further, stated that thought is the objective side of consciousness, whereas the self of human being is known as self-consciousness which happens to be the subjective side of consciousness. Therefore, it may be said that even HOT cannot appropriately explain introspective consciousness. It may be reassuringly told that the self-consciousness of human being while knowing the objective world, it knows itself. There is no other entity in the entire universe, which knows itself.

Thought takes place in response to the memory according to the Advaita Vedānta philosophy. Memory depends upon the disposition as its specific causal condition. However, memory is the immediate knowledge of past. According to Sir William Hamilton, the contents of memory are known within the sphere of consciousness. It is stated that the hypothesis which postulates consciousness without memory violates the fundamental laws of our intellectual being.

Thought has, however, the atomistic character. There are no intermediate stages in both: atom and thought. In any sequence of thoughts, there is always a sudden discontinuous jump from one thought to the next. We are not aware at all of any intermediate stages. If one is so aware, no thinking would be possible. So is the case with atom. When atom makes a jump from one stationary state to another, the actual process cannot be visualized or even imagined.

Thought process has been quantified on the basis of the Buddhist philosophy. One moment of matter is equivalent to seventeen moments of mind. The first three moments are known as *bhavaṅga*-mind which becomes the source of thought. In the *bhavaṅga* state, the mind is vacant as has been the case of dreamless sleep. This state is known as *vithi-mutta* (thoughtless or thoughtfree). The remaining moments take part in a process of thought as a functional state. This has been described as the objective form of a conscious act of mind or thought, which is known as process consciousness (*vithi-citta*). In this, there are three phases – genesis, development and dissolution.

It may be noted that *vithi-mutta* is treated as Being which is opposed to thought (*vithi-citta*). This shows that thought and being are not treated as identical in Buddhist philosophy.[1] The other fact is that there are two elements in every consciousness:

---

[1] Aung, S.Z., 1979, *Compendium of Philosophy*, p. 9.

the constant and the variable.[2] The former may be compared with *vithi-mutta* and the latter happens to be the matter of consciousness. But it also ought to be recognized that "in Buddhism there are several forms of consciousness, each of which will be designated a process of thought whenever it takes place as a fact".[3] This indicates that constant consciousness and variable consciousness are treated as two different elements.

Treating two elements differently in every consciousness does not seem to be appropriate. This is mainly because it creates duality in consciousness, whereas the consciousness itself is unity, but its functions are many. The different functions of consciousness are merely the manifestations of consciousness in itself. In this pathway of manifestations or reflections, the functions of consciousness and consciousness in itself are merely too different phases of the one and the same consciousness. This is the Vedāntic interpretation.

Now the other factor regarding thought is that it is treated as the source of nature. This observation does not seem to be appropriate for the reason that thought becomes the object of self-consciousness, which embodied in human being known as *jīvātman* (self) according to the Advaita Vedānta of Indian philosophy. An inference may, therefore, be drawn that it is the self-consciousness which becomes the source of nature.

While discussing thought as the source of nature, it has been observed that the quantum physics seems to have a tendency to undermine the principle of causation. This has been replaced by the principle of indeterminacy. In this context, it may be mentioned that when the matter itself is causality according to Schopenhauer and in the quantum physics the observer (i.e. human being) is involved, now the question arises, how the causality can be undermined. In fact, the causality has been

---

[2] Aung, S.Z., 1979, op. cit., p. 25.

[3] Ibid.

mentioned in different ways. However, the following facts may also be taken into account while drawing an inference about the causality.

According to the Vedānta school of Indian philosophy, there are three bodies in human being. These are: the gross physical body, the subtle body and the causal body. The causes reside in the causal body and they manifest as effects. These are known through causal consciousness. This shows that whenever human beings are involved, the causes are inherent in the activity. It is rather a well-known fact that the scientists are involved in the quantum physics as the observer. Therefore, an inference may be drawn that the causality operates through the observer in the quantum physics.

i. The cause–effect relationship in the West is the effect–cause relationship in India. The difference may be due to the customary chronological orientation in the West and the ontological orientation in India. Causality or causations is the effectuality or resultness in India.[4]

ii. The internal conviction about the truth of the principle of causality is that there is no phenomenon without its cause. This is mainly because it is derived from one of the innate tendencies (*saṁskāra*) inherent in mind generated by its past experiences. These accumulated *saṁskāra*s are in Indian philosophy the source or our irresistible assumptions and convictions.[5]

The most important concept of quantum mechanics is the concept of oneness. This is a fundamentally new concept. In the total wave function, the identity of individual electron is completely lost. The electrons have submerged themselves as it were in one brotherhood of electrons. The many become one.

---

[4] Organ, T.W., 1988, *The Self and Its Worlds: East and West*, p. 72.

[5] Woodroffe, J., 2001, *The World as Power*, pp. 253-54.

For instance, the one is an abstract space, the many in physical space. The concept of one in many has been supported by the observations of Vijñānavāda school of Buddhist philosophy and the Upaniṣads of Indian philosophy.

However, according to Bohm, the matter and consciousness are projections from the implicate order, which in turn enfolds the entire universe holographically. In that it is stated:

i. Bohm's implicate order is the agent of the universal potentiality of consiousness, then we may at last have found a ship that will sail us beyond the Big Bang, a story that will tell us what happened before "once upon a time".[6]

ii. Bohm's logical notion of the implicate order, which can enfold the primary field and consciousness. Think of the cosmic potentiality of consciousness in the pre-space, where all potentialities are presumed to be in quantum coherence, and it is reasonable to assume the feasibility of just one source, as envisioned by the world's various spiritual traditions.[7]

Now coming to the knowledge aspect of the study, it may be stated that perceptual knowledge concerning the relative existence and knowledge dealing with the absolute reality are discussed in the Advaita Vedānta and Yogācāra Vijñānavāda of Buddhist philosophy. Kant's theory of knowledge is also discussed.

However, according to Kant, there are two main sources of knowledge. In the first source, object is given to us. This is known as the faculty of receiving representations (receptivity of impression). The second one is the power of cognizing by means of the representation. This is referred to as spontaneity in the production of conceptions. However, the main function of sensibility is to receive as object. Except sensibilities, there

---

[6] Bhaumik, M., 2005, *Code Name God*, p. 197.

[7] Ibid., p. 198.

is no other way to receive an object. This object is operated by understanding. It is to be recognized that without interaction between sensibility and understanding, the knowledge of any kind is not possible.

The concept of physical object means for more than what can be given in my sensory experience. From the Kant's point of view, even when we perceive physical objects, it becomes the result of synthesis. This is because it belongs to the very conception of the object.

Space is treated by Kant as the way in which sensibility receives an object as outside us. When we receive an object as arranged, it is called spatial relation. The objects are also received by mind or sensibility in time, which is referred to as inner sense.

External perception takes place when the formal nature of the subject to be affected by the objects and thereby to obtain immediate representations, i.e. perception of them, and consequently only as the form of the external sense in general.

In the Vedānta school of Indian philosophy, the higher knowledge (*parā-vidyā*) has been distinguished from the lower knowledge (*aparā-vidyā*). However, the absolute reality (i.e. *Brahman*) is pure consciousness. This is the most important because it is treated as foundation through which the entire universe is known. It may be stated here that pure consciousness in itself is the absolute reality. Whereas pure consciousness for itself is involved in the worldly affairs which have only relative existence.

The transcendental consciousness seems to be like *Ātman* (absolute reality) in the Indian philosophy. When it descends in human being it becomes self-consciousness because it works through mind. In that, it becomes witness consciousness (*sākṣī*). It illumines the mental states: knowledge, ignorance, pain, etc. This mental states are immediately cognized because of their presence to the witness self.

The experience of witness self is related to mind; for in deep sleep one does not have any experience, but after awakening from sleep one remembers immediately that "I slept well". This is mainly because in the waking state the mind starts working. The sleep state indicates two things: (i) pure consciousness witnesses the sleep; and (ii) the mind recollects immediately that "I slept well" in waking up from sleep. If there was no persistence of pure consciousness witnessing sleep, it would not have been possible for the mind to remember immediately the experience of sleep. It is rather a well-known fact that the mind remembers only those events which have been experiences earlier. This in a way gives supportive evidence to the fact that the mind works in the shadow of past experience. However, without the functioning of the mind, it would be difficult to acquire knowledge. It may be stated that when pure consciousness manifests through mind, it becomes self-consciousness (*jīvātman*).

However, the perceptual knowledge is twofold: external and internal. The former is known by any of the five sensory organs such as hearing, sight, touch, taste and smell. Whereas the latter is the mental perception of pain and pleasure of knowledge, ignorance, love, hate, etc. The cognitive process of external perception has been explained through consciousness, which is immanent in every phase of existence. It is hidden is all physical objects, but is manifesting in every sentient being. In a human being it finds expression as self-awareness, which is the only immediate and direct cognition in the strict sense. An object is known through its association with the immediacy of subject consciousness. The mental mode brings about associations.

Human beings experience daily three states: dreamless sleep, dreaming and waking. When one transcends these states and through modifications reaches the *turīya* state, this consciousness is known as transcendental unity of the self. In this state one is likely to attain the liberation (*mokṣa*).

It may be mentioned here that the *turīya* state transcends the *kāraṇa-śarīra* (causal body) of the Vedānta.

However, there is no denying the fact that the Buddha evolved the philosophy of Anātmavāda (no soul or self). Yet Śāntarakṣita in the *Tattvasaṁgraha* has accepted the self-cognition of the cognition which is by the nature of self-consciousness. Therefore it may be said that the self is represented by self-consciousness which is involved in the internal perception. Whereas the external perception depends on the images of the objects. However, the object of perception happens to be the unique particular meaning thereby an entity that is not shared by anything else. The unique particular is perceived directly (direct perception) without any distortion or delusion. The object of cognition is, however, double in the sense that it is perceived is two moments: (i) the first moment happens to be pure sensation; and (ii) the moment of reflection by which one realizes that one has perception of something (this is blue) on the basis of sensation.

Sense perception is categorized as the entire class of perception to consciousness through the medium of sense organs. Once the object is presented its function is exhausted. So the first presentation is alone authoritative with regard to objective reality.

However, the representative theory of perception indicates that everything happens as an inner episode within the mind. The inner happening in the mind is quite often being justified by the dream experience in which action also takes place.

Now coming to the knowledge of absolute reality. Which is treated in the Buddhist philosophy as emptiness. This has also been described as the Buddha Nature known as *tathatā* (suchness), which is dependently co-arise. It may, however, be mentioned that the concept of emptiness has been compared with the quantum physics, whose field being vacuum is also treated as emptiness. In view of these observations, it is stated that the void (*śūnya*) of Buddhist and the vacuum of the quantum physics are identical. Therefore, an attempt is made to briefly describe the Buddha Nature as *tathatā*, which in unconditioned form is treated as the Absolute Reality. *Tathatā* is the essential nature of consciousness. The self-transparency of *tathatā* in the totality of phenomena is the self-recognition of consciousness in the multiplicity of its forms.

The *ālaya-vijñāna* is the noetic aspect of *tathatā*. When the *ālaya* returns to itself, it becomes the *dharmakāya* of the Buddha, the non-dual (*advaya*) principle, the Absolute.

In order to achieve the stage of *dharamakāya* one has to purify his consciousness by going through the four stages: (i) *kāmāvacāra-citta-bhūmi* (sphere); (ii) *rūpāvacāra-citta-bhūmi*; (iii) *arūpāvacāra-citta-bhūmi*; and (iv) *lokuttara-citta-bhūmi*. The fourth stage is the supramundane consciousness. This stage happens to be the realization of *nirvāṇa*, the Absolute Reality. The supramundane consciousness is a state of eternal bliss.

The changes in *ālaya-vijñāna* are momentary. Each moment on the basis of the Buddha statement has three sub-moments: arising, presence and dissolution. Whereas, according to the Sautrāntikas, there are only two moments: arising and passing away. The first sub-moment (i.e. arising) gets destroyed completely: nothing is left in this preceding moment.

In the two-moments series the main problems are: (i) in the complete destruction of the proceding sub-moment before the succeeding sub-moment, there is not time for any activity to leave its impressions. As a result, it may not be possible to accumulate impressions in the storehouse of consciousness, which is known as the *ālaya-vijñāna*, (ii) Being a homogeneous series, it may not be possible to arise the *karma* because the *karma* is a specific and particularized job. The problem of circularity is also involved in this series.

The cause and effect relationship in the moment-instant, may be explained in a better way by taking into consideration the Chinese version of the *Treatise on Thirty Verses* (*Triṁśikā*) of Vasubandhu. According to Hsuan-tsang, when consciousness is born, its manifestation has two aspects: (i) the perceiving (*darśana*), and (ii) the perceived (*nimitta*) portions. The former discriminates the seeming subject (what can cause), and the latter is discriminated, the seeming object (what is caused). However, there is another functional aspect of consciousness that supports the perceiving and perceived divisions. This is called self-corroboratory aspect (*sva-saṁvitti-bhāga*). It is the realization by the consciousness of itself. If this was lacking, there would be no way of remembering the various manifestations of mind and its activities. This implies that all three portions of consciousness operate simultaneously in the moment-instant. As a result, the moment-instant becomes complete in itself and forms unity because both, subject and object as cause and effect respectively, are included in it. In this case, the series of moment-instant in all probability may turn out to be heterogeneous under which it may be possible to arise the *karma*.

Bibliography

Acharya Narendradeva, 2001, *Baudha Dharma Darshan*, Delhi: Motilal Banarsidass.

Agarwal, M.M., 1991, *Consciousness and Integrated Being*, New Delhi: National Publishing House.

Alston, A.J. (tr.), 1997, *The Method of the Vedānta of Swami Satchidanandendra: A Critical Account of the Advaita Vedānta*, Delhi: Motilal Banarsidass.

Aung, S.Z., 1979, *Compendium of Philosophy*, London: The Pali Text Society.

Aurobindo, Sri, 2001, *The Life Divine*, Pondicherry: Sri Aurobindo Ashram.

———, 2002, *The Synthesis of Yoga*, Pondicherry: Sri Aurobindo Ashram.

Balasubramanian, R., 2004, "Advaita Vedānta on the Problem of Enworlded Subjectivity", in *Phenomenology and Indian Philosophy*, ed. D.P. Chattopadhyaya, L. Embree and J.N. Mohanty, New Delhi: Indian Council of Philosophical Research.

Balsekar, R.S., 1998, *Pointers from Nisargadatta Maharaj*, Bombay: Chetana.

Balsys, B., 2006, *Karma and the Rebirth of Consciousness*, New Delhi: Munshiram Manoharlal.

Barborka, G.A., 1998, *The Divine Plan*, Chennai: The Theosophical Publishing House.

Bart, W.H., 1995, *Philosophy of Knowledge*, vols I and II, ed. H.L. Mansel and John Veitch, Delhi: Ajay Book Service.

Besant, A., 2000, *Man and His Bodies*, Chennai: The Theosophical Publishing House.

Bhadra, M.M., 2004, *A Critical Survey of Phenomenology and Existentialism*, New Delhi: Indian Council of Philosophical Research.

Bhatt, G., 1989, *The Basic Ways of Knowing*, Delhi: Motilal Banarsidass.

Bhattacharyya, K., 1992, *Advaita-Siddhiḥ of Madhusūdana Sarasvatī*, New Delhi: Indian Council of Philosophical Research.

Bhattacharyya, K.C., 1983, *Studies in Philosophy*, ed. G. Bhattacharyya, Delhi: Motilal Banarsidass.

Bhattacharyya, S., 2004, "Phenomenology and Indian Philosophy", in *Phenomenology and Indian Philosophy*, ed. D.P. Chattopadhyaya, L. Embrace and J.N. Mohanty, New Delhi: Indian Council of Philosophical Research.

Bhaumik, M., 2005, *Code Name God: The Spritual Odyssey of a Man of Science*, Penguin Books.

Bhikkhu Bodhi (gen. ed.), 1999, *A Comprehensive Manual of Abhidhamma: The Abhidhammattha Sangh of Ācārya Anuruddha*, Kandy: Buddhist Publication Society.

Bohm, D., 2012, *Wholeness and the Implicate Order*, First Indian Reprint, London and New York: Routledge.

Bohm, D. and F.D. Peat, 1987, *Science, Order and Creativity*, New York: Bantam Books.

Brown, B.E., 1994, *The Buddha Nature: A Study of Thathagatagarbha and Ālaya-vijñāna*, Delhi: Motilal Banarsidass.

Bowne, B.P., 1897, *Theory of Thought and Knowledge*, New York: American Book Company.

Capra, F., 1989, *The Tao of Physics*, London: Fontana Paperbacks.

Catalina, F.V., 1968, *A Study of the Self: Concept of the Sāṁkhya-Yoga Philosophy*, New Delhi: Munshiram Manoharlal.

Chakrabarti, K.K., 2001, *Classical Indian Philosophy of Mind: The Nyāya Dualist Tradition*, Delhi: Motilal Banarsidass.

Chakraborty, N.B. (comp.), 2003, *A Dictionary of Advaita Vedānta*, Kolkata: The Ramakrishna Mission Institute of Culture.

Chang, G.C.C. (gen. ed.), 1982, *A Treasury of Mahāyāna Sūtras: Selection from the Mahāratnakūṭasūtra*, University Park and London: The Pennsylvania State University Press.

Chatterjea, T., S. Basu and A. Chatterjee (eds), 2014, *J.N. Mohanty Lectures on Kant's Critique of Pure Reason*, New Delhi: Munshiram Manoharlal.

Chatterjee, A.K., 1999, *The Yogācāra Idealism*, Delhi: Motilal Banarsidass.

Chatterjee, S. and D.M. Dutta, 1950, *An Introduction to Indian Philosophy*, Calcutta: University of Calcutta.

Chattopadhyay, N.K., 1979, *Indian Philosophy*, Calcutta: Sanskrit Pustak Bhandar.

Chaudhury, S., 1983, *Analytical Study of the Abhidharmakośa*, Calcutta: Firma KLM.

Collins, S., 1982, *Selfless Persons: Imagery and Thought*, Cambridge, New York: Cambridge University Press.

Cross, S., 2014, *Schopenhauer's Encounter with Indian Thought, Representation and Will and Their Indian Paralle*, New Delhi: Munshiram Manoharlal.

Datta, D.M., 1998, *The Six Ways of Knowing*, Calcutta: University of Calcutta (repr. 2018, New Delhi, D.K. Printworld).

Datt, N., 1978, *Mahāyāna Buddhism*, Delhi: Motilal Banarsidass.

Dyczkowski, M.S.G., 2006, *The Doctrine of Vibration*, Delhi: Motilal Banarsidass.

Ergardt, J., 1986, *Man and His Destiny*, Leiden: E.J. Brill.

Flanagon, O., 1992, *Consciousness Reconsidered*, Massachusetts: MIT Press.

Ganguly, S. (tr)., 1992, *Treatise in Thirty Verses on Mere Consciousness*, Delhi: Motilal Banarsidass.

Garfield, J.L., 1995, *The Fundamental Wisdom of the Middle Way: Nāgārjuna's Mūlamadhyamakakārikā*, New York/Oxford: Oxford University Press.

Godman, D. (ed.), 1992, *Be As You Are: The Teachings of Sri Ramana Maharshi*, New Delhi: Penguin Books.

Griffiths, P.J., 1999, *On Being Mindless*, Delhi: Sri Satguru Publications.

Grimes, J., 1992, *The Naiṣkarmyasiddhi of Sureśvara: A Monograph*, Delhi: Sri Satguru Publications.

Gupta, B., 2003, *Cit-consciousness*, New Delhi: Oxford University Press.

Gupta, R.K., 1986, *Exercises in Conceptual Understanding*, I.P.Q. Publication no. 11, Pune: Department of Philosophy, University of Poona.

Haldar, A., 2001, *Some Psychological Aspects of Early Buddhist Philosophy Based on Abhidharmakoṣa of Vasubandhu*, Kolkata: The Asiatic Society.

Hanh, T.N., 2008, *Understanding Our Mind*, New Delhi: Harper Collins.

Hawking, S.W., 1988, *A Brief History of Time*, London: Bantam Press.

Heil, J., 2017, *Philosophy of Mind*, New York: Routledge.

Hegel, G.W.F., 1998, *Phenomenology of Spirit*, tr. A.V. Miller, New Delhi: Motilal Banarsidass.

———, 2002, *Phenomenology of Mind*, vol. I, tr. J.B. Baillie, New Delhi: Cosmo Publications.

Hoffe, O., 2010, *Kant's Critique of Pure Reason: The Foundation of Modern Philosophy*, Dordrecht, Heidelberg, London, New York: Springer Verlag.

Hopkins, J., 2006, *Reflections on Reality*, Delhi: Motilal Banarsidass.

Hume, D., 1951, *A Treatise of Human Nature*, vol. I, London: J.M. Dent and Sons and New York: E.P. Dutton & Co.

Indich, W.M., 2000, *Consciousness in Advaita Vedānta*, Delhi: Motilal Banarsidass.

Iyer, K., 1991, *Vedānta or Science of Reality*, Bangalore: Adhyatma Prakashan.

Jha, G. (tr.), 1986, *Tattvasaṁghraha of Śāntarakṣita with Commentary of Kamalśīla*, vol. II, Delhi: Motilal Banarsidass.

John, H., 2017, *Philosophy of Mind*, repr., New York and London: Routledge.

Joshi, M.M., 2006, "Life, Mind and Consciousness", in *Life, Mind and Consciousness*, the paper read at a seminar, Kolkata: Ramakrishna Mission Institute of Culture.

Kalupahana, D.J., 1992a, *The Principles of Buddhist Psychology*, Delhi: Sri Satguru Publications.

———, 1992b, *Mūlamadhyamakakārikā of Nāgārjuna*, Delhi: Motilal Banarsidass.

Kant, I., 1950, *The Critique of Pure Reason*, tr. J.M.D. Meiklejohn, London: Dent and Sons.

Kapani, L., 2013, *The Philosophical Concept of Saṁskāras*, Delhi: Motilal Banarsidass.

Kher, C.V., 1992, *Buddhism as Presented by the Brahmanical Systems*, Delhi: Sri Satguru Publications.

Kochumuttom, T.A., 1999, *A Buddhist Doctrine of Experience*, Delhi: Motilal Banarsidass.

Koesternbaum, P., 1971, "Religion in the Tradition of Phenomenology", in *Religion in Philosophical and Cultural Perspective*, ed. J.C. Feaver and W. Horosz, New Delhi: East-West Press.

Kothari, D.S., 2002, "Atom and Self", Meghnad Saha Medal Lecture 1978 delivered at INSA; New Delhi, 5 October 1979. This is published by F. Ahmad (ed.) in *Collection of Lectures Delivered by D.S. Kothari*, New Delhi: New Age International.

Krishnamurti, J., 1997, *Reflections on the Self*, ed. Raymond Martin, Chicago: Open Court.

———, 2007, *Choiceless Awareness*, California: Krishnamurti Foundation of America.

Laksmithathachar, M.A., 2009, "Study of Consciousness from the Point of View of Viśiṣṭādvaita Philosophy", in *Understanding Consciousness: Recent Advances*, Kolkata: Ramakrishna Mission Institute of Culture.

Larson, G.J., 2003, "The Anthropic Principle: Life Cosmos and Consciousness", in *Philosophy and Science: An Exploratory Approach to Consciousness*, paper read at the Seminar held at the Ramakrishna Mission Institute of Culture, Kolkata, 8 and 9 February 2002, Kolkata: Ramakrishna Mission Institute of Culture.

———, 2009, "The Notion of 'Consciousness' as Witness in Indian Philosophy and Modern Science", in *Life, Mind and Consciousness*, paper read at a Seminar held at Ramakrishna Mission Institute of Culture, Kolkata during 16-18 January 2014, Kolkata: Ramakrishna Mission Institute of Culture.

Levy, J., 2004, *The Nature of Man According to the Vedānta*, Boulder, CO: Sentient Publications.

Levy, P., 2019, *A Physics of Possibilities: Explore of the World of Quantum Spirituality*, Mumbai: Jaico Publishing House.

Limaye, S.V. (tr.), 2000, *Mahāyānasūtrālaṁkāra by Asaṅga*, Delhi: Sri Satguru Publications.

Macy, J., 1991, *Mutual Causality in Buddhism and General Systems Theory: The Dharma of Natural Systems*, Albany, NY: SUNY Press.

Manju, 1986, अद्वैतवाद और शून्यवाद, Delhi: Eastern Book Linkers.

Masih, Y., 2002, *A Critical History of Western Philosophy*, Delhi: Motilal Banarsidass.

Matilal, B.K., 1986, *Perception: An Essay on Classical Indian Theories of Knowledge*, Oxford: Clarendon Press.

———, 1997, *Logic, Language and Reality*, Delhi: Motilal Banarsidass.

Medhidhammaporn, P., 1995, *Sartre's Existentialism and Early Buddhism: A Comparative Study of Selflessness Theories*, Bangkok: Buddhadhamma Foundation.

Merleau-Ponty, M., 2005, *Phenomenology of Perception*, New York: Routledge.

Misra, V.N., 2014, *Science of Consciousness: A Synthesis of Vedānta and Buddhism*, New Delhi: Munshiram Manoharlal.

———, 2017, *Saṁsāra and Nirvāṇa: A Unifying Vision*, New Delhi: D.K. Printworld.

———, 2019, *Phenomenal Consciousness and Mind–Body Problem in East–West Perspective*, New Delhi: D.K. Printworld.

Mittal, K.K. (ed.), 1990, *Perspectives on Karma and Rebirth*, Delhi: University of Delhi.

Mohanty, J.N., 1995, "Some Aspects of Indian Thinking on Being", in *The Question of Being: East–West Perspective*, ed. Sprung Mervyn, Delhi: Sri Satguru Publications.

Mookerjee, S., 1993, *The Buddhist Philosophy of Universal Flux*, Delhi: Motilal Banarsidass.

Mukerji, A.C., 1938, *The Nature of Self*, Allahabad: The Indian Press.

———, 1957, *Self, Thought and Reality*, Allahabad: Indian Press.

Mukhopadhyaya, M.M.G., 2004, "The Intrinsic Nature of Consciousness and Its Different Manifestations as Envisaged in Different Systems of Indian Philosophy", in *Life, Mind and Consciousness*, Kolkata: Ramakrishna Mission Institute of Culture.

Nicholson, G., 1962, *Illutrations of Being: Drawing upon Heidegger and upon Metaphysics*, New Jersy/London: Humanities Press.

Organ, T.W., 1988, *The Self and Its Worlds: East and West*, Selingrove: Susquehanna University Press; London and Toronto: Associated University Press.

Panda, N.C., 2008, *Māyā in Physics*, Delhi: Motilal Banarsidass.

Pandit, M.L., 1993, *Being as Becoming: Studies in Early Buddhism*, New Delhi: Intercultural Publications.

———, 2008, *The Buddhist View of Knowledge and Reality*, New Delhi: Munshiram Manoharlal.

———, 2012, The *Philosophical and Practical Aspects of Kāśmīra Śaivism*, New Delhi: Munshiram Manoharlal.

Potter, K.H., 1998, *Encyclopedia of Indian Philosophy*, vol. III: *Advaita Vedānta upto Śaṅkara and His Pupils*, Delhi: Motilal Banarsidass.

Powell, A.E., 2000a, *The Causal Body and the Ego*, Adyar (Chennai): The Theosophical Publishing House.

———, 2000b, *The Astral Body*, Adyar (Chennai): Theosophical Publishing House.

Prasad, H.S., 1990, "The Buddhist Doctrine of Karma", in *Perspectives on Karma and Rebirth*, ed. K.K. Mittal, Delhi: University of Delhi.

Prichard, H.A., 1909, *Kant's Theory of Knowledge*, Oxford: The Clarendon Press.

Pruden, L.M. (tr.), 1991, *Abhidharmakośabhāṣyam*, vol. I by Louis La Vallée Poussin, Berkeley, CA: Asian Humanities Press.

Radhakrishnan, S., 2002, *Indian Philosophy*, vol. II, New Delhi: Oxford University Press.

———, 2005, *The Dhammapada*, New Delhi: Oxford University Press.

———, 2009, *The Principal Upaniṣads*, New Delhi: Harper Collins.

Rajagopal, L.V., 1993, *A Critique of Vedānta*, New Delhi: Munshiram Manoharlal.

Ram, K., 1995, *Integral Non-Dualism*, Delhi: Motilal Banarsidass.

Ramana Maharshi, Sri, 1999, *Absolute Consciousness*, tr. G.L.M. Martin, Bangalore: Ramana Maharshi Centre for Learning.

———, 2002, *Self-Abidance: Sat-Darshanam*, tr. G. Kameshar, Bangalore: Ramana Maharshi Centre for Learning.

Ranasinghe, C.P., 1957, *The Buddha's Explanation of the Universe*, Colombo: Lanka Bauddha Mandalaya Fund.

Rangaswami, S., 2012, *The Roots of Vedanta*, New Delhi: Penguin Books.

Reat, N.R., 1990, *Origins of Indian Psychology*, Berkeley, CA: Asian Humanities Press.

Rene, G., 1981, *Man and His Becoming According to Vedānta*, New Delhi: Oriental Books Reprint Corporation.

Rinpoche, T., 2001, *Transcending Ego: Distinguishing Consciousness from Wisdom: A Treatise of the Third Karmpa*, Delhi: Sri Satguru Publication.

Rosenthal, D.M., 2005, *Consciousness and Mind*, New York: Oxford University Press.

Roy, K., 2013, *Subjectivity in Science: Interpretations of the Cartesian Project*, Kolkata: Ramakrishna Mission Institute of Culture.

Sadhu, Santinatha, 1938, *The Critical Examination of the Philosophy and Religion*, vol. II, Amalner: Pratap Seth.

Safaya, R., 1976, *Indian Psychology*, New Delhi: Munshiram Manoharlal.

Saksena, S.K., 1971, *Nature of Consciousness in Indian Philosophy*, Delhi: Motilal Banarsidass.

Sarasvati, Madhusudana, 2007, *Bhagavadgītā with the Annotation Gūḍhārtha Dīpikā*, tr. Swami Gambhirananda, Kolkata: Advaita Ashrama.

Sarbadhikari, A., 1991, *Mill's Self Regarding Acts: An Analysis*, Shimla: Indian Institute of Advanced Study, in association with Munshiram Manoharlal, New Delhi.

Sartre, J.-P., 1984, *Being and Nothingness*, tr. Hazel E. Barnes, New York: Washington Square Press.

———, 2012, *The Transcendence of the Ego*, First Indian Reprint, London: Routledge.

Sastri, S.S.S. and C.K. Raja (tr.), 1992, *Bhāmatī of Vācaspati*, Madras: The Adyar Library and Research Centre.

Sayadaw, L., 1997, *The Manuals of Buddhism*, Delhi: Sri Satguru Publication.

Seal, B., 1985, *The Positive Sciences of the Ancient Hindus*, Delhi: Motilal Banarsidass.

Searle, J.R., 2004, *Mind: A Brief Introduction*, New York: Oxford University Press.

Sharma, C.D., 2003, *A Critical Survey of Indian Philosophy*, Delhi: Motilal Banarsidass.

Shah, N.J., 1967, *Akalanka's Criticism of Dharmakirti's Philosophy: A Study*, L.D. Series II, Ahmedabad: L.D. Institute of Indology.

Shrivastava, S.N.L., 1968, *Śaṅkara and Bradley: A Comparative and Critical Study*, Delhi: Motilal Banarsidass.

Sinari, R.K., 2007, *The Paradox of Being Human*, New Delhi: Indian Council of Philosophical Research.

Singh, S.P., 2004, *Vedic Vision of Consciousness and Reality*, New Delhi: PHISPC-Centre for Studies in Civilizations.

Sinha, J.N., 1971, *A History of Indian Philosphy* vol. III, Calcutta: Sinha Publishing House.

———, 1999, *Indian Realism*, Delhi: Motilal Banarsidass.

———, 2006, *Indian Philosophy*, vols I-III, repr., Delhi: Motilal Banarsidass.

———, 2008, *Indian Psychology: Cognition*, vol. I, Calcutta: Sinha Publishing House.

———, 2008, *Indian Psychology*, vol. III, Delhi: Motilal Banarsidass.

Sparham, G. (tr.), 1993, in collaboration with Shotara, *Ocean of Eloquence: Tsongakhapa's Commentary on Yogācāra Doctrine of Mind*, New York: SUNY Press.

Sri Ananda Acharya, 1985, *Tattvajñānam or the Quest of Cosmic Consciousness*, Hoshiarpur: Vishveshvaranand Vedic Research Institute.

Srinivasan, G., 1994, *Insights into Inward Consciousness*, New Delhi: Indian Council of Philosophical Research.

Stcherbatsky, T. (tr.), 1978, *Madhyānta-Vibhaṅga*, New Delhi: Oriental Books Reprint Corporation.

———, 1983, *The Central Conception of Buddhism*, Delhi: Motilal Banarsidass.

———, 1996, *Buddhist Logic*, vol. I, New Delhi: Munshiram Manoharlal.

———, 2003, *The Conception of Buddhist Nirvāṇa*, Delhi: Motilal Banarsidass.

Suzuki, D.T., 1999, *Studies in the Laṅkāvatārasūtra*, Delhi: Motilal Banarsidass.

———, 2000, *Outlines of Mahāyāna Buddhism*, New Delhi: Munshiram Manoharlal.

Swami Atmapriyananda, 2006, "Bhavamukha: Sri Ramakrishna's Unique Contribution to the Science of Consciousness", in *Consciousness: A Deeper Scientific Search*, the paper read in a seminar held at the Ramakrishna Mission Institute of Culture, Kolkata.

Swami Bhajananda, 2009, "Knowledge and Consciousness: An Integral Approach", in *Understanding Consciousness: Recent Advances*, paper read at a seminar held at the Ramakrishna Institute of Culture, Kolkata, 18-20 January 2008, Kolkata: Ramakrishna Mission Institute of Culture.

Swami Gambhirananda (tr.), 2000, *Brahmasūtra Bhāṣya of Śrī Śaṅkarācārya*, Kolkata: Advaita Ashrama.

——— (tr.), 2003, *Chāndogya Upaniṣad*, Calcutta: Advaita Ashrama.

——— (tr.), 2004, *Taittirīya Upaniṣad with Commentary of Śaṅkarācārya*, Kolkata: Advaita Ashrama.

——— (tr.), 2007a, *Muṇḍaka Upaniṣad*, Kolkata, Advaita Ashrama.

——— (tr.), 2007b, *Bhagavad Gītā of Madhusudana Sarasvati*, with the annotation *Gūḍhārtha Dīpikā*, Kolkata: Advaita Ashrama.

Swami Jagadananda (tr.), 2000, *Upadeśa Sāhasrī of Śrī Śaṅkarācārya*, Madras: Sri Ramakrishna Math.

Swami Jitātmānanda, 1993, *Holistic Science and Vedānta*, based on the book *Quantum Questions* by K. Wilber, New York: Shambhala Publications; 1984, Bombay: Bhartiya Vidya Bhawan.

Swami Madhavananda (tr.), 1997, *The Bṛhadāraṇyaka Upaniṣad with Commentary of Śaṅkarācārya*, Calcutta: Advaita Ashrama.

———(tr.), 2000, *Vedānta-Paribhāsa of Dharmarāja Adhvarīndra*, Calcutta: Advaita Ashrama.

Swami Mukhyananda, 2006, *Sri Shankaracharya: Life and Philosophy:*

An Elucidative and Reconciliatory Interpretation, Kolkata: Advaita Ashrama.

Swami Muni Narayana Prasad, 1998, *Muṇḍaka Upaniṣad*, New Delhi: D.K. Printworld.

———, 1999, *Praśna Upaniṣad*, New Delhi: D.K. Printworld.

———, 2004, *Kaṭha Upaniṣad*, New Delhi: D.K. Printworld.

———, 2006a, *Chāndogya Upaniṣad*, New Delhi: D.K. Printworld.

———, 2006b, *Karma and Reincarnation*, New Delhi: D.K. Printworld.

———, 2009a, *The Taittirīya Upaniṣad*, New Delhi: D.K. Printworld.

———, 2009b, *Īśāvāsya and Māṇḍūkya Upaniṣads*, New Delhi: D.K. Printworld.

Swami Nikhilananda (tr.), 1997, *Vedānta-Sāra of Sadānanda*, Calcutta, Advaita Ashrama.

——— (tr.), 2000, *The Māṇḍūkya Upaniṣad with Gauḍapāda's Kārikā and Śaṅkara's Commentary*, Calcutta: Advaita Ashrama.

——— (tr.), 2008, *Self Knowledge of Śrī Śaṅkarācārya*, Chennai: Sri Ramakrishna Math.

Swami Satprakashananda (tr.), 1974, *The Goal and the Way*, Madras: Sri Ramakrishna Math.

———, 2001a, *Methods of Knowledge According to Advaita Vedānta*, Kolkata: Advaita Ashrama.

———, 2001b, *Mind According to Vedānta*, Madras: Sri Ramakrishna Math.

———, 2004, *The Universe, God and God-Realization from the Viewpoint of Vedānta*, Chennai: Sri Ramakrisna Math.

Swami Swahananda (tr.), 2001, *Pañcadaśī of Sri Vidyaranya Swami*, Chennai: Sri Ramakrishna Math.

Swami Tattwananda (tr.), 2002, *The Quintessence of Vedānta of Śrī Śaṅkarācārya*, Kalady, Ernakulam: Sri Ramakrishna Ashrama.

Swami Turiyananda (tr.), 2007, *Vivekacūḍāmaṇi of Śrī Śaṅkarācārya*, Chennai: Sri Ramakrishna Math.

Swami Virupakshananda (tr.), 2003, *Sāṁkhyakārikā of Īśvarakṛṣṇa*, Chennai: Sri Ramakrishna Math.

Swami Yogeshwaranand Saraswati, 1987, *Science of Soul*, Rishikesh: Yoga Niketan Trust.

Swami Yogindrananda, 2005, *Pramāṇavārtikam of Dharmakīrti*, vol. II, Varanasi: Chowkhamba Vidyabhawan.

Taimni, I.K., 1987a, *Glimpses into the Psychology of Yoga*, Madras: The Theosophical Publishing House.

———, 1987b, *Science and Occultism*, Madras: The Theosophical Publishing House.

———, 1998a, *The Secret of Self Realization*, Chennai: The Theosophical Publishing House.

———, 1998b, *Self-Culture in the Light of Ancient Wisdom*, Chennai: The Theosophical Publishing House.

———, 1999, *The Science of Yoga*, Chennai: The Theosophical Publishing House.

———, 2005, *Man, God and the Universe*, Chennai: The Theosophical Publishing House.

Thanh, T.M., 2008, *The Mind in Early Buddhism*, New Delhi: Munshiram Manoharlal.

Thibaut, G. (tr.), 1994, *The Vivaraṇaprameya Saṁgraha of Vidyāraṇya*, Delhi: Sri Satguru Publications.

Tilak, B.G., 2000, *Śrīmad Bhagavad-Gītā Rahasya*, Poona: Tilak Brothers.

Timalsina, S., 2006, *Seeing and Appearance*, Aachen, Germany: Shaker Verlag.

Tiwary, M. (ed.), 1988, *Nāmarūpa-Paricchedo*, Delhi: Uttaranchal Cooperative Group Housing Society.

Tola, F. and C. Dragonetti, 2004, *Being as Consciousness*, Delhi: Motilal Banarsidass.

Wilber, K., 2002, *The Spectrum of Consciousness*, Delhi: Motilal Banarsidass.

———, 2004, *The Ātman Project*, Varanasi: Pilgrims Publishing.

Williamson, R.K., 1984, *Introduction to Hegel's Philosophy of Religion*, Albany, NY: State University of New York Press.

Woodroffe, J., 2001, *The World as Power*, repr., Madras: Ganesh and Company.

Index

PRINTWORLD